Imagining Men

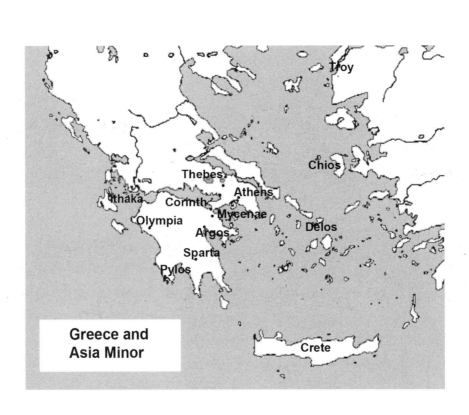

Greece and
Asia Minor

IMAGINING MEN

Ideals of Masculinity in Ancient Greek Culture

Thomas Van Nortwick

Praeger Series on the Ancient World
Bella Vivante, Series Editor

PRAEGER

**Westport, Connecticut
London**

Library of Congress Cataloging-in-Publication Data

Van Nortwick, Thomas, 1946–
    Imagining men : ideals of masculinity in ancient Greek culture / Thomas
Van Nortwick.
        p. cm. — (Praeger series on the ancient world, ISSN 1932–1406)
    Includes index.
    ISBN-13: 978–0–275–98812–8 (alk. paper)
1. Masculinity—Greece—History—To 1500.   I. Title.
II. Title: Ideals of masculinity in ancient Greek culture.
    DF93.V36   2008
    305.310938—dc22   2008017742

British Library Cataloguing in Publication Data is available.

Library of Congress Catalog Card Number: 2008017742
ISBN: 978–0–275–98812–8
ISSN: 1932–1406

First published in 2008

Praeger Publishers, 88 Post Road West, Westport, CT 06881
An imprint of Greenwood Publishing Group, Inc.
www.praeger.com

Printed in the United States of America

The paper used in this book complies with the
Permanent Paper Standard issued by the National
Information Standards Organization (Z39.48–1984).

10 9 8 7 6 5 4 3 2 1

For Mary

Contents

Series Foreword

The lives of ancient peoples may seem far removed, socially, linguistically, and especially technologically, from the concerns of the modern world. Yet the popularity of historical subjects on both the big and little screens—*Troy, Alexander, 300*, HBO's *Rome*, the many History Channel programs—demonstrates the abiding fascination the ancient world continues to exert. Some people are drawn to the dramatic differences between the ancient and modern, others seek to find the origins for contemporary cultural features or the sources to provide meaning to our modern lives. Regardless of approach, the past holds something valuable for all of us. It is literally the root of who we are, physically through our actual ancestors and culturally in establishing the foundations for our current beliefs and practices in religious, social, domestic, and political arenas. The same ancients that we study were themselves drawn to their own pasts, often asking questions similar to the ones we pose today about our past.

The books in the Praeger Series on the Ancient World address different topics from various perspectives. The ones on myth, sports, technology, warfare, and women explore these subjects cross-culturally, both within the ancient Mediterranean context—Egypt, Mesopotamia, Greece, Rome, and others—and between the ancient Mediterranean cultures and those of the Americas, Africa, and Asia. Others, including the volumes on literature, men, sexuality, and politics and society, examine their topic more specifically within a Greek or Greek and Roman cultural framework.

All renowned scholars committed to bringing the fruits of their research to wider audiences, each author brings a distinctive new approach to his or her topic that differentiates them from the many books that exist on the ancient world. A major strength of the first group of books is their multicultural breadth, which is informative in its comprehensive embrace and provides numerous opportunities for comparative insights. Likewise, the books in the second group explore their topics in dramatically new ways: the inner life of male identity, the contributions of both women and men to the social polity, the ancient constructions of concepts of sexuality and eroticism.

Each volume offers amazing windows into aspects of ancient life. Together, the series provides an invaluable overview of how ancient peoples thought about themselves and the world, how they conducted their lives, and how they expressed their views in creative terms. Enjoy the journey into the past that each one provides.

Bella Vivante
Series Editor
Praeger Series on the Ancient World

Preface

The ancient Greeks were intensely curious about the differences between men and women. Their literature is full of works that explore the ways of experiencing the world that they attributed to each gender. In the pages that follow, I explore one side of that duality, ancient Greek models for masculinity, as they are reflected in Greek literature in the period from 750–400 B.C.E. My interest is in asking how assumptions about manhood and masculine identity shaped the perception of questions about the meaning and value of a man's life in ancient Greek society. To put it another way, I will be looking at how the question "what kind of man am I?" implies "who am I?" and points further to "where do I fit in the larger order of things?" or "what are my obligations as a man to others?" and so forth. How the Greeks answered these kinds of questions for themselves has had a profound effect on the history of Western civilization, and their conclusions are still influential today.

The major sources for the ideas I will be exploring are mythical stories that the Greeks told about their past in the form of poems, both epic and lyric, and plays. My procedure is to make my way through these works of art, interpreting them as reflections of Greek ideas about manhood. In doing so, I try as best I can—given the uneven quantity of historical material that has survived from ancient Greece—to understand the stories in their wider historical and cultural context.

One danger of my approach is that I will of course be looking at the material from my own contemporary perspective and thus run the risk of distorting ancient cultures to fit modern preoccupations. To this charge I plead guilty ahead of time. I, at least, am indeed looking from my own perspective as a middle-age, North American white male. I don't see how such a view might be avoided, but at the same time I do not think that means I can't have objectivity about the material. And in any event, looking at ancient literature as a way of learning about ourselves seems a legitimate—I would even say laudable—goal.

That being said, we will in fact see that ancient Greek models for masculinity, like all cultural constructions, are to some degree a product of their particular time and place and are not necessarily identical to our own. For example, our contemporary ideas about manliness, reflected in action movies and westerns, generally prohibit so-called real men from displaying high emotion, with the exception of anger. John Wayne doesn't cry. By contrast, Achilles, the epitome of manliness in Homer's *Iliad*, weeps openly and at length over the loss of his friend Patroclus. Likewise, the practice of pederasty by Athenian males in the classical period (500–400 B.C.E.) was not thought to reflect effeminacy, in contrast to the modern tendency to associate homosexuality with a lack of manliness.

The concept of the heroic life, which lies at the center of all ancient speculation about the shape and meaning of a masculine life, comes to its richest expression early, in Homer's *Iliad* and *Odyssey*, composed between 750 and 700 B.C.E. Homer's models establish indelibly, in the crucible of war and the perils of survival in a hostile world, some central ideas about how to evaluate the life of males. Greek lyric poets reflect those ideals as well as new political and social structures evolving in Greek civilization from 650–500 B.C.E. From 500–400 B.C.E., Athenian dramatists explore and reinterpret received ideas about the heroic life in the context of the first democratic society, testing older assumptions about masculinity against the later communal values of the city-state. Although I mainly describe mythical patterns of maleness found in poetic sources, the histories of Herodotus and Thucydides and the speeches of Attic orators do sometimes offer a more straightforward view of ancient masculinity. The orators are especially valuable, as they must convince a large body of regular Athenian citizens and cannot afford to stray too far from received wisdom about the proper behavior for men.

Anyone using these kinds of sources to get at societal ideals must tread carefully. The *Iliad* is crucial for our understanding of Greek ideas about masculinity, but Achilles surely does not represent the ideal of masculine behavior for ordinary, nonheroic men. Homer, like most ancient poets, creates a character who helps us understand the boundaries that define a masculine life by constantly—and often egregiously—transgressing them. The same can be said for the most famous heroes of Greek tragic drama, Oedipus, Herakles, or Philoctetes, who often show us how to behave properly by spectacularly failing to do so. Aristophanes, the one Greek comic playwright whose work survives, provides another kind of exaggerated portrait. In his plays, appropriate manly behavior is often reflected in the funhouse mirror of overtly effeminate characters, always the target of jokes.

In pursuing Greek ideas about manliness from our modern perspective, we need to keep in mind the distinction between gender, a cultural construct organized around the polarity of masculine/feminine, and sex, a biological category defined by male/female. Today we understand that a human being, whatever his or her sex, can exhibit both masculine and feminine patterns of behavior. Greek artists also acknowledged this distinction, although sometimes with an emphasis different from ours. They explore the question of what it is to be a man by creating in their characters a tension between what we would now call masculine and feminine characteristics. Homer's heroic male can reach full maturity only by incorporating qualities that the Greeks defined as feminine. Likewise, some of the most arresting models for exploring the life of males in fifth-century tragic plays are women. Clytemnestra, Electra, and Medea all transgress in their behavior and attitudes the traditional territory of males in Athenian culture of the fifth century B.C.E. Through these often frightening characters, the dramatists created powerfully vivid representations of masculine ideals.

One final caution: as is the case with any study of ancient Greek civilization, the evidence we have at our disposal is limited in several ways. First, the written remains from this period are almost exclusively produced by and for the elite upper classes. The lives of ordinary Athenian artisans or farmers are almost entirely invisible, not to mention the experience of slaves and resident aliens, who may have made up as much as half the population of fifth-century Athens. People of lower status, socially and/or economically, may sometimes be glimpsed through the distorted lens of Aristophanic comedy, but this portrait must be used with great care. Second, the vast majority of written material after 500 B.C.E. is from Athens. Again, Spartans do appear in these accounts, but always from the strongly biased perspective of Athenian cultural and political imperialism.

All of these issues bring us back eventually to the fundamental question, for the Greeks and for us, "what does it mean to be a man?" As I have said, my inquiry will prompt speculation about the characteristic shape and course of a man's life, and how a man finds meaning as he journeys through it. The plan of this book reflects these connections between identity and the life cycle. For this reason, I begin with the definitive fact of mortality. Indeed, the central question to which all serious Greek thought responds in one form or another is, "What does it mean to be a creature who knows he must die?" Because notions of an afterlife were not prominent in the Greek heroic view of human existence, the only chance for survival came in the form of fame, which supplied a kind of hedge against the oblivion of death. Thus the proximity of death increased the urgency to become known, to do and say whatever was considered valuable in the eyes of one's fellows. Given this dynamic, it follows that in Greek thought (as in our own), a crucial moment in the life of males comes when they confront the finite nature of their existence and must adjust their understanding of themselves and their place in the world to reflect that realization.

The remaining chapters explore the nature, dimensions, and meaning of a life seen from a masculine perspective. This book is organized topically, with chapters on critical stages in the life cycle—youth, old age, and death—on the function of male identity within the family, and in the relations both between men and women and between men and gods. Each chapter focuses in particular on a few works of art that reflect the ideals being treated. At the end of the book, I include a brief list of further reading for each chapter in the hope that readers will be stimulated to learn more about this topic. All translations of Greek texts are my own.

ACKNOWLEDGMENTS

Many of the ideas in this book have come out of my teaching at Oberlin College. Thus it would be appropriate—if I could remember all of their names—to begin by thanking personally all of those intelligent and curious young people who have shared the reading of ancient Greek literature with me over the past 33 years. One of the many pleasures of writing this book has been in recalling a snippet of conversation or a friendly argument with one of them. If one of you should happen to read this, thanks for the memories. So, too, I owe much to my colleagues in Classics who have talked with me about the poems and plays that form the backbone of this study. Thank you, Nate Greenberg, Jim Helm, Jenny Lynn, Kirk Ormand, Ben Lee, and Drew Wilburn, for your intelligence, your patience, and the pleasure of your company. I'm sure you'll recognize ways in which you have made the book better. The mistakes, needless to say, are mine, not yours.

I owe a great debt of gratitude to Karen Barnes, Administrative Assistant in Classics, who over the past 22 years has helped me in so many ways to be a better teacher. Alice Nordquist, one of those wonderful students, helped me in the early stages of this project with bibliographical research. I am grateful to my old friend, Bella Vivante, for offering me the chance to contribute to the series of which this book will be a part. Special thanks are due to Kirk Ormand—who is writing another entry in the series—for his helpful strategizing about how to approach the material, and Drew Wilburn, for much patient tutoring about mapmaking.

My wife, Mary Kirtz Van Nortwick, read the entire manuscript, caught many errors, and made valuable suggestions for improving my writing. Her intelligence, her own experience and skill as a teacher and scholar, and her loving patience have made this book much better than it might have been. The book is dedicated to her with love and gratitude.

Historical Timeline

3000 B.C.E.	Beginning of Minoan civilization in Crete.
2200–1400	Crete becomes the dominant power in the Aegean.
1600–1400	Strong Cretan influence in Greece.
1400–1200	Mycenaean civilization on mainland of Greece.
	Earliest mythical sources for Homer's *Iliad*.
1300?	*The Epic of Gilgamesh* (standard Babylonian version).
1250–1150	Unrest across the Mediterranean.
1200–1150	Mycenaean palaces and their civilizations destroyed.
1184	Traditional date for the fall of Troy.
1050–950	Greeks from mainland (Ionians, Dorians, Aeolians) move east to colonize Asia Minor.
800–700	Rise of aristocratic oligarchies throughout mainland Greece.
776	Traditional date for founding of Olympic games.
725?	Homer, *Iliad* (Chios?, Asia Minor).
700?	Homer, *Odyssey*.
	Hesiod, *Theogony*.
	Homeric Hymn to Aphrodite.
680–640?	Archilochus of Paros, the first Greek lyric poet.
	Homeric Hymn to Demeter.
	Homeric Hymn to Apollo.
650–600	Rise of tyrants in Ionian Greek settlements in Asia Minor.

	Mimnermus of Colophon (Asia Minor), Greek elegist.
	Ibycus of Rhegium (Sicily), Greek lyric poet.
630–550	Solon, Athenian poet and politician.
600–500	Tyrants rule in Athens.
560–490	Anacreon, of Teos (Asia Minor) lyric poet.
546–545	Persians conquer Greeks in Asia Minor.
525	Birth of Aeschylus.
508–507	Reforms of Cleisthenes in Athens.
499–494	Unsuccessful revolt of Greeks in Asia Minor from Persians.
496?	Birth of Sophocles.
490	First Persian invasion of Greece under Darius.
	Battle of Marathon.
480	Second Persian invasion of Greece under Xerxes.
	Buildings on the Athenian Acropolis destroyed.
	Battle of Thermopylae.
	Battle of Salamis.
	Birth of *Euripides*?
479	Battle of Platea; Persians driven from Greece.
472	Aeschylus, *The Persians,* the earliest surviving Athenian tragedy.
467	Aeschylus, *Seven Against Thebes.*
461–429	Pericles the dominant force in Athenian politics.
461	The political reforms of Ephialtes, ally of Pericles.
460	Birth of Thucydides?
458	Aeschylus, Oresteia trilogy: *Agamemnon, The Libation Bearers, The Eumenides.*
456	Death of Aeschylus.
448	Sophocles, *Ajax?*
447	Pericles begins reconstruction of buildings on the Athenian Acropolis, including the Parthenon (Temple to Athena).
440s	Herodotus reads his *Histories* (of the Persian wars) in Athens?
441	Sophocles, *Antigone?*

431	Peloponnesian War between Athens and Sparta begins.
	Euripides, *Medea.*
430	Outbreak of the plague in Athens.
	Euripides, *Children of Herakles*?
429	Death of Pericles from the plague.
427	Sophocles, *Oedipus Rex.*
421	Peace of Nicias, between Athens and Sparta.
415	Athens launches a naval expedition to Sicily.
413	Defeat of Athenians in Sicily.
411	Oligarchic revolution in Athens.
	Active conflict between Athens and Sparta resumes.
	Aristophanes, *Lysistrata.*
410	Democracy restored in Athens.
409	Sophocles, *Philoctetes.*
406	Death of Euripides.
	Death of Sophocles.
405	Sparta defeats Athens at Battle of Aegispotami.
404	Peloponnesian War ends; Sparta imposes peace terms on Athens.
401	Sophocles, *Oedipus at Colonus* produced posthumously.
399	Euripides, *Bacchae* produced posthumously.

One

Introduction: Men, Death, and the Meaning of Life

Death is the mother of beauty.

—Wallace Stevens

Men are rational; women are emotional. Men are naturally aggressive; women are more passive. These ideas and myriad others related to them are embedded in modern Western culture. Since the advent of the feminist movement of the 1970s, such assertions have come under heavy scrutiny: Are they true? If they are true, what are the causes for the differences between men and women? Are they based on biological differences between the sexes, or are they the product of political or ideological choices within cultures? If they are not true, why do they continue to influence our thoughts and actions? The debate about these questions continues and the outcome is not trivial. At stake are fundamental decisions ranging from economic ones about the distribution of resources in our society (equal pay for equal work) to those addressing the essential nature and worth of human beings (what does it mean to be a man?).

What follows here is not intended to settle these questions. My aim is more modest: to fill in one part of historical background for these issues by exploring the earliest expression of traditional ideas about "masculinity" that we know in the civilization of the Greeks during the period 750–400 B.C.E. Almost all of our common ideas about masculinity and manliness are very old. The earliest stories we have from the Mediterranean basin, composed around 2000 B.C.E., already reflect ideas about the nature of a masculine life that persist to this day. These ways of thinking are tenacious. Why they have been so sturdy is another question that I explore in this book.

We can begin to trace the shape of a characteristically masculine life from the perspective of the ancient Mediterranean by looking at two of the earliest examples of the hero story, *The Epic of Gilgamesh*, a Mesopotamian poem from around 1600–1100 B.C.E., and Homer's *Iliad*, which was probably composed around 750 B.C.E. on the island of Chios, off what is now Turkey but was then inhabited by Greeks. These narratives present many of the essential elements of a masculine life as it was understood around the Mediterranean in that period. Both stories reflect what we would now call a *developmental* understanding of such a life, dramatizing the ways in which a man must adjust his perspective as he moves through his life. Hero stories are often about growing up; both *The Epic of Gilgamesh* and the *Iliad* call attention to the role of human mortality in defining the meaning of a masculine life.

THE ARC OF A MAN'S LIFE I: THE HERO STORY

Gilgamesh, the King of Uruk and hero of *The Epic of Gilgamesh,* has just lost his best friend, Enkidu, to a wasting disease:

I am going to die!—am I not like Enkidu?!
Deep sadness penetrates my core,
I fear death, and now roam the wilderness. (*The Epic of Gilgamesh* IX. 3–4)[1]

Gilgamesh's response to his friend's death is typical of grieving figures in ancient literature and in our own time. When someone we love dies, all we can feel at first is *absence.* The warm, lively presence we loved was embodied, and now that body is cold and lifeless, gone and yet still here. So we must have funerals, ways of helping ourselves let go of the dead. In our grief, a part of us wants to go with the dead person, to cling to the body as the only available essence of the one we loved. Life goes on, we are told, but we do not want to go with it. In this sense, when someone we love dies, a part of us dies, too. Because Enkidu was a "wild man," someone who ran with the animals and drank from their watering hole, Gilgamesh now roams the wilderness, unable to release his friend to death.

But something else has happened to Gilgamesh. For the first time, he understands—viscerally and not simply as an idea—that he will die, the definitive experience that marks him as human. That his realization comes just when it does is also important. To see why, we need to look at some earlier parts of the story. Just before Enkidu's death, he and Gilgamesh kill Humbaba, the monster of the Cedar Forest. Flushed with their triumph, they return to Uruk to bask in glory, declaring themselves the bravest and boldest of men. Ishtar, the goddess of sexuality, is drawn to all this male force and asks Gilgamesh to be her consort. He declines, citing a number of her previous lovers, all of whom have met a bad end. In her anger, Ishtar arranges to have the Bull of Heaven, another fearsome monster, attack the two men. They team up to kill this creature as well and seem to reach the pinnacle of male power. Enkidu tears off the bull's hind quarter and flings it in the face of the goddess, a fatal mistake. She retaliates by demanding that the father of the gods punish the men for their arrogance, and he makes Enkidu fall ill and die.

In this sequence of events we can trace some important connections. The killing of Humbaba is a typical heroic act in the mythical tradition of the ancient Mediterranean. Human civilization, in this perspective, is the product of imposing human control over the raw power of nature. Monsters embody the natural disorder that threatens human culture, and heroes who kill monsters are therefore revered as the guardians of human civilization. So Gilgamesh and Enkidu, by killing the monster, hold the disorderly power of nature at bay and are rewarded with glory. Glory, in turn, is purely a product of human civilization, something preserved by human recordkeeping.

So far, all is well. But because they seem to be able to control the world and its creatures through their acts, and because these acts are rewarded with glory, heroes are often tempted to see themselves as omnipotent, like the gods. Impatient of any limits on their expression of power, they over-reach, only to be brought back to their right size by an encounter with the ultimate limit, death. Gilgamesh's anguished realization, quoted previously, marks the moment when he first fully understands himself as human. His fear and the journey it provokes will take him far away from Uruk, across the Waters of Darkness to the Land of Dilmun, where he will consult Utnap-ishtim, the only human to have been granted immortality, about his plight. But Gilgamesh cannot beat death, and he returns home. His last words mix resignation with a new wisdom:

Go up, Urshanabi, onto the wall of Uruk and walk around.
Examine its foundation, inspect its brickwork thoroughly—
is not (even the core of) the brick structure of kiln-fired brick,
and did not the Seven Sages themselves lay out its plan?
(*The Epic of Gilgamesh* XI. 314–317)

Walls delimit cities, always the heart of human civilization in the ancient Mediterranean. When Gilgamesh finally accepts his mortality, he has be-come fully human, ready to live inside the city walls.

The Gilgamesh epic, in the version quoted here, was composed in Mesopotamia sometime between 1600 and 1100 B.C.E. Although relatively short, the story shows us an essential pattern in the shape of a man's life as the civilizations around the Mediterranean saw it: youthful energy leads to self-assertion and impatience with limits; maturity inevitably brings re-minders that life is finite: friends and loved-ones die, physical changes be-come harbingers of the human inability to stop time. Eventually there comes a reckoning: either a man changes his perception of himself as unlimited, or his inflexibility, fueled by pride, arrogance, or fear, destroys him. Ancient mythical narratives about heroes are the best place for learning how these cultures understood the arc of a man's life, because in these stories the hero always pushes at or even transgresses the boundaries that define how human life fits into the larger order of the universe. By crossing boundaries, heroes reflect where those limits were thought to be.

And once we see limits, we see meaning. Like the ancient Greeks, who have left us a rich record of their thoughts on this subject, we tend to see form as prerequisite to meaning, and formlessness as meaningless. The Greek word for the universe, *cosmos*, simply means "order." Form is in turn defined by limit or boundary: to define means to "put a boundary around." I often enlist my students in a thought experiment. I ask them first to imagine themselves waking up one morning to discover they are ageless, all-knowing, and all-powerful. Essentially, they are to try thinking of themselves as Greek gods. The next question is, how would they spend their time? The initial responses always involve saving the world from disease, famine, and bigotry, all laudable aims to be sure. What would they do for the next, say, million years? It soon becomes clear that the unlimited existence of the gods does not bear much inspection because it is finally meaningless. The only way gods such as these could experience a meaningful existence is to inject themselves into the limited, mortal world of death and change (which is exactly what Homer's gods do).

In the second part of my thought experiment, I ask the class to imagine themselves waking to discover that they have only 24 hours to live. Now the question of what to do becomes quite urgent. Do they take the red-eye to Los Angeles to make amends in person to the brother from whom they've been estranged for years? Or perhaps they will try to engage in nonstop dissipation, doing all the things they've been afraid to try for fear of societal censure. Whatever choices they make are freighted with enormous meaning, because the boundary of their mortal lives is so close.

Shape, then, marked by limit, creates meaning. Implicit in the idea of boundary is an inside and an outside. To put it another way, meaning demands a *context*, something larger within which it resides. Now we can begin to see how issues of personal identity and meaning in life intersect. I understand the creature "I" to exist within certain boundaries: spatial, temporal, psychic, and spiritual. I am "myself" within the boundaries of my self. To understand the meaning of my life I must first know where I end and the rest of the cosmos begins. Viewed from this perspective, a human life has meaning within a context. Thus the ultimate sources of meaning in a human life are somehow beyond it, transcendent, the gods, nature, fate. We can see how a figure who crosses the boundaries of human existence becomes a vehicle for exploring issues of meaning. The "Land of Dilmun," which lies on the other side of the "Waters of Darkness," stands in the Gilgamesh epic for the land of the dead, beyond the reach of ordinary mortals. It is not a surprise to find that Gilgamesh goes to the Land of Dilmun to discover "the secret of life and death."

Achilles Grows Up

Homer's *Iliad*, the first work of Greek literature we have, gives us a rich model for how a man moves from adolescence to maturity. Although approximately 15,000 lines long and divided into 24 "books," or chapters, the poem covers only about 50 days toward the end of a 10-year war, which the Greeks of the classical period believed to have occurred sometime around 1200 B.C.E. (although the usual date given for the composition of the poem itself is 750–725 B.C.E.). The Greek army, led by Agamemnon, has besieged Troy, a fortified city on the shores of the Bosporus, in an attempt to recover Helen, wife of Menelaus, from Paris, her Trojan abductor. Menelaus is the party most directly aggrieved, but the poem's principal Greek hero is Achilles, the son of Peleus, a mortal from Thessaly, and Thetis, a divine sea nymph.

The plot of the poem is complex, encompassing a large cast of characters, but for our purposes, the story of Achilles may be summarized briefly. In book 1, Achilles and Agamemnon quarrel over a captured woman, Briseis. Agamemnon has brought a plague on the camp by refusing initially to release to her father his own concubine, the daughter of Chryses, a local priest of Apollo. Achilles calls an assembly of the warriors and asks Agamemnon to release the daughter of Chryses, so that Apollo will relent. Agamemnon agrees to let the girl go, but he demands that he be compensated by receiving Briseis, Achilles's captive woman. The dispute ends when Achilles leaves the camp of the Greek army, furiously vowing not to return to the battle. He then goes to the seashore and calls to his mother, who lives under the sea. She comes to him and he complains bitterly of his treatment at Agamemnon's hands, asking his mother to persuade Zeus, the principal god of the Homeric pantheon, to punish his fellow Greeks for not honoring him as they should. Thetis readily agrees and heads for Mount Olympus, where the gods live, and Zeus in turn nods his assent. Meanwhile, Agamemnon sends two subordinates to collect Briseis.

Books 2–8 tell how the Greeks attempt to do without their best fighter, as Achilles stays apart from the battle, brooding in his hut by the sea. By the end of book 8, Zeus's plan to punish the Greeks has succeeded to the point that the Trojans have pinned the Greek army against the sea, and it looks as though they will overrun the camp the next morning. As book 9 opens, Agamemnon, desperate to save the army, sends an embassy of three Greek soldiers, Odysseus, Ajax, and the aged Phoenix, who has been a familiar of Achilles since the latter's infancy.

The members of the embassy each address Achilles, trying to convince him to return to battle, for the Greeks are on the brink of defeat. The appeal fails, as Achilles, in one of the most famous speeches in the poem, refuses to accept Agamemnon's terms for his return. Not until the Trojans set fire to the Greek ships will he reenter the battle. The three men dejectedly return to the Greek camp, and the next morning the battle resumes, with the fortunes of the Greeks looking increasingly grim (books 10–15). One by one, the principal Greek warriors are wounded and withdraw from the fighting. The Trojans, led by their leader Hector, move closer and closer to the ships, until at the end of book 15, Hector grabs the stern of a Greek ship and calls for fire.

Book 16 opens with Patroclus, Achilles's close friend, coming to plead with him to return to battle. Still he refuses. Patroclus then asks for Achilles's armor, so he can impersonate the great warrior and stall the Trojans. Achilles agrees, Patroclus arms himself, and we return to the battle, where the Trojans are fooled for a brief time into thinking that Achilles has returned. Patroclus kills many Trojans, including Sarpedon, a Trojan ally who has given a big speech earlier in the poem, and then is killed himself by Hector. Book 17 is taken up with a fight over the corpse of Patroclus, with the Trojans wanting to desecrate it, and the Greeks desperate to preserve it for burial. At the beginning of book 18, Achilles learns of Patroclus's death, goes to the edge of the battlefield, and shouts in such a terrifying way that the Trojans abandon the corpse, and the Greeks can bring it safely off the battlefield. Achilles collapses in grief, tortured by guilt over his responsibility for his friend's death, and then vows not to stop fighting until he has avenged Patroclus by killing Hector.

Achilles is given new armor by his mother Thetis, as Hector took his original set as a trophy after killing Patroclus. The armor was made for Thetis by Hephaestus, the smith god, and is impregnable. He reenters the battle and cuts a gory swath through the Trojan ranks, heading relentlessly toward Hector (books 19–22). The climactic duel occurs in book 22. Achilles kills Hector and displays the corpse for his comrades, who stab it repeatedly. Book 23 is taken up with the funeral of Patroclus, whose body has been magically preserved by Thetis, followed by athletic games in his honor. The final book begins with Priam, Hector's father, traveling at night to ransom his son's body. Achilles has been obsessively dragging the corpse around the tomb of Patroclus, tied to the back of his chariot. Zeus sends Thetis to tell Achilles he must release the body to Priam, and Achilles agrees. In their exchange, Priam and Achilles console each other for the deaths of their loved ones, the body is released, and the poem ends with the burial of Hector at Troy.

Behind this complex story lies a significant narrative pattern: (1) The hero separates from his customary position or status; (2) destruction or disruption of some sort ensues; and (3) the hero returns, often bringing some special knowledge to share with his fellow mortals. This threefold pattern is one of the most common structures in hero stories from many different cultures. The particular form of the story highlights the hero's separation/isolation from his fellow mortals, his special status as one who can go places and do things that ordinary mortals cannot, and the special gift he brings back with him, which may transform him and/or his fellows and the world.

In the *Iliad*, the central plot, focused on Achilles, repeats the pattern of withdrawal, destruction, and return three times:

> W1: Achilles leaves the Greek camp in book 1;
> D1: Many Greek warriors die as a result of Achilles's absence;
> R1: Patroclus returns to battle in book 16, wearing Achilles's armor;
>
> W2: Achilles refuses to return to battle himself in book 16;
> D2: Patroclus is killed;
> R2: Achilles goes to the battle field and screams;
>
> W3: Achilles refuses to eat, bathe, sleep, or have sex until he kills Hector;
> D3: Hector is killed;
> R3: Achilles pities Priam and releases the body of Hector.

Each repetition of the pattern raises the stakes of Achilles's acts, for himself and others. His first withdrawal is over an issue of personal honor, and results in the deaths of some of his comrades. The second withdrawal, as he clings stubbornly to his prideful position, results in the loss of Patroclus.

The final withdrawal, in which he forswears the ordinary emblems of human culture—food, bathing, sleep, and sex—symbolizes his desire to be entirely apart from humanity. The result is not only the death of Hector but also a profound change in Achilles's understanding of his place in the world.

The Hero and His Mother

Tracing Achilles's progress through the story will bring us to some seminal ideas about how the Greeks—and other cultures around the Mediterranean—thought about the shape of a man's life. We return to the first book of the poem, where Achilles argues with Agamemnon and storms out of the Greek army's camp, and Agamemnon then sends three soldiers to Achilles's hut to retrieve Briseis. The men are afraid of Achilles's anger, but he treats them kindly and tells Patroclus, who has withdrawn along with his friend, to give the girl to them. Next we find Achilles in a telling situation:

The girl went with them, unwilling. But Achilles
withdrew from his comrades, sitting apart
at the edge of the gray sea, looking at the vast deep.
Stretching out his hands he prayed to his mother. (Homer, *Iliad* 1. 348–351)

Unable to get his way, the hero asks his mother for help. To be at once separated from other men and attached to his mother marks Achilles, in the common understanding of Greek culture, as immature. To reach full manhood, heroes in Greek and other Mediterranean literature always need to separate from their mothers and come to terms in some way with wisdom that is associated with the world of their fathers. Gilgamesh moves from the nurture of his mother, Ninsun, to the wisdom of a surrogate father, Utnapishtim. Aeneas, the hero of Virgil's Latin epic, the *Aeneid,* must escape the dangerous attentions of his mother, Venus. Having done so, he then travels to the underworld to learn from his father Anchises the secrets of the universe and his own place in the glorious future of Rome. And of course there is the disastrous counterexample of Oedipus, who, instead of separating from his mother, ends up marrying her and fathering children, having already killed his father.

Thetis will indeed give Achilles unquestioning support in the poem. This is the principal role of mothers in the heroic tradition. We observe, however, that this devotion and validation, although they may make Achilles feel loved, in fact work against his progress toward mature manhood. With Zeus protecting him and supporting his vengeful response to Agamemnon, he cannot learn what he must about his own essential nature as a man. Not until the very end of the poem, when Zeus forces Thetis to conform to his wishes by convincing Achilles to give up Hector's body, does Achilles completely separate himself from his mother's world and move toward the hard wisdom represented by his absent father, Peleus. By doing so, he finally reaches the full measure of his manhood.

What Achilles learns is the answer to the principal question the *Iliad* aims to address: what does it mean to be a man? The inquiry begins with the quarrel in book 1. The dispute is over honor or status, *time* in Greek, which, in the value system of the *Iliad*, is usually represented by possessions. Agamemnon, as the political leader of the expedition, claims to have the support of Zeus, who honors kings, while Achilles demands that he be given the most honor (in this case, a captive woman, who is treated as a possession here, not a human being) because he is the best fighter. Behind all of this wrangling lies another fundamental question: how do we evaluate a human life? As the story progresses, this question comes more and more to be articulated through the figure of Achilles.

The Hero and His Second Self

Because his mother is divine and his father mortal, Achilles is a useful figure for exploring these questions. By his very nature, he straddles the boundaries between humans and gods; because he is semidivine, he expects to be immortal, and in many ways acts more like a god than a man, assuming he should be able to do what he wants, impatient with others who do not see the world as he does. To express Achilles's divided nature and his struggles to resolve it, the poet of the *Iliad* creates in Patroclus an *alter ego*, or second self, for his hero. The second self is essentially a figure who represents parts of the hero that he is denying or has somehow lost touch with, usually through arrogance and pride. Enkidu is such a figure for Gilgamesh, and in fact the relationship between the two Mesopotamian heroes is similar in many ways to that between Achilles and Patroclus. The device survives into modern literature, in stories like Robert Louis Stevenson's *Dr. Jekyll and Mr. Hyde* and Joseph Conrad's *The Secret Sharer.*

We are accustomed in modern times to think of the process dramatized by the interaction between the hero and his second self as an *internal* struggle between different parts of a person's mind or psyche. Freud's model of the unconscious mind, and later adaptations of it by Jung and others, have defined the dynamic as psychological. Writers from the ancient world, by contrast, tend to *objectify* this process, projecting one part out onto a separate figure, rather than representing humans as having levels of consciousness. The modern perspective is more familiar to us and may seem to offer a more sophisticated way of understanding human behavior, but objectifying the struggle as ancient writers do has the virtue of making the outlines of the different parts sharper and clarifying the way the interactions relate to the character of the hero.

The most important aspect of the second self figure is that he (or she: Dido plays that role for Aeneas) represents parts of the hero with which he has somehow lost touch. In this sense, the second self is not identical to the hero, but *complementary*. Enkidu, for example, is a "wild man," who begins by living with animals, in tune with the rhythms of nature, whereas Gilgamesh is a creature of civilization, hungry for fame and the status it brings. Likewise, whereas Achilles is arrogant, demanding that he get his way, Patroclus is a model—rare enough, in the *Iliad*—of humility, concerned for the welfare of his fellow Greeks, uninterested in his own glory. During Achilles's prideful withdrawal and rejection of the embassy, Patroclus is virtually invisible, quietly attending to his friend. Only when a crisis is near after the failure of the embassy in book 9 does he become more prominent.

As the fighting wears on the day after the embassy, and things are going badly for the Greeks, Achilles sends Patroclus to inquire about a fallen Greek warrior. Homer calls this moment "the beginning of evil" for Patroclus, alerting us that something important is afoot: Nestor, a garrulous old fighter from a generation earlier than the present heroes, drags Patroclus into his tent and delivers a characteristically longwinded speech about the suffering of the Greeks and the need for Achilles to give up his withdrawal from battle. This kind of appeal is bound to succeed with Patroclus, and once he has the young man's attention, Nestor makes the fateful suggestion that, if Achilles still refuses to help his friends, then Patroclus should borrow his armor and go out in his place. Now the role of Patroclus as a kind of substitute for Achilles becomes more concrete.

As we have seen, Patroclus eventually does go into battle in Achilles's armor and is killed by Hector, the principal Trojan warrior. We might say that Patroclus is sacrificed to Achilles's arrogance and pride, which keep him from returning himself to help his fellow Greeks. And because as a second self Patroclus carries inside himself the part of Achilles that can relate to others—his compassion and humility—his death can be understood as a kind of spiritual suicide by Achilles: to serve his own ego, the hero kills off another part of himself and becomes even more isolated than before.

The Hero As Boundary Crosser

With the death of his second self, mortality comes closer to Achilles. Before, the men dying were perhaps friends, but not intimate reflections of himself. His response to loss is to move yet further away from his fellow Greeks. When the news of Patroclus's death is brought to Achilles, he falls to the ground and covers himself with dirt; later he announces to his fellow warriors that he will neither eat nor sleep until Hector is dead; when Thetis comes to him later, in book 24, to deliver Zeus's orders, she complains that he has not been sleeping with a woman. By abstaining from all of these typical human activities, Achilles is, according to the symbolism of early Greek poetry, signaling his withdrawal not just from his fellow Greeks, but from all human life.

These gestures characterize Achilles first of all as someone who is grieving. As we have seen in the case of Gilgamesh, the loss of someone close typically causes those who grieve to withdraw from human contact. He tries in some sense to stay with the dead person, moving away from life and toward death, abstaining from taking part in ordinary human society. Achilles's movement toward death is symbolized in various ways in the poem. When Thetis comes to comfort him after Patroclus's death, she holds his head as a grieving figure would hold the corpse of someone who has died; when he refuses to eat, Athena infuses him with nectar and ambrosia, the same substances used by Thetis to preserve Patroclus's corpse from decaying.

Achilles moves away from human experience in more than one way. Nectar and ambrosia, of course, are also the food of the gods. As he draws closer to death, Achilles seems at the same time to make contact with the divine part of himself. In the course of his bloody rampage in pursuit of Hector, he shows absolutely no compassion for others, killing savagely. Unlike the Judeo-Christian God, Greek divinities are not compassionate, nor are they usually guardians of justice. They are immortal and all-powerful, and because they can never be harmed in any permanent way, they have no incentive to restrain their emotions or actions. They want what they want and will have it. Other creatures who defy them are destroyed. These qualities are precisely those that characterize Achilles's behavior as he chases Hector.

Achilles's savagery has yet another dimension. When he finally catches Hector in book 22, the Trojan hero begs for humane treatment: let the two of them agree that the victor in their duel will give the body of the other man back to his own people for burial. Achilles will hear nothing of it. There can be no agreement between men and lions, wolves and lambs, he says. He only wishes that his fury would drive him to hack off Hector's flesh and eat it raw. Now he approaches another definitive boundary, between men and animals.

In all of these dimensions, we see Achilles performing the characteristic function of Greek heroes, crossing over boundaries that usually define human life: life/death; human/god; man/beast. By doing so, Achilles helps us to see and think about those boundaries and therefore about what it means to be a human being. And because he acts always with the support of his mother, he exemplifies a failure to reach maturity as a man. Thetis intercedes to secure the support of Zeus, ensuring that her son's desire for vengeance will be fulfilled. We have seen that when Hector takes Achilles's armor from Patroclus, Thetis persuades Hephaestus, the god of fire, to make impenetrable replacements. Guilty and full of self-loathing after the death of his friend, Achilles vows to his mother to die a glorious death, but not before he kills many Trojans, and especially Hector. Her answer is immediate and unequivocal: his desire for blood is appropriate, and she will bring him the armor he needs to fulfill it.

The Hero and His Father

In none of these choices do we hear anything about Achilles's mortal father, Peleus, living back in Thessaly. This omission would seem to be striking in a patriarchal culture and again suggests something unfinished in Achilles's development as a man. The last book of the poem addresses this problem. Achilles's obsessive abuse of Hector's corpse prompts an assembly of the gods. Zeus hears arguments for and against the hero and decides that Hector's corpse must go back to the Trojans to be buried properly. He sends two messengers to effect his will, one to Priam, Hector's father and king of Troy, to get the old man to travel to Achilles's hut to ransom the body, and another to Thetis, summoning her to Olympus from under the sea. The latter mission is particularly important for our purposes. Once Thetis arrives, the other gods offer her a seat and a drink. She accepts, is given her instructions by Zeus, and goes immediately to her son to tell him to let Priam have the body. He in turn assents with no protest.

These negotiations represent a significant shift in the poem. The offer of a seat and a drink in early Greek literature is a symbolic gesture of consolation to someone who is grieving. By accepting the tokens, the grieving figure accepts the loss of his or her loved one, and reenters human society, ending the withdrawal that accompanies grief. Thetis has been lamenting the short life destined for Achilles since his birth. As a goddess, she has no need to accept mortality and sees her son's short and finite life as especially painful. By accepting the consolation of the gods, she acquiesces in the mortality and coming death of her son, who is fated to die soon after Hector is buried. Once she has made this gesture, she is co-opted into the patriarchal plans of Zeus and ceases to support Achilles in his resistance to his true nature.

We have seen that Achilles, too, feels oppressed by the limitations of mortality and has been acting as if he were in fact a god himself. One reflection of his resistance to his fate is that he has been clinging to the body of Hector and refusing to let it be buried. He was also reluctant to let Patroclus's body go, so much so that the ghost of his friend came to him at the beginning of book 23 to beg him to relent:

You sleep, Achilles, and have forgotten me.
You were not careless of me while I lived, only in death.
Bury me as quickly as possible, so I can pass through the gates of Hades.
The souls keep me at bay, images of the dead,
nor do they ever let me mingle with them across the river,
but I wander, just as I am, around the wide gates of Hades.
Give me your hand, as I am wretched, for never
will I leave Hades, once I have been given to the funeral fire. (Homer, *Iliad* 23. 69–76)

Hector, like Patroclus, seems to reflect something of Achilles. When he is killed in book 22, he wears the armor of Achilles, through which the death blow is struck, suggesting again a symbolic suicide. By denying burial to the two men, Achilles is keeping their souls from their final rest in the Underworld. But because each man, according to the symbolism of the second self, also carries something of Achilles, his acts seem to show him holding out against his own fate, or more specifically, against his own mortality.

Achilles's Reconciliation to Mortality

When Priam arrives at the hut of Achilles, he kneels and grabs the knees of his son's killer, in a gesture of supplication, and kisses his hands:

Remember your father, Achilles—though you are godlike—
a man like me, on the threshold of old age.
I suppose his neighbors, living all around,
wear him down, nor is there anyone to ward off ruin and death.
But that man, hearing that you are alive,
rejoices in his heart, and every day hopes

to see his dear son coming back from Troy;
yet I am ill-fated: though I fathered great sons
in wide Troy, I tell you not one has been left for me.
Fifty there were, when the sons of the Achaeans came;
twenty-one were from one womb, and
all the rest were born to me from women in the palace;
raging Ares loosed the knees of many,
but one alone there was, who guarded the city and the people;
you killed him yesterday, as he stood in defense of his father's land,
Hector. Because of him I have come to the ships of the Achaeans
to ransom him from you, and I bring boundless treasure.
Revere the gods, Achilles, and pity me,
remembering your father. For I am even more pitiable,
having dared to do what no other mortal has done,
To draw to my lips the hand of the man who killed my son. (Homer, *Iliad* 24. 486–506)

All the strands of Homer's complex plot begin to come together in this speech. By enlisting Thetis in his plans to retrieve Hector's body, Zeus, "the Father of gods and humans," has neutralized her as a force working against his patriarchal regime, and, by extension, the evolution of Achilles toward manhood. Priam, meanwhile, by urging Achilles to see him as a substitute for the latter's father, Peleus, invites him to begin to move away from his mother and toward a different way of seeing himself and his place in the larger order of the universe. Finally, by releasing the body, Achilles ceases to deny his own mortal nature, and in so doing he separates from his divine mother and can accept the hard wisdom that defines his mortal father's world: he, like all humans, must die.

This evolution is confirmed in the two great speeches Achilles makes during the exchange with Priam. In the first, he urges the old man to bear up under his grief. This is the lot of all mortals, he says, to live in sorrow, while the gods never suffer. He continues:

Two jars sit on the threshold of Zeus;
one contains evil gifts, the other good.
He to whom Zeus who loves thunder gives a mixture,
meets evil one time, good the next.
The man to whom he gives only from the jar of miseries,
he makes wretched, and evil hunger drives him across
the bright earth; he wanders, honored by neither gods nor men.
(Homer, *Iliad* 24. 527–533)

The view of human life here is radically different from what we have seen in the poem until now. The competitive, hierarchical model on display in books 1–23 emphasizes what separates one man from another. In book 1, Achilles insisted that as he was the best fighter, he should get the biggest share of the spoils, whereas Agamemnon claimed primacy because of his political position. Now Achilles can see only what connects one man to another, their powerlessness to change or refuse the gifts of the gods. And of course the most significant "gift" of all is human mortality.

Achilles builds the second speech around another mythical image, Niobe, the woman who compared herself to the goddess Leto, mother of Apollo and Artemis. The goddess had two children, she said, but she had twelve, six boys and six girls. In response to this outrage, Apollo killed all the boys, and Artemis all the girls. Niobe is turned to stone, a rock in the mountains, but in her grief she weeps still, in streams that run down the face of the rock. Before and after this vignette, Achilles urges Priam to eat and drink, for even Niobe, in her unending grief, remembered to eat. We see that this speech, like the first, is an attempt to console Priam for his loss, urging him to sit and take nourishment with Achilles. That the two take a meal together signals that they have both accepted consolation for the death of those they loved and have decided to rejoin human society. The poem ends quietly, with the burial of Hector in Troy, followed by a great banquet in the palace of Priam.

Separation and Return; Mortality and Manhood

In the story of Achilles as Homer tells it, we see two narrative patterns at work, the separation and return of the hero, and the separation of a boy from his mother and his evolution into a man. Homer's complex poem brings the two patterns together so that each illuminates and enriches the other. The first implies change followed by a reassertion of stability. The hero travels, literally or figuratively, to some new place, encounters experience unavailable to ordinary mortals, and returns to share this experience in a way that may change the world. The second pattern seems to require a linear, one-way journey from childhood to maturity, from the protecting nurture of the mother to the more perilous world of the father. But as Achilles's journey shows us, the movement into his father's world is in fact a "return," from the young man's illusion of a self-created life fueled by human achievement to the community of human suffering, symbolized by the shared limit of death.

Seeing how the two patterns reinforce each other allows a fuller understanding of how the Greeks conceived of a masculine life. The obsession with competition, which characterizes so much of the *Iliad,* is an enduring feature of Greek culture, visible in their athletic games, their sometimes treacherous politics, and even in their dramatic festivals, which featured not just performances, but a contest between three playwrights. The emphasis on *separation,* in both the hero story and the model of a lifecycle, reflects this central preoccupation. To grow up, a man must stand apart not only from his mother but from his fellows. Human achievement, according to this perspective, is always to be measured in *difference,* who is the fastest, the most handsome, the richest. The quarrel between Achilles and Agamemnon highlights this way of looking at human achievement. Not only do the two men compete for the most honor, symbolized by possessions, but they see their contest as a zero-sum game. That is, they—and all the other warriors—assume that there is a finite amount of honor available, so that if one man gets more, then someone else gets less.

Achilles, with his semidivine nature and abundant physical gifts, would seem to be an example of a man fully equipped for success in this system. And yet, Achilles does not prosper in the world of the poem. As he pursues honor and status among his fellows, he becomes more and more isolated, the price of distinction in a competitive society. In response to Patroclus's death, he veers away from all human society, becoming at once more godlike and more bestial in his actions. The pursuit of distinction, the effort to separate himself from other men, which the society of the poem seems at first to validate, leads Achilles toward a dismal self-involvement, powered by guilt and self-pity. At the beginning of book 24, after the funeral games for Patroclus, we see the fruits of his quest for greatness:

The games broke up, and the soldiers scattered,
returning to the swift ships. They thought of eating,
and to enjoy sweet sleep. But Achilles,
remembering his dear friend, wept, nor did sleep,
all-subduing, take him; rather he turned here and there,
longing for the manliness and strength of Patroclus,
all they dared together, all they suffered,
crossing through battles and the punishing waves.
Remembering these things, he let fall a swelling tear,
lying now on his side, and then on his back,
and then face-down. Then standing up
he would wander aimlessly along the shore, nor did dawn,
shining over sea and land, escape his notice.
But then he would yoke his swift horses to the chariot,
and bind Hector to be dragged behind the chariot,
and dragging him three times around the tomb of Patroclus,
he would stop again by his hut, and leave the body
face-down on the sand. (Homer, *Iliad* 24. 1–18)

Here we see Achilles in a self-created hell, trapped by his own feelings, looking for relief by abusing the corpse of his enemy. But because the poem has symbolically connected Hector and Achilles through the latter's armor, this savagery is also directed inward, a vivid picture of self-loathing. The only escape for him from his torment is to let go of his desire to escape the inherent limits of human life, and "return" to humanity. By letting go of the corpse, he lets go of his impossible dreams of glorious separation; the body of Hector also reflects Achilles's own mortal existence, embodied in the fragile vessel of flesh. By letting Hector's soul find rest, he frees his own soul.

THE ARC OF A MAN'S LIFE II: TENSIONS IN THE LIFECYCLE

A man's life, as it is dramatized in the outsized, heroic acts and thoughts of Achilles, reflects most of the characteristic tensions inherent in the Greek conception of masculinity. To grow up, a boy must find a way to separate from the protected world of childhood, which is represented by his mother. Going out from the household, run by women, into the public world of men requires him to achieve some distinction among his peers. This imperative fits well, as we have said, with the Greek tendency to elevate competitive virtues—strength, beauty, fighting skill, speaking ability—above virtues such as compassion and cooperation. These competitive, or *agonal* (from *agōn*, meaning "struggle") features of Greek society would have been useful in the period from 750–500 B.C.E., when Greeks lived primarily in small, tribal kingdoms, on the mainland of Greece or along the coast of what is now Turkey, where we think the Homeric epics might have been originally composed. All the warriors of Homer's *Iliad* are themselves minor kings of their individual cities. The topography of the Greek mainland in particular favors such small, independent kingdoms, dominated as it is by mountains, making travel and communication over land difficult.

At the same time, Achilles's difficulties suggest a keen awareness of the penalty for overvaluing competitive virtues and accomplishments. First of all, there is the obvious problem of living with others in any kind of communal setting, which would require cooperation. This particular challenge is explored, as we will see, intensively in Athenian tragic drama, in which there is a characteristic clash between the perspective of the hero, often embodying traditional heroic values, and the chorus, representing in many cases the values of the emerging democracy. Joseph Roisman has recently offered the following ideology of manhood as it can be found in the orators of the fifth and fourth centuries B.C.E. in Athens:

The typical positive male image in the speeches is that of an adult male (*anēr*), a loyal and useful citizen or leader of his *polis* (city-state), free in origin and way of life, willing to rank public interest over personal needs, courageous in war and politics, competitive within approved boundaries, helpful to friends and community, zealous of honor, considerate in the use of power, fulfilling familial duties, truthful, hardworking, careful, practical, intelligent, guided by reason, and able to control his appetites. The bad or wicked Athenian was disgraceful and treated others hubristically (insolently), aggressively, and inconsiderately. He gave way to pleasures or any desires that a man was supposed to control, which often led to sexual misconduct, wasting of resources, violence, or other forms of wrongdoing. He was self-centered in his relations with family, or the city, or even a destroyer of his *oikos* (household) or the state. He was slavish in origin or character, and cowardly or rash on the battlefield, in the political arena, or in his interaction with other men.[2]

As we have said, the hero illuminates the bounds of propriety by crossing over them.

But Achilles's problem goes beyond the clash between the individual and society. The function of the second self figure in the *Iliad* suggests that to pursue distinction among one's fellows through competition can lead to a crisis *inside* the hero, as the drive to win stifles a capacity and need for relationships, for connection to others. The personal hell that Achilles inhabits at the beginning of book 24 is, in this perspective, the reward for total victory.

Demeter and Persephone: A Different Voice

The *Iliad* gives us a rich understanding of certain key elements in a man's life, as the Greeks saw it. There are women in the story of course, but they are always under the control of men, and their lives appear in the shadow of masculine imperatives. Thetis falls in line with Zeus's plans in spite of her attachment to her son; the concubines over whom the heroes fight in book 1 are essentially chattel, goods interchangeable with horses or tripods; even the women in the Trojan royal family, Hecuba, the queen, Andromache, Hector's wife, and Helen, Paris's wife and the cause of the entire war, although sympathetically drawn and full of interest as human beings, are finally part of the property that men must protect. To appreciate fully the lifecycle implications of Achilles's journey, we need to look at a story that reflects the Greeks' view of a *woman's* life, the abduction and return of Persephone, daughter of the goddess Demeter, by Hades, god of the Underworld. The fullest version of this ancient myth is found in a poem from the seventh century B.C.E., the *Homeric Hymn to Demeter.*

The *Homeric Hymns* are a collection of 34 poems, two to five being 300–600 lines apiece, the rest much shorter. The poems are composed in dactylic hexameter, the meter of Homeric epic, and the language and style of the earliest of the hymns is close to Homer's. These similarities may explain why the collection came to be associated by the fifth century B.C.E. with the author of the *Iliad* and *Odyssey.* We now think, however, that although the earliest of these poems, the *Hymn to Aphrodite*, might be contemporary with the Homeric epics, the rest of the collection was composed later. The poems are called hymns because they are each addressed to a particular Greek god or goddess and use language associated with hymns of praise in the classical period. Each of the four longer hymns, to Demeter, Apollo, Hermes, and Aphrodite, tells a story or stories about the deity that reflects central ideas about him/her in Greek religious practice. As far as we can tell, the poems were not part of any formal religious ceremony, although each has material that might be related to cult practice.

In the case of the *Hymn to Demeter,* the religious context is the mystery religion, practiced at a shrine in Eleusis, a few miles from Athens, for more than a thousand years. Those initiated into the cult were apparently sworn to secrecy, so how exactly the narrative about Demeter and her daughter Persephone fits into the cult practice can never really be known. In any event, the parts of the story most helpful to our inquiry reflect a myth common in many places around the Mediterranean for nearly a thousand years before our hymn, of the fertility deity who is angered by someone, and in retaliation causes famine on the earth. We will also see that the *Hymn to Demeter* shares some significant narrative patterns with both *The Epic of Gilgamesh* and the *Iliad.*

Marriage as Rape and as Death

The story the hymn tells is of the abduction of Persephone, daughter of Demeter, the goddess of grain and agricultural fertility generally, by Hades, the god of the Underworld. After the prologue, we see Persephone and her playmates, all probably understood to be in their early teens, playing in a meadow filled with flowers. When Persephone plucks a narcissus flower, the earth opens up and Hades rolls out in his chariot, snatching her up as she screams and tries to resist, and plunging back into the Underworld. Demeter hears her daughter's cries for help, but too late. She eventually hears what happened to Persephone from Hekate, a minor hearth goddess, and Helios, the Sun god, who sees everything. The abduction was apparently authorized by Zeus, Hades's brother and Persephone's father, who prevailed on Gaia, the goddess of the earth, to send up the deadly narcissus as a trigger for the abduction.

That Zeus arranged for the removal of his daughter to the Underworld suggests two things right away: (1) Hades's snatching of Persephone, brutal though it may seem to us, is sanctioned by the patriarchal regime of the father of the universe; and (2) the abduction reflects in some way the marriage of a young girl—marriages in Greece were invariably arranged by the parents of the bride and groom. So we seem here to have a story that implicitly compares the experience of a young girl's marriage not only to a forcible abduction, but to a kind of death. The question arises immediately of how the author invites us to evaluate these events. Judging the tone of a poem composed 2,000 years ago is an uncertain project to be sure, and we should proceed with caution. Still, it is hard not to see the abduction as a violent imposition of male prerogatives on an unwilling and relatively helpless girl.

In response to the loss of her daughter, Demeter tears off her headband and veil, the traditional symbols of a woman's modesty and/or chastity, and roams the earth in distraction, refusing to eat, drink, or bathe. She returns to Hekate, who offers consolation, and Helios, who confirms that it was Zeus who sanctioned the abduction, and then counsels her to give up lamenting the loss of Persephone:

But cease your lament, goddess; you ought not
hold on in vain to unquenchable wrath. For among the gods
Hades, leader of many, your own brother from the same seed,
is not an unworthy husband. He won honor
when first the three-fold division was made.
He lives among those over whom he was allotted rule.
(*Homeric Hymn to Demeter* 82–87)

Helios serves as an apologist here for the male regime of Zeus: Demeter ought to let go of her grief and rejoice that Persephone will have such a powerful husband.

Nevertheless, Demeter remains angry at Zeus and leaves the company of the gods on Olympus. She disguises herself as an old woman, travels down to the earth, and sits by a well near Eleusis. The daughters of the king of Eleusis see her when they arrive at the well to fetch water and ask her who she is and why she has ended up in the countryside. She replies that she was forcibly abducted from Crete by pirates, but escaped them when they landed on the tip of the Attic peninsula, south of Eleusis, and wandered for days before arriving at the well. She asks the girls if they know of anyone in town who needs an old woman to work in the house, to clean or nurse children. They reply promisingly and head home to ask their mother, who agrees to hire the old woman. Once she has arrived at the house of the king, Demeter is offered a seat and a drink, both of which she initially refuses. After a special nonalcoholic drink is prepared and a special coverlet placed on the chair, she sits and drinks. Metaneira, the queen, hires her to nurse her son Demphoön, and the disguised goddess accepts.

Grief and Withdrawal

We see some familiar elements in the story. In response to Persephone's abduction, Demeter behaves like a typical grieving figure, mimicking the fate of her daughter, as Gilgamesh mimics the death of Enkidu by roaming the wilderness in animal skins. She tears off her veil, the symbol of her modesty, as if she too were raped, and duplicates her daughter's removal to a "lower" station by leaving Olympus and living among mortals as a servant, even telling a false story about being abducted herself. She refuses to eat, bathe, sleep, or have sex (she makes herself into an asexual old woman); and this reaction, of one grieving, confirms that Persephone's abduction is to be seen as a kind of death. The consolation scene, where the goddess is offered a seat and a drink, seems on the other hand to suggest that Demeter accepts consolation for the loss of Persephone and is ready to give up her grief. Also evident here is a doubling of the heroic withdrawal theme, as Persephone is "withdrawn" from her customary place among goddesses, and Demeter leaves Olympus. Once the pattern appears, we look for the second phase of destruction, followed by some kind of return.

The destruction in the wake of withdrawal comes in stages. Demeter nurses the child with nectar and ambrosia, and places him, magically protected, in the fire at night, all with the intent of making him immortal. The plan fails because Metaneira spies on the nurse and discovers, to her horror, Demophoön in the fire. Once found out, Demeter throws the child angrily to the floor, reveals herself as a goddess, and tells the terrified mother that her interference has cost her son immortality. She demands that a temple dedicated to her be built to honor her so as to appease her wrath.

The goddess seems to have been trying to replace Persephone with another immortal child. This gambit may explain why the consolation of Demeter appears at first to be successful: she could let go of her desire for Persephone if a substitute were available. (Exactly what significance the special nature of the drink and coverlet have, we cannot finally know, although it is tempting to see some reflection of the cult practices of the Eleusinian mysteries here.) After being discovered, Demeter still refuses to return to Olympus, staying in her new temple in Eleusis, and she raises the stakes for mortals (and for gods: if there are no mortals, the gods have no one to worship them and offer sacrifices) by refusing to let any crops grow on the earth. The destruction caused by Demeter's withdrawal expands now, from the local consequences in Eleusis to starvation for the entire human race and consequent disruption of the gods' tribute. Clearly, Demeter is not yet ready to give up her grieving for Persephone.

Demeter's behavior is beginning to cause significant trouble for the gods, and Zeus sends Iris to try to get her to relent and return to Olympus. This embassy fails, as do those of several more deities. Zeus then sends Hermes to Hades, telling his brother that he must send the girl back to her mother, so that she will allow fertility to return to the earth. Hades obeys his brother, but craftily gets Persephone to eat a pomegranate seed. The poet tells us this trick ensures that Persephone will spend at least some time in the Underworld, and Hades, when sending her off, envisions himself continuing as her husband, and her being worshipped as mistress of the dead. One common folk tale has it that anyone who eats with the dead must stay in the Underworld. Although the poet says nothing about Persephone refusing food up until this point, it may be that the seed is the first food the girl has accepted since being abducted, so that the gesture reflects some acceptance on her part of her connection to Hades and the "death" of her childhood. The pomegranate is also associated with blood, death, and sex, so that Persephone's eating of it may symbolize her initiation into sexuality as a "bride."

The joyous reunion of mother and daughter follows. After they embrace, Demeter questions Persephone closely about whether she accepted food from Hades. If she did not, then she can remain with her mother above the earth; if she did eat, then she must spend one-third of the year, the winter, with her husband in the Underworld, and two-thirds with her mother. Persephone then retells the story of her abduction and admits eating the seed, but swears that Hades forced her to eat it against her will. Persephone's description of the eating of the seed differs somewhat from what the poet tells us earlier, when Hades is said to feed her *lathrē*, "secretly," not forcibly. The question of Persephone's own desires in the matter is thus left somewhat unresolved, one part of a rather complex characterization of the young girl's motives in the poem.

Zeus confirms that Persephone will have to spend one-third of the year with her husband in the Underworld. Demeter agrees and allows the crops to return. The poem ends with Demeter instructing the mortals in Eleusis about how her rites are to be conducted in the temple, and the picture of mother and daughter happily living on Olympus. The similarities to the story of Achilles in the *Iliad* are clear enough here. An angry figure withdraws, causing great suffering, and initial attempts to appease him/her fail. Likewise, the "return" phase of the pattern brings about for both Achilles and Demeter a rejoining of their customary society. Grief and consolation are central to both stories. Perhaps more important for our purposes, however, are the similarities and differences between Achilles and Persephone as models for growing up.

Persephone Grows Up

To move toward mature adulthood, young Greek men were to leave home and the sheltering nurture of their mothers and engage in the public world of their fathers in politics, war, or work. The comparable journey for a girl was from the house of her parents to the house of her husband, not from private to public but from one private venue to another, from the control of one male to that of another. Nevertheless, marriage is seen as a critical moment in the maturing of a girl. By looking at how the poem represents this moment and its consequences for Persephone in the context of its traditional narrative patterns, we can see at least one example of how the Greeks saw the shape of a woman's life.

I have said that tone is difficult to establish in a poem so far removed in time, but it seems clear that this part of Persephone's "marriage" to Hades is meant to emphasize the fear of a young girl when she is removed from her childhood home and thrust into a relationship with a more powerful male. We might say that this version of the myth is told from the point of view of the mother and daughter, not the husband and his allies. Whereas separation from the mother was seen by the Greeks as critical to the maturing of a young man, this poem suggests that for Greek girls, separation from the mother could be traumatic and potentially damaging. Like other young girls, Persephone is given away to her husband by her father, but here she is tricked by the alluring flower, and snatched away against her will. The setting for the abduction, young girls frolicking in the countryside, is in fact a typical situation for abduction or rape to occur in Greek myth.

Patriarchy is portrayed as potentially tyrannical in the poem and is reinforced by male solidarity. Helios is kind to Demeter in her grief, but urges her to be grateful that Persephone has such an admirably powerful husband. Demeter herself, of course, as a goddess, has her own kind of power. Her attempt to appropriate Demophoön, the royal prince of Eleusis, as a substitute for her lost daughter might in fact be seen as a parallel "abduction." But since we understand that Demophoön will not be harmed but helped by his time in the fire, Demeter's nursing is characterized—at least for us if not for the child's mother—by gentleness, not by the violence of Persephone's abduction. Likewise, from the point of view of both gods and mortals in the story, for him to have become immortal would not make Demophoön a victim, as Persephone's fate does her. In fact, were Demeter to have been successful, Demophoön's transformation would have reversed Persephone's in one sense, for he would go from a limited, death-bound existence to immortality, whereas she goes from carefree immortality to the land of the dead.

The eventual compromise reached by Zeus and Demeter suggests that, for a young girl as opposed to a young man, the bond with her mother must be preserved to some extent and that the demands of the husband be balanced by the need for continuing connection to the mother. To put it another way, separation must be balanced by attachment. Whereas the young heroic male initially defines himself by how autonomous he is, how free to impress his will out into the world, Persephone's example seems to accord more weight to what we might call *relational* values in assessing a successful evolution into maturity. Here we need to think about the importance of the underworld as a symbol in this poem. We have seen that at first, being forcibly torn from her mother feels like a death to Persephone, and Demeter's griev-ing response confirms this understanding. She is, after all, going to live in the land of the dead. At the same time, the significance of the pomegranate seed as her first meal with her husband makes a further connection between sexuality and death.

This latter relationship demands further thought. Adult sexuality would mean the "death" of childhood, so this is one more way that Persephone's marriage to Hades clearly marks that boundary. And of course the meta-phorical identification of sex and death is both a very old feature of Western culture that persists to this day. But if we think about Persephone's expe-rience in the light of male patterns of maturing, we come immediately to the central importance of mortality as a source of meaning in human life generally. If Persephone were to stay exclusively with her mother, she would be essentially leading the life of a god, changeless and carefree. As we have seen, this existence is viewed by the Greeks as not only unavailable but even meaningless and morally trivial: if your life never ends, nothing you do mat-ters. Making some accommodation with the fact of mortality—which is one way to view Persephone's time in Hades with her husband—is just as impor-tant for women as for men, in this story at least.

Another way to think about the function of mortality in the meaning of human life is as an issue of *responsibility.* In the lives of both men and women, as Greek myth seems to present them, a critical moment in the journey to maturity comes with the reestablishment of *attachment* to others. In each case, the bond with one's mother offers unconditional love and affirmation of the child's desires, but the function of that bond within the larger context of maturation is different for each. For men, responsibility to others appears as movement beyond the illusion of heroic autonomy and isolation, beyond a self-involvement that is supported by the mother's unquestioning support and love, to a reaffirmation of one's membership in and responsibility to the human race, a perspective associated with the father; for women, respon-sibility to one's husband and his world must be followed by a reassertion of responsibility to care for oneself, as represented by the bond with one's mother. The danger for a man in failing to complete the journey to maturity is in losing touch with his compassion, his attachment to the community of fellow mortals; the danger for a woman is in losing touch with herself, of being entirely subsumed by her obligations to her husband.

Nature and Culture, Masculine and Feminine

Another telling difference between the stories of Achilles and Demeter is the role of the natural world and its rhythms in each. When Demeter is deprived of her daughter, the entire earth is rendered sterile; Persephone goes to the land of the dead at the end of the fall, and returns in the spring, a reflection of the death and rebirth of the earth and all that grows there. This feature of the Demeter and Persephone story is not surprising, for in the patriarchal culture of ancient Greece, women were thought to be more closely connected to the world of nature than men. And because, as we have seen, human civilization was understood to be the product of the imposition of human intelligence on the power of nature, the actions of Zeus and Hades might be thought of as "civilizing" Persephone. The hymn would be, in this perspective, the same kind of story as is portrayed by Gilgamesh and Enkidu conquering the monster of the Cedar Forest.

But we have seen that the poem presents the "marriage" from the perspective of a young girl, not that of the dominant patriarchal culture, so we are not encouraged to see the events as the triumph of human civilization over nature. Hades and Zeus do not appear heroic in the story. On the contrary, Demeter is the heroic figure, withdrawing, causing destruction, and returning with bounty. And because the whole earth and all its inhabitants are her beneficiaries, we are justified in seeing a comprehensive message in the poem: for the cosmos to be fruitful and harmonious, there must be a balance between the masculine urge to impose order on the powers of nature, and through that order to articulate new meaning, and the feminine need to preserve connection and continuity. This model for the universe reflects on a large scale what ancient civilizations saw as the desirable shape for an individual human life.

CONCLUSION: THE LIMITS OF HEROISM

We have said that the hero story is the best place to look for the ideals that ancient Mediterranean societies used to define the arc of a man's life. In looking at *The Epic of Gilgamesh* and Homer's *Iliad*, we have also confirmed that although the hero's life shows us the contours of masculinity, it does so through an outsized figure, whose excesses are revealing but not naturalistic. Of particular importance for us is the recognition in those stories that the fully mature male must embody both masculine and feminine traits, as those civilizations defined them. The competitive drive to distinguish oneself from others, if it is not tempered by connection to others, is both destructive and self-destructive. At the same time, the carefree, unlimited existence of the gods, although it often seems to represent the ultimate fulfillment of human desires, is shown in the hero story to be finally meaningless and morally trivial. Only the existence of limits on human action and thought creates meaning.

The kind of story we have been looking at, insofar as it relates to the human lifecycle, represents symbolically, not naturalistically—the *Iliad* covers only 50 days or so—issues that arise in what we would now think of as the period from young adulthood to middle age. Achilles begins, in book 1, with the perspective of an adolescent boy, tied to his mother and self-involved. His eventual encounter with, and acceptance of, limit, especially that of human mortality, is a stage that we now see as a kind of gateway to middle age. Childhood on the one hand, and old age on the other, are not usually included in the perspective of the hero story. We must look elsewhere for evidence of how the ancient world understood these parts of a man's life. We will begin at the beginning.

NOTES

1. Translations of *The Epic of Gilgamesh* are from Kovacs 1985.
2. Roisman (2005), 7.

Two

Young Men

The special delights of childhood, the innocent pleasures enthroned by the Victorians, are not much in evidence in the literature of classical antiquity. More common are stories about divine babies like Hermes with special powers, who spring from their mother's loins and into the adult world in a single bound:

And then Maia bore a child, ingenious, wily,
a thief, cattle rustler, leader of men,
spy in the night, doorway watcher, who would soon
reveal wondrous works among the deathless gods.
Born at dawn, he was playing the lyre at noon,
and stealing the cattle of farworking Apollo by dusk. . .
After he jumped from his mother's immortal womb,
not long did he linger in his holy crib;
springing up he went after Apollo's herd,
leaping over the threshold of the high-roofed cave. (*Homeric Hymn to Hermes* 13–23)

Apollo, too, makes a bold entrance:

Apollo jumped into the light, and the goddesses shrieked.
Then, noble Apollo, the goddesses bathed you in clear water,
reverently, with pure intent, and wrapped you in a white mantle,
gossamer and fresh, with a golden swaddling band tied around.
Nor did his mother nurse Apollo of the golden sword,
but Themis fed him nectar and lovely ambrosia
from her own hands, and Leto was glad, since
she bore a strong son who wields the bow.
But when you finished the immortal food, Phoibos,
not long did the golden band hold you as you struggled,
nor did the bonds restrain you, but their ends came loose.
(*Homeric Hymn to Apollo* 119–129)

From these and other stories, we may conclude that, in contrast to the sentimentalizing picture of childhood found in nineteenth-century Europe and America, those infants who were thought by the Greeks to be especially blessed could skip over the shortcomings of childhood altogether, assuming adult powers. In the strongly patriarchal cultures of the ancient Mediterranean, it is perhaps not surprising that the state most prized was that of the adult male, the time when a man was most able, physically and emotionally, to exhibit control over himself and his world. As usual, the nonliterary sources for attitudes toward childhood and adolescence are almost entirely from the elite classes in Athens of the fifth and fourth centuries B.C.E. In that democratic city-state at least, we find a tendency to judge children against the standards for adults. Plato and Aristotle usually group children with women, slaves, and animals as inherently inferior, physically weak, morally incompetent, and mentally incapable.

COMPETING TO SURVIVE: HERMES THE SUPERBABY

These attitudes do not, of course, mean that Greeks did not love their children or want them to be happy in their youth, only that the experience of male children at least was judged primarily as a preparation for the ideal of manhood rather than an existence interesting in and of itself. Thus the most compelling narratives about youth from the ancient world usually show adolescent males moving toward the threshold of adulthood. One partial— and charming—exception is the *Homeric Hymn to Hermes*, a sixth century B.C.E. poem quoted previously. Hermes is, as we noted, quick to assume the powers of older males, but he can also slip back into his infancy if it suits his nefarious purposes. After having invented the lyre by noon on his first day, slipped out in the night, stolen Apollo's sacred herd of cattle, sacrificed some and eaten a few others, he wafts magically back through the keyhole of the door to his cave:

In haste glorious Hermes came to his crib,
wrapping the swaddling around his shoulders
like a little baby, playing with the covers with
his hands and knees and keeping the lovely
lyre on the left side of the crib. (*Homeric Hymn to Hermes* 150–153)

His mother, the nymph Maia, is neither fooled nor amused. Where has he been? Apollo is going to tie him up and drag him away. At this rate, he'll end up living the life of a bandit. He is nothing but trouble! Hermes answers in what would be recognizable to any modern parent as the voice of a teenager. Why is she treating him like an ignorant child? He is not scared of her. On the contrary, he is the only one in the family (of two, effectively: Zeus is the absent father) who knows how to get them out of their cave in the sticks and onto Mount Olympus with the other gods, where everyone is rich. He will go to his father and demand to be treated like his big brother Apollo! If Zeus does not give him what he wants, he will become the king of thieves. Apollo better not try to stop him, or he'll steal the tripods and lots of other things from his sanctuary at Delphi. Just watch!

While they argue, Apollo discovers that his cattle are missing. He tracks the thief back to his cave and bursts in, demanding justice. Hermes dives under his blankets, but to no avail. Apollo wastes no time:

Listen kid, lying there in your cradle, show me the cattle,
and quick! Or you and I will soon part ways, and it won't be nice.
I'll throw you straight into dusky Tartarus, bitter and
gloomy, with no way out! And don't think your mother
or father will get you back into the light. No!
You'll wander around down there, king of the babies.
(*Homeric Hymn to Hermes* 254–259)

Hermes is not cowed:

Son of Leto, those are harsh words you speak.
And you've come here looking for cattle from the fields?
I haven't seen them or heard anything, not a word.
I don't know anything to tell, and wouldn't get a reward for telling.
Do I look like a cattle rustler to you?
This isn't my business; I have other things to do.
Sleep and my mother's milk, that's what I care about,
having blankies and warm baths.
I hope nobody finds out where this charge came from!
It would be pretty surprising for the gods to hear that
a newborn baby got through the doorway
with cattle from the fields. You're talking nonsense!
I was born yesterday; my feet are tender and the ground is rough.
If you want, I'll swear a big oath on the head of my father:
Not guilty!
And I haven't seen anybody else stealing your cattle either,
whatever cows are anyway. I've only heard rumors.
(*Homeric Hymn to Hermes* 261–277)

Apollo is amused, but not fooled. As he scoops up his baby brother and heads toward Olympus, Hermes sends forth an "omen" from his belly. We are well outside the normal bounds of heroic verse here. The remainder of the poem is taken up with an audience before Zeus on Olympus, where Hermes gives another masterful speech, and Apollo again comes across as the stolid dupe of his younger brother's clever thievery. Zeus is delighted by his new-found son and orders the two siblings to resolve their differences amicably. Hermes gains his objective of moving into the company of the gods on Olympus in return for the lyre and the music it makes.

Hermes is the only baby protagonist of an entire poem in Greek literature. On the one hand, we do have a fleeting glimpse of a child's existence; at the same time, the ironic humor in the story comes from the distance between the expectations raised by his looking like a baby and his fully adult cleverness. The portrait is not really about Hermes the baby, but mirrors instead—in a humorous way—the story of a young man's arrival at the threshold of adult-hood. The poem's focus on competition, however, puts us in contact with a central element in all models of Greek masculinity, childhood being no ex-ception. From the beginning of his life, a boy born to Athenian parents faced judgment and might be found wanting. Newborn babies had to be formally accepted into the family by the head of the household (*kurios*). The factors influencing judgment are not specified in any particular case, but probably included gender—girls would be rejected more often—and optimum family size. Two ceremonies marked this acceptance, the *amphidromia*, "walk-around," in which, on the fifth or seventh day after birth, the father carried his son around the hearth and sacrifices were performed, and the *dekaté*, "tenth day," a somewhat more festive celebration on the tenth day after the birth. This occasion was open to outsiders and included more sacrifices, as well as dancing and feasting.

As he progressed toward manhood, the Athenian male continued to encounter official rites of passage, presided over by his father and other adult males. Entries into the *phrata*, "tribe," and *genos*, "clan," larger groups to which the family was affiliated by blood, were ritual occasions and seemed to occur at a fairly young age, although the exact age is not known. The *koureion*, "barber shop," a ceremony that seems to refer to the cutting of hair, possibly the topknot that tended to mark boys as opposed to men in Athens, probably took place at around the age of 14, and after around 500 B.C.E. was associated with a son's being enrolled by the father in the *phratra*. When a young man reached the age of 18, he could vote in the assemblies, but could not yet serve on juries or be a member of the Council of 500. Starting in the fourth century B.C.E., boys who had reached their 18th birthday were required to enroll in a two-year paramilitary training regimen, the *ephebeia*, working with physical trainers and weaponry instructors in the first year, and serving as guards on frontier posts in the countryside of Attica in the second year. The full extent of the duties in the program is not known, but may have included some ritual duties as well.

The evidence for these various rituals and civic milestones in the life of Athenian boys is not always secure, but for our purposes, what is important is the recurrent need to meet standards administered by other males. The constant pressure to measure up reflects, in turn, the relentlessly competitive nature of Greek masculinity. Boys also competed with each other in various ways at religious festivals, in choral contests, and of course in athletics, the last of these venues celebrated in the odes written by the Theban poet Pindar to commemorate the winners at various athletic festivals in Greece, at Olympia, and other sites around the mainland. Particular skills would be on display, but the underlying goal was always to learn and display mastery of one's body and, by extension, the capacity for controlling other people and things, an emblem of adult masculinity. Stories about this struggle for boys almost always feature the father as the first standard against which they are measured.

THE EDUCATION OF PRINCES I: HOMER'S *ODYSSEY*

The first and most famous story of a son's apprenticeship is in Homer's *Odyssey*. The first four books of the poem focus on Telemachus, the son of Odysseus, the king of Ithaka, born just before the latter's departure for the

Trojan War. Now, 20 years later, his mother Penelope is besieged by suitors, who assume that Odysseus—still not back from the war—is dead. He is, in fact, trapped on a remote island, the captive paramour of a nymph, Calypso. Athena, Odysseus's special protector, convinces her father Zeus to her favorite. Meanwhile, she will go to Ithaka to rouse Telemachus from his late adolescent funk. She will urge him to confront the suitors, who are eating up all of Odysseus's stores, and send him to Pylos and Sparta to find out about his father's condition and to win fame for himself. She arrives at the royal house disguised as Mentes, an old friend of Odysseus. Telemachus, brooding among the suitors, is the first to see her:

Godlike Telemachus saw her first of all;
for he sat among the suitors, troubled in his heart,
imagining that his dear father would appear from somewhere,
making the suitors scatter all through the house,
and so would win honor and rule over his possessions.
Sitting with these thoughts among the suitors, he saw Athena.
He stepped straight to the doorway, angry in his heart
that the stranger was left standing at the entrance. Standing close
he took her right hand, received the bronze sword
and addressed her, speaking winged words:
"Welcome, stranger. You will be treated well among us.
When you have tasted food, you can say what you need."
(Homer, *Odyssey* 1. 113–124)

The scene is full of imperatives for Telemachus. Because his father is gone, there is no male head of the household, and the greedy suitors have moved in to profit from the resulting disorder. As the king's son, Telemachus should step in and restore order, but he seems powerless, stuck in his gloomy fantasies of Odysseus lying dead on some deserted beach. Athena could have appeared to him as herself and surely gotten some action. That she chooses to disguise herself as a man emphasizes for us that her mission is at least in part about nudging Telemachus over the threshold into manhood, where he can summon the necessary authority to assert control over the suitors and his inheritance as a man. Whatever he finds out about his father, Telemachus must leave adolescence and enter male adulthood. If his father is dead, he must be ready to step up as the leader in Ithaka; if Odysseus returns alive, Telemachus must be ready to stand beside him and help him rout the suitors. Athena wants him to do two things, as we have seen: confront the suitors and travel to Pylos and Sparta. Both are loaded with significance for Telemachus's journey toward manhood.

The showdown with the suitors does not go well. After talking with the stranger, Telemachus goes up to his bedroom:

Then Telemachus went where his lofty bedroom had been built
for him, in a protected spot off the lovely courtyard,
and there he went to bed, turning over many things in his mind.
Eurykleia, the daughter of Ops, Peisander's son,
went with him, devoted to him, carrying flaming torches. . .

She bore bright torches for him, for she always loved him
very much, and nursed him when he was a baby.
(Homer, *Odyssey* 1. 425–429; 434–435)

Everything here signals Telemachus's lingering youth, the snug bedroom,
closed off from the main part of palace, his nurse lighting the way. The next
morning, he calls the first assembly since his father's departure. On his way,
we hear that he was accompanied by two "swift-footed hounds." In Homeric
epic, when a man is in his rightful position of masculine authority, he is accompanied by two male servants. Telemachus can manage only dogs so far
and is not ready to be in charge, as the events in book 2 of the poem make
clear. His speech in the assembly begins with a recounting of the suitors'
disgraceful behavior in the royal house, lounging around all day, eating and
drinking from the household stores. We might expect him then to threaten
retaliation, but instead, he is abject:

There is no man such
as Odysseus here, who could drive destruction from the house.
We are not the sort to drive anything off now. We'd be
shameful weaklings, and lacking in strength to defend.
I would chase them off myself, if the strength were in me. (Homer, *Odyssey* 2. 58–62)

He then begs the suitors to leave them alone and tearfully throws the scepter,
another symbol of masculine authority, to the ground.

Homer's portrait of Telemachus so far has made it clear that, although the
royal household desperately needs male leadership, he is not yet man enough
to play that role. The second part of Athena's plan will address this deficiency.
She helps Telemachus commandeer a ship and crew, so that he can sail down
the coast of the Peloponnesus to Pylos, where Nestor, Odysseus's comrade
from the Trojan War, is king. From there, he will travel overland to Sparta,
the home of Menelaus and his queen, Helen. In both places, he will meet
veterans from the war at Troy, comrades of Odysseus there. From them, he
will hear stories about his father's exploits at Troy and learn more about how
to be a man; by making himself known to them, he will gain the recognition
that is prerequisite for fame in the heroic culture of the poem.

Telemachus prays to the unknown deity who came to the palace to help
him. Athena, now in the disguise of "Mentor," another wise male counselor,
comes to him and pledges her support, saying he looks like someone who
can do what must be done:

Telemachus, you will be neither a coward nor unthinking,
if the broad strength of your father has been instilled in you,
such a man was he for accomplishing by words or deeds.
Nor then will your journey be in vain or unfinished.
But if you were not born from that man and Penelope,
then I do not expect you to achieve your goals.
For few sons are equal to their fathers,
more are worse; and few indeed are better.
But since you will be neither a coward nor unthinking,

nor has the mind of Odysseus entirely given out in you,
then there is hope for your plans to succeed. (Homer, *Odyssey* 2. 270–280)

She goes on to advise him to ignore the rash suitors and their plans for now and to concentrate on his journey. She will be with him, and his departure will be soon:

For such a companion am I for you, like a father,
who will outfit a fast ship for you, and go along myself. (Homer, *Odyssey* 2. 286–287)

Now the goddess's agenda becomes clearer still. To succeed, Telemachus must be the equal of his father; although few are able to reach this standard, he looks as if he might have what it takes. For now, Athena will stand in for Odysseus, leading him forth toward Pylos. She will be, in fact, Telemachus's "mentor." His adventures will offer many more such models.

One prominent negative example is already available in the suitors who are greedy, gluttonous, and oblivious to the standards for proper behavior. Their presence serves as a cautionary tale to Telemachus. In the poem's first scene, they party on with no regard for the stranger who has arrived at the palace door. It is left to Telemachus to properly receive the guest and offer food and drink. Hospitality is a major measure of moral worth in the *Odyssey*. Zeus is the god who looks after guests, and in this story those who fail to perform their duties as hosts or as guests—the relationship is reciprocal—usually suffer. That Telemachus steps up to fill the void left by the dissolute suitors is already a hopeful sign. He is careful to first offer the stranger food and drink and then ask who he is, where he is from, and what he needs.

The suitors' faults are many, but chief among them is their lack of self-control, symbolized concretely by gluttony and sexual exploitation of the palace servants. As we will see, Odysseus, by contrast, is famous for his self-mastery, able to keep his own counsel and refrain from indulging his appetites when they would make him vulnerable. This quality is given prominence right at the beginning of the poem, in the prologue:

Sing to me of the man of many turns, oh Muse, who
suffered much, when he destroyed Troy's holy citadel.
The cities and minds of many men he came to know,
and endured many pains on the sea and in his heart,
protecting his life and the homecoming of his companions.
But he did not save his companions, hard as he tried,
for they were destroyed by their own blind folly,
fools, who ate the cattle of Helios, Hyperion's son.
The god took away their day of homecoming. (Homer, *Odyssey* 1. 1–9)

We notice a surprising similarity implied here between the suitors, who are irredeemably bad, and the loyal companions of Odysseus, whom we might expect to appear in a more positive light. But as we have seen, control of oneself, which in turn becomes the basis for control of other people and things, is a fundamental requirement for manhood in Greek culture. That Odysseus's excellence eventually isolates him, as his companions fall victim to their unrestrained appetites in the course of the trip home, highlights another aspect of his masculinity. He surpasses all others and so is alone. The tension between a competitive drive for excellence and the need for communal interdependence is somewhat muted in the *Odyssey* because of the relatively top-down, aristocratic societies it describes. By contrast, as we will see, Athenian tragic drama, the dominant verbal art form during the emergence of the world's first democracy, focuses rather insistently on this inherent problem in the ancient Greek valorizing of competition.

Telemachus's Journey: Finding His Father

Telemachus and his crew sail through the night toward Pylos, on the southwestern coast of Greece. Athena sits beside her young charge and smoothes the way across the water. Making land the next morning, they immediately come upon Nestor, the king of Pylos, who is in the midst of a sacrifice to Poseidon, god of the sea. There is some irony here, in that we know—as Telemachus does not—that Poseidon is angry at Odysseus for blinding his son, Polyphemus the Cyclops, and will make Odysseus's homecoming as difficult as he can. At the same time, by participating respectfully in the rites, Telemachus may unwittingly help his father's case. In any event, establishing and maintaining proper relationships with the gods are prime responsibilities of Homeric males in positions of authority, so the visit immediately offers instruction.

As they approach the Pylians, Athena goes in front and coaches Telemachus. Go right up to the king, she says, and ask direct questions—this is no time for undue modesty. But Telemachus is still unsure of himself. How should he approach an elder? He has no experience with such discourse. We are reminded that his father has been absent since his infancy, and there has been no other male in authority from whom he could learn. Athena reassures him: he will make the right choices, guided by his own intelligence and also by "some god." As it happens, Peisistratus, the oldest son of the king, approaches them first, leading them to a seat and giving them a cup of wine. The young man is himself a model of decorum, addressing Athena:

Offer a prayer now, my guest, to the lord Poseidon.
For arriving here you've come upon his feast.
But when you've poured a libation and prayed, as is proper,
give the cup of honeyed wine to this man,
to pour out, since I think he'll offer a libation
too. All men have need of the gods. But
this one is younger than you, the same age as I.
Therefore I will give you the golden goblet first. (Homer, *Odyssey* 3. 43–50)

Deference to one's elders and knowledge of the proper rituals for right relations to the gods are requisite qualities for a young man entering on his masculine inheritance. Athena prays to Poseidon, then hands Telemachus the cup, and he prays "in the same way." His education is fully underway.

Next, Telemachus observes Nestor presiding over a meal, another occasion in Homeric poetry for the display of proper form. Once all have finished,

Nestor asks the strangers who they are, where they're from, what they want. Telemachus replies with his own lineage, then goes directly to a request for information about his father. Here Homer uses the word *kleos* for "information." By doing so, he creates a second level of meaning. Telemachus wants to know, on one level, what the "report" is on his father. But the second—and more frequent—meaning of *kleos* is "fame," the basis for a hero's reputation. Telemachus is after concrete information about what has happened to his father, but also about how to be a hero—more particularly, how to be like his father.

Nestor replies with a long story, characteristic for him, about how the various Greek warriors made their way home from Troy. As it happens, he knows nothing about Odysseus's fate after he left Troy. He does say more than once how crafty Odysseus was at Troy and that he deferred to the authority of Agamemnon, the overall leader of the Greek expedition by not leaving for home against the leader's wishes. And the speech does highlight what is perhaps the most pressing imperative for Telemachus, to act against the suitors. Nestor recalls—in this speech and then in a second, pressed by Telemachus for more details—how Orestes, Agamemnon's son, avenged his father's murder by Aegisthus, Agamemnon's cousin and the illicit lover of his mother Clytemnestra.

The story of Agamemnon's murder and the revenge exacted on Aegisthus and Clytemnestra by the king's children forms the basis for several plays in Athenian tragedy. There the agency of Clytemnestra in the murder and the subsequent horrors of matricide are brought into prominence. In the *Odyssey*, Clytemnestra, although a model for the bad wife, does not join Aegisthus in the murder of Agamemnon. The focus here is on the danger of a wife "going bad" when left alone by an absent warrior, and on the role of the good son in avenging the murder of his father. This set of events is present all through the poem, a paradigm against which to measure the behavior of both Penelope and Telemachus.

After another elaborate sacrifice the next morning, to Athena this time, Telemachus leaves his sailors in Pylos and heads overland for Sparta, accompanied in the chariot by Peisistratus. Athena makes her excuses and leaves the two boys to make the journey alone. The visit has been an education for Telemachus in many ways. Although he did not learn much about his father's present situation, he has witnessed and participated in several communal events at Pylos. Each has modeled for him the functioning of a healthy society in the world of the poem, with a strong male, like Odysseus a veteran of the Trojan War, taking the lead, and his son behaving in the proper way toward both his family and guests. The *Odyssey* is full of scenes of feasting and other communal rituals that display, or in some cases imply by their omission, proper relations between members of the community and strangers and their hosts. The import of such scenes goes beyond the highlighting of good manners. Ultimately, what is on display is the flow of power and responsibility through human societies. And in a patriarchal culture, this process demands an empowered male, in control of himself and secure in his position, as the source of authority from which power proceeds. Nothing about the chaos in Ithaka has offered this model to Telemachus, and so he must go elsewhere to find it.

Sparta, too, is in the midst of important ceremonies, in this case, wedding celebrations for both the daughter and the son of Menelaus. Hermione, the child of Menelaus and Helen, is to be the bride of Achilles's son, Neoptolemus; and Megapenthes, whose mother is a slave, is marrying a local girl. Another facet of a healthy family is on display here, as we see Menelaus and Helen celebrating the arrival of their children at the threshold of adulthood, something not available to Telemachus as long as his father is missing. As in Pylos, so here hospitality to strangers is a prominent theme. When the two boys arrive from Pylos, Sthenelaus, one of Menelaus's retainers, asks Menelaus whether he should welcome the newcomers or send them elsewhere. The question brings a strong rebuke from the king:

> You were not a fool before, Sthenelaus, son of Boethius,
> but now you're babbling like a little child.
> Surely we two enjoyed many feasts as guests
> of other men on our way back here; may Zeus
> prevent such misery hereafter. Come now, unharness
> the horses of the strangers, and bring the men here to feast.
> (Homer, *Odyssey* 4. 31–36)

The connection between immaturity and failure as a host is clear. Telemachus now receives another generous welcome, with food, bath, and then carefully polite questions from his host.

In contrast to his procedure at Pylos, Telemachus here does not immediately reveal his name. Menelaus recounts more stories of heroes returning from Troy, ending with a lament that he has been able to discover nothing about whether Odysseus is still alive or has died before reaching home. These words cause Telemachus to weep into his cloak, and although Menelaus concludes that his guest is the son of Odysseus, he decides to wait to let the boy identify himself. As it happens, Helen appears and immediately remarks that the visitor bears a striking resemblance to Odysseus. Menelaus now agrees, at which point Peisistratus confirms that although Telemachus is too discreet to say so, this is indeed the son of Odysseus. The point of all this reticence becomes clear when both Menelaus and Helen relate stories about Odysseus at Troy, each emphasizing how Odysseus surpassed all others in both self-control, restraining his comrades in the Trojan Horse when they wanted to cry out, and control of others, through disguise and deceit. In withholding his name, Telemachus may, as Peisistratus implies, simply be shy. But we will learn later in the poem that Odysseus consistently withholds his name when he arrives at a new place while trying to find out as much as he can about his hosts. Knowledge is power in the *Odyssey,* and Telemachus is apparently coming into his inheritance as an empowered male.

By far the largest section of the interlude in Sparta is taken up by another story from Menelaus, which he tells in response to Telemachus's direct request for information about Odysseus. On his journey home from Troy, Menelaus found himself blown far off course, making land eventually on Pharos, an island off the coast of Egypt. There he was stranded, as the gods kept the winds from blowing, angered because he had not made sufficient sacrifices to them. After 20 days, with food running out, Eidothea, a kindly sea nymph, appeared and took pity on him. She recommended that he ambush her father, Proteus, "The Old Man of the Sea," a follower of Poseidon. This creature, it seemed, could tell Menelaus how to get home and what the situation was in Sparta. But to make him do so, Menelaus and his men had to grab him and hold on, while he tried to escape them. What would make him especially hard to handle, she said, was his ability to change shape:

He will try to become every kind of creature that
moves on land; he will try to become water and blazing fire.
(Homer, *Odyssey* 4. 417–418)

Her warning was accurate: once in their grasp, Proteus changed into a lion, a snake, a leopard, a boar, then into water and finally a tree. The Greeks hung on, and eventually the creature gave them the information they wanted, including a report on the fates of three Greeks returning from Troy, the last being Odysseus.

Telemachus finally learns through this story that his father was last seen languishing on an island, the prisoner of another sea nymph, Calypso. One of Athena's two aims for Telemachus's mission seems to be fulfilled with this revelation. The second goal, for him to win glory for himself, will have to wait. Meanwhile, Menelaus's report on his adventures offers another model of manliness. As we have seen, civilization, as the Greeks understood it, was the product of imposing human order on the powerful forces of nature. Ancient Mediterranean mythology is full of stories about male heroes who found or preserve civilized order by taming some kind of monster. Gilgamesh and Enkidu kill the monster of the Cedar Forest; the Babylonian hero Marduk creates the earth by cutting Tiamat in half; Apollo founds his oracle in Delphi over the rotting remains of a serpent he has killed; Zeus establishes the Olympian regime by defeating Typhoeus, a storm god. Menelaus's taming of Proteus is squarely in this tradition: Proteus embodies the powerful and fluid multiplicity of nature; by controlling him, the Greeks extract knowledge about their future, how they can return to their human civilization. And, of course, the suitors, agents of chaos in the palace, would be an apt target for civilizing by Telemachus.

As Telemachus and Peisistratus prepare to return to Pylos at the end of book 4, the narrative shifts back to Ithaka, where we hear of Penelope's great distress at learning that her son has slipped out of the palace to make his journey. She, at least, is not ready for Telemachus to grow up, whatever Athena's plans may be. Her anxious response is natural enough for a mother but also recalls Thetis's nurture of Achilles, which, as we have seen, does not usually advance her son's progress toward manhood. Mothers in the heroic literature of Greece are an especially powerful example of the "detaining woman," whose seductive powers work to keep the hero from accomplishing his mission. Odysseus faces several such obstructive females, Calypso, Circe the witch, and the alluring Sirens. Like all heroic males, Telemachus must leave the potentially smothering attentions of his mother and come to terms with the world of his father. The journey to Pylos and Sparta is the first stage of this process, when Telemachus makes indirect contact with his father through the stories he hears. The second phase begins when he again reaches Ithaka.

Telemachus's Journey: Becoming His Father

After book 4, Telemachus recedes from view while Homer introduces us to Odysseus. Books 5–15 of the *Odyssey* recount all of Odysseus's adventures as he makes his way back to Ithaka. At the beginning of book 15, we see Telemachus again in Sparta, ready to make his way back to Pylos and then sail home. As it happens, he and his father arrive at almost the same time, as Telemachus's journey to manhood comes into phase with Odysseus's plans for routing the suitors. The reunion of father and son will take us to a new level in Telemachus's progress toward manhood. He will continue to learn from his father, but he must also begin to put his knowledge to use in the service of Odysseus's campaign to drive the suitors out of Ithaka. As this plot unfolds, a tension between father and son, which has been muted while Odysseus has been away, comes to the surface.

The imperative for Telemachus to grow into manhood implied, as we have seen, two possible outcomes. If Odysseus did not return, he had to be ready to step into the role of male head of the household in Ithaka, deciding his mother's future and disposing of the suitors. If Odysseus did survive, he would need to be ready to help his father address the chaos in the palace. When the second alternative comes to pass, it presents some problems, as it might begin to seem crowded at the top of the chain of command. The eventual resolution of this potential conflict comes at a climactic moment in the story. Meanwhile, father and son must meet face-to-face.

After landing, Telemachus does not head straight for the palace but, on the advice of Athena, detours to the humble country dwelling of Eumaeus, Odysseus's faithful swineherd. Odysseus himself has been guided by the goddess toward Eumaeus, but he is disguised as an old beggar, so that once he arrives at the royal palace, he will be able to observe the suitors without raising suspicion. The beggar has already made himself at home with Eumaeus when Telemachus arrives. The swineherd's greeting is effusive:

The swineherd stood up, amazed,
and the bowls, in which he had been mixing
sparkling wine, fell from his hands. He went to his lord,
and kissed his head and both his shining eyes,
and his hands. And he let fall a swelling tear.
As a father warmly welcomes his son,
who has returned from abroad after ten years,
his only son, full-grown, over whom he has suffered much,

so did the noble swineherd embrace and kiss
godlike Telemachus, as if he had escaped death. (Homer, *Odyssey* 16. 12–21)

Homer creates a curious kind of double vision here. Eumaeus is, for a moment, another surrogate father for Telemachus. At the same time, Telemachus is said to be his "lord" (*anax*), the word we would expect to be used of Odysseus. Telemachus continues his apprenticeship but also begins to have some of the authority of a grown man.

Telemachus enters the hut and encounters Odysseus, still disguised. After some preliminary niceties, Eumaeus says he will put the stranger in Telemachus's care. Having observed Nestor and Menelaus, Telemachus is now offered the chance to be a host himself. He declines at first, citing the chaos at the palace. The beggar expresses sympathy for the young man's plight but asks why he has not thrown the louts out of his house. Telemachus's new authority comes under scrutiny on two levels here, inside the frame of the story from Odysseus, and outside from us, as we are reminded of the example of Orestes, the "good" son of Agamemnon, who punished his mother's nefarious suitor, Aegisthus. In his answer to the beggar, Telemachus says he cannot by himself, being an only child, overcome the large number of suitors. He tells Eumaeus to go to the palace and let Penelope know that he is back safely.

So far, Telemachus displays much the same attitude toward the chaos in the palace as he did in the poem's opening scene, when Athena visited him disguised as "Mentes." He is disgusted but unable to take action. After Eumaeus sets off, Athena appears to Odysseus and says it is time to reveal himself to his son, so that he can be of help in the campaign against the suitors. She herself, she says, will be right beside them. Now comes the big moment. Athena restores Odysseus to his former stature, dark hair, standing straight, jaw square. Telemachus is taken aback:

You appear to be different, stranger, younger than before;
your clothes are different, too, and your skin has changed.
Surely you are some one of the gods, who hold wide heaven.
Be gracious, so we can give you sacred offerings,
and golden gifts, well-made. But be merciful to us. (Homer, *Odyssey* 16. 181–185)

Odysseus demurs: he is no god, but rather the very father over whom Telemachus has suffered so many pains. Odysseus kisses his son tearfully.

Telemachus is not convinced. This man cannot be his father, for without a god's help no mortal could change from old to young as he has. No, he must be a god, practicing magic. Indeed, answers Odysseus, it was a goddess, Athena, who transformed me: I am your father. Finally, Telemachus relents and the two embrace. There are more signs here of Telemachus's maturity. His skepticism in the face of Odysseus's claims reminds us of no one more than his father, famously reserved and cautious in the presence of strangers. This caution is another example of self-control. Presented with a man who claims to be his father, whom he has not seen in 20 years, Telemachus restrains himself, waiting for more proof.

In the plotting that ensues, Odysseus again calls on Telemachus to exhibit self-control. He will go to the palace, disguised again as the beggar, to reconnoiter. No matter how badly the suitors mistreat him, Telemachus must hold his temper. In doing so, Telemachus will continue to walk in his father's footsteps. The beggar himself will be attacked, verbally and physically, while in the palace; and Odysseus will hold himself in check, enduring seeming humiliation while he waits for the right moment to strike back.

Although he has been showing some signs of increased maturity since Pylos, the meeting with his father seems to have a striking effect on Telemachus. From now on, he will be much more assertive, both with his mother and with the suitors. The change is already evident in his first meeting with his mother after returning to the palace. In response to her affectionate but anxious questioning, he is firm:

Mother, do not stir up a lament, nor move the heart
in my chest, now that I have escaped utter destruction.
But climbing to the upper rooms with your maids,
go and wash, putting clean clothes on your body,
and offer to complete hecatombs to all the gods,
that Zeus might grant vengeance for what has been done to us.
I meanwhile will go to the place of assembly, so I
can summon my guest, who has followed me here.
Him I sent ahead of me with my godlike companions,
and told Peiraios to lead him to his house,
to give him honor and friendship, until I should come. (Homer, *Odyssey* 17. 46–56)

These are not the words of the tentative young man we met in book 1. Telemachus has stepped into the role for which Athena was preparing him. This is the first of several occasions when he asserts himself in talking to his mother. As the story moves to its climax, we also see him as the proper host, putting the suitors in their place when they abuse the beggar, but holding himself enough in check not to throw the revenge plans awry.

Penelope's future is linked explicitly to Telemachus's maturing, as we discover in book 18. Appearing before the suitors, she toys with them, recalling what she says were Odysseus's words to her when he left for Troy. If he had not yet returned from the war by the time Telemachus was grown up and sporting a beard, she should marry whomever she wished. This injunction adds another element to the so far submerged tension between father and son. Now Telemachus's coming to manhood is driving Penelope toward a decision about her future that implies abandoning hope of Odysseus's return and her departure from the palace.

Everything comes to a head in the contest in book 21 to string Odysseus's bow. Penelope, guided by an interview with the beggar and Odysseus's earlier instructions, decides to stage a contest for her hand. Whoever can string Odysseus's bow, which he left behind when leaving for Troy, and shoot an arrow through a row of axeheads will be her new husband. In a move that makes those of us familiar with Freud a little nervous, Telemachus declares that he will give it a try. Three times he fails, but on the fourth, he would have succeeded, Homer tells us, but Odysseus warns him off with a shake of his head. It is a delicious moment. Telemachus grumbles:

Blast! I must be a coward and feeble too,
or I'm too young and my hands cannot defend
against another man, when he starts a quarrel.
Never mind; you who are stronger than I am,
try the bow, and let's finish the contest. (Homer, *Odyssey* 21. 131–135)

The physical act of stringing the bow carries a heavy symbolic load. The linear progress of Telemachus toward manhood and the circular return of Odysseus to the status he enjoyed before leaving for Troy, as king, husband, father, and son, collide here. If Telemachus strings the bow, then Odysseus's return is—at least symbolically—too late. His son has moved into the position that manhood demands of him and has displaced his father. (Hello again, Dr. Freud.)

The emotional, psychological tension inherent in the father-son relationship reappears in the bow itself, as Telemachus strains to replace his father. We experience the scene on two levels at least, the surface of the plot, with Telemachus working in concert with his father, and the more submerged, unacknowledged sphere of intergenerational competition. When Telemachus obeys his father's warning, the two levels come back into phase: the bow can now eventually go to the beggar and the revenge plot proceed; Odysseus can reassume his powers, with his son still in the supporting role. When the male hierarchy is stabilized, the lessons in self-control that Telemachus has been learning reflect in an uncomplicated way his assumption of masculine maturity: by holding back with the bow, the son demonstrates the responsibility to a larger whole—in this case the royal household in Ithaka—that must always temper the self-assertion that fuels competition.

Conclusion: Harmony in the Palace

The rest of the story, as the *Odyssey* tells it, reaffirms the solidarity represented in the stringing of the bow. Odysseus and Telemachus, backed by Athena, kill the suitors and reassume control of the royal household. Odysseus and Penelope are reunited—after some hesitation on her part worthy of her mate—and the ghosts of the suitors are shown making their dismal way to Hades. Odysseus then goes to see his father Laertes, who has been relegated by the suitors to a wretched patch of land in the countryside. Instead of identifying himself to the old man immediately, Odysseus decides to test his own father, lying about his own return and reducing Laertes to groveling in the dirt. Although he does then relent, Odysseus seems gratuitously cruel here, and his behavior has never been adequately explained by commentators. For our purposes, we can at least say that the abuse gives us one last glimpse of the antagonism between males that is always near the surface in the competitive world of Greek masculinity, especially between fathers and sons. The last scene of the poem has Laertes, Odysseus, and Telemachus lined up side-by-side against the families of the suitors. Zeus and Athena then short-circuit this confrontation and the poem ends somewhat abruptly. We are left with that final tableau of three generations of males working in concert to defend the household, a visual representation of the restored harmony between generations.

In Telemachus's journey to manhood, we see some aspects of masculinity that the Greeks associated particularly with the transition from boyhood to manhood. The first is the centrality of the father-son relationship. Especially in a strongly patriarchal society, the good father offers to his son a model for how to move into the adult world, balancing the drive for dominance with the need for cooperation as a basis for social order. In the *Odyssey*, we first see Telemachus encountering and absorbing lessons from stories told about Odysseus by others: Nestor, Menelaus, and Eumeaus. At the same time, the societies of Pylos and Sparta, with their display of appropriately ordered meals, sacrifices, and their hospitable treatment of strangers, all presided over by strong males, show the young man what is missing in Ithaka. After book 16, the son may observe his father directly, while simultaneously putting what he has learned to work in the service of restoring the male hierarchy, and thus the harmony of the larger society, in Ithaka.

Among the qualities associated with masculine maturity in the *Odyssey*, the most prominent is that of self-control, as a method of self-protection in a potentially hostile world, and as the prerequisite for controlling other people and things. Learning to curb self-aggrandizement is especially crucial to young men, whose energy and lack of experience make them vulnerable to the overreaching that both Penelope's suitors and Odysseus's companions display. The use of knowledge as a means of manipulation and control is also particularly prominent. Odysseus is the master of this skill, always withholding knowledge about himself and learning as much about others as he can. The young man must balance his need for knowledge with discretion.

We see Telemachus progressing in just this way in the course of his journey from Ithaka to Pylos and Sparta and back again. In Pylos, his first stop, he reveals his name immediately, eager for news about his father; in Sparta, both Menelaus and Helen speculate that he might be Odysseus's son, but he declines to identify himself. Eventually Peisistratus reveals his name. Back in Ithaka, in response to his mother's anxious request for information on his trip, he refuses to talk right away, telling her to go upstairs and bathe first. Once the plotting to overthrow the suitors is underway, he is completely reliable as a keeper of secrets, from his mother, from the servants, and of course from the suitors.

The *Odyssey*'s emphasis on self-control and control of others as the most important elements of masculinity seems to contrast markedly with the lessons offered by the *Iliad* and its hero. There, passionate expression is the norm, especially in Achilles. His rage is the focal point for the plot, a frighteningly powerful force elsewhere found only in gods, not mortals. But the differences may not be as significant as they seem at first. Achilles is in fact a prominent example of one kind of immaturity in males, in his solipsism and refusal to accept limits on his own power. This tendency to narcissistic selfishness is abetted by his mother, who supports him in his prideful withdrawal and later thirst for vengeance. Like Telemachus, he must move away from his mother's protective nurture and come to terms with the world of his father. The lessons of the father in the *Iliad* also urge self-restraint, articulated specifically in the speech of Priam to Achilles in book 24, when the old man begs his son's killer to take pity on him and release the body of Hector. Priam's appeal is founded on his plea that Achilles remember his father, Peleus, who, like Priam, is missing his son.

The different masculine ideals we observe in the two poems has partly to do with the differing goals of the two narratives. The *Iliad,* as the first example we have of a *tragic* story, has as its goal the acceptance by the hero of human mortality. The *Odyssey,* by contrast, is the first *comic* narrative we know of, the goal of which is for the hero to survive at all costs. The hero of each story must exemplify those traits that will allow him to succeed according to the terms set by the form of the story. Thus Achilles, who is semidivine, represents the human urge to deny the natural limits imposed by time and nature, most particularly the limit of mortality: his mother is immortal, so why can't he, too, escape death? Odysseus, on the other hand, exemplifies the equally human desire to control other people and things, so as to survive. The less anyone knows about him, the smaller the chances of his being under his or her control. Disguise and deceit are seen as appropriate weapons for the comic hero, whereas the same qualities in the tragic hero only lead further away from the moment when he faces the ultimate truth about his own nature.

But these distinctions aside, to be a man Odysseus (and Telemachus) must, like Achilles, find a balance between his own needs and desires and the good of larger social groups of which he is a part. The secrecy and disguise work well in giving Odysseus the leverage to negotiate the challenges of his trip home and to defeat the suitors. But to finally restore harmony to his household, he must win back the confidence of Penelope. His attempts to do so after the slaughter of the suitors are at first unsuccessful. She is not ready to give herself to him without one last test: is he really Odysseus or just another of the many imposters who have tried to win her?

Odysseus, we learn, built his house around the trunk of an olive tree, which served as an anchor for his existence—appropriately enough, as the olive is the symbol of his divine patron, Athena. The very bed that he and Penelope sleep on uses the trunk as one of the bedposts. Penelope, in the presence of Odysseus and Telemachus, tells the servants to move the bed outside into the courtyard. Odysseus angrily objects: What man has moved his bed? How could he do it? He then tells the story of how he built the house and the bed, as justification for his anger and disbelief. Penelope is now convinced and receives him as her husband.

This is the first moment in the entire story that Odysseus loses his famous self-control. Penelope, unlike any of his most dangerous foes, has succeeded in forcing Odysseus to give in to his emotions. Manipulating others in the service of survival has served him well but to fully restore his household, he must allow himself to be vulnerable to those he loves. Although self-control is necessary for achieving mature manhood, when carried to an absolute extreme, this quality brings isolation and stifles the ability to function in society. The tension between individual excellence and communal health is always at the heart of Greek ideals of masculinity. In the aristocratic societies of the Homeric epics, which reflect the civilizations out of which they came, the tension is present but finally resolved. When we turn to the emerging Athenian democracy of the fifth century B.C.E., the balance is yet more precarious as the newly empowered citizens wrestle with what form their society will take. The mirror for this struggle is Athenian tragic drama.

THE EDUCATION OF PRINCES II: SOPHOCLES'S *PHILOCTETES*

The relationship between fathers and sons remains a central focus of Greek literature down through the fifth century B.C.E. Agamemnon and Orestes, Ajax and Eurysaces, Herakles and Hyllus all tread the stage of Athenian drama. Oedipus's troubles with both his father and his sons have left an enduring mark on Western culture. But the play most useful for our purposes here is Sophocles's late masterpiece, *Philoctetes,* produced in 409 B.C.E., three years before the playwright's death and five years before the final defeat of Athens by Sparta in the Peloponnesian War. The action takes place on Lemnos, an island in the Aegean Sea between Troy and the mainland of Greece, during the late stages of the Trojan War. The background for the play is that Philoctetes, a Greek warrior on his way to the war, stumbles inadvertently into the sanctuary of a god on the island of Chryse. He is bitten by a snake and, from that time on, suffers from a wound on his foot that will not heal. The smell of his wound and the sound of his cries of pain repulse his fellow warriors, and, led by Odysseus, they maroon him on Lemnos, a deserted island, and proceed to Troy.

Ten years have passed when the play opens. It seems that a captured Trojan seer has told the Greeks that they will never take Troy without Philoctetes and the bow of Herakles, which was left to Philoctetes when Herakles died. Neoptolemus, meanwhile, the son of Achilles by a captive woman from the island of Skyros, has come to Troy after his father's death to collect his father's effects. The great warrior's arms are no longer available, however, as they were won in a contest between Odysseus and Ajax. In response to the prophecy, Odysseus takes Neoptolemus to Lemnos to help him use deceit to get the bow from Philoctetes. At first, the young man goes along with the scheme, lying to Philoctetes and gaining his trust. But eventually, after Philoctetes invokes the spirit of Achilles in begging him not to deliver him into the hands of his enemies, Neoptolemus decides he cannot participate in the deception and is prepared to help Philoctetes escape the island in defiance of Odysseus. The standoff is resolved when Herakles, now a god, appears to tell

Philoctetes that he must return to Troy, be healed of his wound, and help in the taking of the city.

Sophocles clearly had both Homeric epics in mind when writing his play. The *Iliad* and Achilles in particular form a kind of penumbra behind the *Philoctetes*. In both works, the hero is kept out of the Trojan War for a significant time, and his absence is part of a divine plan. Achilles and Philoctetes share an implacable anger toward Agamemnon, Menelaus, and the other leaders of the Greek expedition. In both works, missions to the absent hero to convince him to return to the battle fail, and the agency of a dead friend (Patroclus; Herakles) ultimately persuades each to relent. Finally, the weakness of both heroes is represented by a wound in the foot. Achilles dies from it and Philoctetes is cured.

The spirit of Achilles is also present in his son, Neoptolemus. Sophocles uses the contrast between the young man's fiery but somewhat naïve temperament and the manipulative Odysseus as a focus for some reflection on intellectual trends in Athens at the end of the Peloponnesian War. The rise of the Sophists, traveling teachers who came to Athens after 450 B.C.E. and who challenged older, aristocratic ideas about human nature, is ironically refracted here. Odysseus, the older and more established man, uses arguments borrowed from the Sophists to try to convince Neoptolemus to lie to Philoctetes; the younger man channels his father's more traditional values.

If the plot of the play is Iliadic, the themes recall the *Odyssey*. Although the hero is a disabled warrior, everything finally hinges on the choice Neoptolemus must make as to which of two father figures, Odysseus or Achilles, he will take as his model. Like Telemachus, he has been sent on a mission by someone with greater authority and, presumably, greater wisdom, in the course of which he must make certain choices that will mark his crossing of the threshold of adult manhood. For him, as for Telemachus, everything will finally hinge on his disposition of a hero's bow. These parallels, however, only highlight major shifts in the way the play treats themes found originally in the *Odyssey*. And those shifts reflect in turn the intellectual and social revolution occasioned by the establishment of the world's first democracy in Athens.

It is well beyond the scope of this book to give a full account of Athenian social and political innovations between 550 and 400 B.C.E. The evolution away from an aristocratic society based primarily on tribal affiliations toward one in which power was distributed more widely throughout the populace, based on geographical location rather than blood ties, had an impact still felt today all around the world. For our purposes, a sketch will have to suffice. In Athens, as in other city-states on the mainland of Greece, monarchy had given way, in the period from 900–650 B.C.E., to aristocratic oligarchy based on blood ties. From 650–550 B.C.E., that oligarchy was challenged in turn by a series of individual leaders, called "tyrants" by the Greeks, who appealed for power to the newly emerging merchant class rather than to landed aristocrats. The last such leader in Athens, Cleisthenes, sponsored crucial reforms in Athens, which undermined the power of blood ties and opened the way for the democracy that developed in the years 500–450 B.C.E.

As the last phase of the development of Athenian democracy was unfolding, the Greeks repulsed two invasions of the Greek mainland, in 490 and 480 B.C.E., by the kings of Persia. The terrifying and also exhilarating experience of twice defeating what looked like a vastly superior force, led by an absolute monarch, was definitive for the Greeks of the fifth century B.C.E., and especially the Athenians. Athenian democracy, the collective power of (relatively) free men who were learning to govern themselves in a new way, had overcome a society founded on the complete dominance of the mass of its people by a few autocrats. The excitement and pride generated by these triumphs rippled through all of Athenian culture, reflected in the friezes carved on the great temple of Athena on the Athenian Acropolis. More practically, the importance of the Athenian navy in the second victory brought new prestige and new political power to the sailors, adding impetus to the redistribution of political power in the democracy.

Along with these sweeping changes in the way power was distributed in Athenian society came new speculation about the nature and meaning of human experience in the larger context of the universe as the Greeks understood it. In particular, there was an intense debate among Greek intellectuals about the sources of human excellence. Were the qualities associated with excellence inherited through blood ties, or could a person learn to be excellent, given the right instruction? As might be expected, the *aristoi*, or "best men," who had ruled the city-state through alliances based on blood ties before the advent of democracy, favored the idea that excellence could only be inherited. The newly empowered citizens of the democracy would have preferred that the skills and talents required for success be available to those who were willing to work to acquire them. Here we encounter the Sophists, a group of traveling teachers who came to Athens and other cities in the fifth century B.C.E. to offer their services to those wishing to learn how to be successful. Behind all of this ferment lies the question of what it means to be human, as opposed to other mortal creatures on the one hand and the gods on the other. That the Greeks were so insistent in pursuing these issues is one reason why their civilization has remained of vital interest to Western cultures ever since.

The most enduring vehicle for the intellectual revolution accompanying the growth of democracy in Athens was tragic drama. The venue for this, the first dramatic form we know of in Western civilization, was the annual festival in honor of the god Dionysus in Athens. Typically for the culture out of which they came, the plays were created as part of a contest. Three playwrights' works were chosen for the annual competition, each submitting three tragedies and a satyr play. The last, as the title suggests, was a satirical response to some tragic story. We possess the written scripts for 32 tragedies, 7 each by Aeschylus and Sophocles, and 18 by Euripides, plus one satyr play, the *Cyclops* of Euripides. For those three playwrights—and they are only the best known—we have records indicating slightly less than 300 titles. Of the complete plays we do have, 24 are apparently the result of a selection made during the early Roman Empire for schools. The nine remaining plays, all by Euripides, were found in a manuscript dating from the thirteenth century B.C.E. Thus we may now have about 10 percent of the plays composed by Aeschylus, Sophocles, and Euripides, a precious legacy.

The form of the plays underwent some evolution—from the earliest known in the late sixth century B.C.E. to the last play of Euripides, the *Bacchae*, produced in 399 B.C.E.—but the basic elements remained the same. Two and eventually three actors interacted with a chorus of 12 to 15 in an outdoor space consisting of a circular area known as the "orchestra," or "dancing place," behind which was a rectangular stage (*skéné*). Behind the stage was an architectural backdrop with central doors, usually understood to represent the façade of some kind of dwelling. A cranelike device, *mēchanē*, was attached to the roof of the central building, from which special entrances could be made by gods or other extraordinary creatures. (The phrase in Latin, *deus ex machina*, "god from the device," refers to this kind of divine entrance from above.) On either side of the stage were two paths, *eisodoi*, leading to the orchestra, through which entrances and exits could be made. The Athenian Theater of Dionysus, in which all the plays we have were first produced, was a natural amphitheater with seats built into a hillside. All scenes are understood to take place outside, although the central doors could be opened to provide a glimpse of an interior. Vigorous physical action was minimal onstage, with messenger speeches used to describe such events, which were understood to occur offstage. Because the plays were part of a public festival, the audience is thought to have been widely inclusive. There is some debate about whether women attended the performances, but the prevailing view is that they did. In any event, Athenian tragedy was surely the most public and inclusive of any art form from classical antiquity, an apt vehicle for exploring the implications of the newly emerging democracy.

All speech in these plays was written in poetry, with dialogue between actors usually in simpler metrical forms thought to be closer to ordinary speech, and choral songs, accompanied by dancing and some form of musical instrument, in more complex lyric stanzas. The choral odes were usually divided into two or three parts, with the first two, called "strophe" and "antistrophe," having identical metrical forms, and the third, called an "epode," in a different meter. Long choruses could have more than one triad of stanzas. The identity of the chorus varied from citizens to soldiers to ecstatic religious followers and from young to old. Choruses were always entirely male or entirely female, never mixed. All actors, whether they were playing male or female parts, were male.

Certain features of this complex art form are especially germane to us here. The stories on which the plays were based are—with the exception of Aeschylus's *Persians*, produced in 472, right after the second Persian invasion—set in the mythical past, not in democratic Athens. Stories from the cycle of myths surrounding the Trojan War were popular, as well as those following the fortunes (or misfortunes) of the family of Oedipus in Thebes. The old stories, of course, could be used to reflect obliquely on the present. In particular, the heroic protagonists, played by the individual actors, often represent older, aristocratic attitudes and values, whereas the chorus might give voice to the communal perspective and values emerging as a part of the political and social changes occasioned by the beginning of democracy. Thus the plays could become laboratories for exploring the tensions resulting from the political, social, and intellectual revolution in classical Athens.

Sophocles's *Philoctetes* was first staged at the end of that revolution, when the Athenians had already been through more than 20 years of war with Sparta, during most of which the city was overcrowded with farmers forced into the city from the surrounding countryside. A plague had ravaged the city in 429–428, killing Pericles, the first hero of Athenian democracy, and further exacerbating the societal tensions already present. The intellectual ferment of which the Sophists were a part had continued unabated, and the experiment in democracy had been colored by the emergence of more radical politicians after the death of Pericles. (The term *demagogue*, meaning someone who leads the *demos*, or body of citizens, in unscrupulous ways, originates from this period in Athenian politics.) In response to the radical democrats, other more conservative elements in the citizen population forced a short oligarchic revolution in 411, in an attempt to push the political setup back to a more conservative form, transferring some power back from the full body of citizens to a smaller, more aristocratic group. Although this effort failed after only a year, it reflects the continuing tensions in Athenian society as a result of the changes of the past 75 years.

Sophocles himself was briefly associated with the revolution of 411, although he quickly withdrew his support when it became clear that what looked like a principled readjustment was in fact simply a power grab. Nevertheless, this vignette is consistent with the sense one gets from his plays that he was uncomfortable with the more radical democrats, whom he saw as using rhetorical virtuosity often associated with the Sophists to manipulate political debate and action. This bias comes through clearly in the portrayal of Odysseus in the *Philoctetes*. In Sophocles's *Ajax*, produced nearly 40 years earlier, Odysseus shows compassion toward his enemy Ajax, convincing Agamemnon and Menelaus to allow the great warrior's body to be buried properly despite his hostility to them and to him. Here, Odysseus is a ruthless, deceiving schemer from the start. He has brought Neoptolemus with him on his mission to capture the bow because he knows that his own part in the stranding of Philoctetes on Lemnos 10 years before will make the wounded man distrust him. But the son of Achilles, a hero renowned for his completely straightforward candor, will be able to win Philoctetes's trust.

Odysseus stresses from the outset that Neoptolemus is to think of him as a mentor, someone to whose wisdom and experience the younger man must naturally defer. The father-son relationship is to be the model. (Since the *Philoctetes*, unusually for Athenian tragedy, has no women characters, the focus on male-male relationships is even more intense.) Odysseus identifies him as "child" (*pais*) of Achilles, the most powerful of the Greeks, and Philoctetes as "son of Poias." Such a form of address is not unusual in Greek literature; but for Odysseus's first mention of these two principal characters, the explicit invocation of the father seems striking and suggests that he wants that dynamic to be in the air as he manipulates his young charge.

The lesson Neoptolemus is to learn from Odysseus is how to use deceit to gain one's ends:

Neoptolemus:	What, then, do you want me to do?
Odysseus:	You must deceive the soul of Philoctetes with words.
	(Sophocles, *Philoctetes* 54–55)

Such behavior is not natural to Neoptolemus, but the mission must be completed:

Odysseus:	But you must learn this, how to become
	a thief of the unconquerable weapon.
	I know, my child, that is not natural for you
	to say such things, or contrive such mischief.
	But the prize of victory is sweet to win;
	take heart: later we will be known as just men.
	Now, for a brief shameless part of one day,
	give yourself to me, and for the rest of time
	you will be called the most scrupulous of men.
Neoptolemus:	Those words that I hate to hear,
	child of Laertes, I hate to carry out.
	For I am not suited by nature to perform
	any kind of crafty deceit.
	Nor, they say, was the father who begot me.
	But I am prepared to take this man by force
	rather than trickery. Surely a man with one foot
	could be overpowered by men like us.
	I know I was sent to be your accomplice, and
	I do not want to be called a traitor. Yet I prefer,
	my lord, to fail while doing what is right
	than to win through deceit.
Odysseus:	Son of an excellent father, I was young once too,
	And had a quiet tongue with an active hand.
	But now when I enter a contest, I see that among men
	the tongue always wins, not the deed.
	(Sophocles, *Philoctetes* 77–99)

This exchange captures the essence of the relationship between Odysseus and Neoptolemus. The older man looks only to the ends, the apprentice to the means. By playing on Neoptolemus's deference to his elders, Odysseus hopes to convince him to put aside his scruples for a brief time in the service of a worthy prize. Words, for the older man, are tools to be used without worrying about how they reflect either what is true in fact. Neoptolemus, by contrast, considers that relationship to be the essential guide to a man's moral worth. A man is to be judged by his acts, which should be consistent with his words.

Further richness is added to this clash by the Homeric background. Odysseus is celebrated in the *Odyssey* for his skill at using deceit to gain leverage over others and, in particular, his ability to manipulate others through words. Lying is not considered to be morally culpable in that poem, as long as it occurs in the service of getting the hero back in charge in Ithaka. In the *Iliad*, however, the tone is different. Liars and sneaks do not fare well there. And the most famous objection to exactly what Odysseus is urging on Neoptolemus is voiced by Achilles in book 9 of the *Iliad*, speaking to Odysseus:

Son of Laertes and seed of Zeus, crafty Odysseus,
I must speak out without regard for your feelings,
how I think and how it will be accomplished,
so you do not sit beside me chattering, one after the other.
For hateful as the doorway of Hell is that man,
who hides one thing in his heart, and says another. (Homer, *Iliad* 9. 308–313)

We are not surprised to find this man's son feeling nervous about using deceitful words to manipulate others.

Sophocles dramatizes intergenerational issues, and the father-son relationship in particular, with all of their implications for the ideals of masculinity, through a complex set of filters—political, social, and intellectual. The clever and admirable deceit of Homer's Odysseus becomes, amidst the political and intellectual ferment of late fifth century Athens, a cause for shame, the tool of men who would lead others into dishonorable acts through misleading words. The lessons by which Odysseus could once guide Telemachus across the threshold of manhood are precisely those that repulse Neoptolemus and drive him instead to honor Achilles's spirit of open expression. The great moment in the *Odyssey*, when the hero's son puts the bow into his father's hands, is replayed here, but with Philoctetes standing in for the father. As in Homer's poem, the hero's son secures the reestablishment of proper order by passing the bow to a seemingly diminished creature. As the beggar in the *Odyssey* will in fact effect the overthrow of the hero's enemies with the bow, so here Philoctetes will vanquish Troy.

Given the political power struggles in late fifth-century Athens, it is no surprise that Odysseus could be cast as a villain in Sophocles's play. But the shift from oligarchic to democratic rule would in any event challenge traditional models for masculinity, because the emphasis in aristocratic societies on the ability to control others through individual excellence would be undermined by the imperative to share power with one's fellow citizens. We are back to the familiar tension in Greek culture between the competitive quest for excellence and the necessity for cooperation as the basis for any social system. In the Homeric epics, the product of an aristocratic culture, individual excellence dominates; in democratic Athens, the needs of the group become more prominent. What we know of Athenian schools in the fifth century B.C.E. suggests that a stress on discipline and punishment tended to outweigh the teaching of skills. This bias was certainly due in part to the need for soldiers, but it may also reflect Athenian understanding that, for their democracy to survive, young men had to learn to temper their competitive drives.

There was one other vehicle for instructing young men in their progress toward adulthood in Athenian culture of the fifth century B.C.E. It was a commonly accepted practice in the elite classes for an older man (*erastes*, "lover") to take a younger male lover (*eromenos*, "beloved"). This relationship was understood to be reciprocal, in that the older man would receive sexual favors, and the younger man would be guided by an older mentor; the power dynamics were mixed in that the older man was expected to court the younger. Parents of young men apparently often approved of such unions, for having a powerful lover could raise the boy's social standing.

To explore this social arrangement in detail is beyond the scope of this book. We do know that, for an adolescent boy, being a sexual partner for an older man was not considered evidence of diminished masculinity. Homosexual relations were not understood by Athenians to be a sign of a fundamentally different sexual makeup, as they tend to be by modern societies. Older men who took younger lovers were often married and behaved in ways we would now identify with heterosexual men. Rather, the emphasis, not surprisingly, was on whether the male was an active or passive sexual partner. To be penetrated by another male of lower or even equal societal standing was a sign of weakness—the issue of control of one's body appears here again. We may have a hint about how Odysseus would like to see his relationship with Neoptolemus in the opening lines of the *Philoctetes*, when he addresses the young man as child of Achilles. "*Pais,*" the word Odysseus uses for "child," is the standard term applied to the younger beloved in Athenian society.

CONCLUSION

The works we have explored in this chapter show some by now familiar imperatives for young men: (1) the need to move away from the nurture offered by their mothers and toward a harder wisdom found in the world of their fathers; (2) the importance of self-control as a basis for the control of other forces, human and nonhuman, in the universe; and (3) the primacy of the father as a model for how to negotiate the challenges of a masculine life. Telemachus and Neoptolemus both approach the threshold of adulthood by learning from father figures. In both cases, the young men must manage their youthful energies so as to balance the quest for individual excellence with the need for cooperation with others as the basis for the healthy functioning of human society. In the aristocratic, heroic cultures of the *Iliad* and *Odyssey*, individual excellence is somewhat less problematical, as we have seen, than in the democratic Athenian city-state. Even so, the portraits of Achilles and Odysseus in the Homeric epics imply a recognition that success in the intensely competitive societies of the Greek epic also carries the risk of personal isolation.

The advent of Athenian democracy brought with it increased anxieties among thoughtful citizens about how to accommodate the forces of aristocratic individualism within a system that distributed political power—and thus social leverage—across a much broader segment of the society. By the late fifth century B.C.E., Sophocles worried that the new ideas about human excellence that had appeared as part of the intellectual ferment accompanying political change had gone too far in devaluing old models for human excellence. By valorizing Neoptolemus's choice to follow his father's example and not that of Odysseus, the young man reaches back to an older, more aristocratic model of masculinity as a check against the sophistic excesses of Odysseus.

These tensions persist, as we will see, in the Greek ideal of mature masculinity. Once a man had entered the realm of adult males, he had to negotiate the boundaries of individual self-assertion and communal responsibility in a larger arena, within which he carried heavy new responsibilities. The first level of organization to be managed was still the family, but now the young adult male would be expected, as father and husband, to establish his own branch, with himself as the controlling authority. This arena necessarily brought the young male into a new and challenging relationship with women, whose inner nature was, in the Greek patriarchal perspective, both powerful and fundamentally different from that of males. And because women were also believed to be closer to the raw forces of nature than were males, controlling their power was, for the adult male, part of the larger project of creating human civilization itself.

Three

Men and Women

The greatest glory for women is to be least talked of by men, either in praise or blame.

—Thucydides, *Histories* 2.45

For the ancient Greeks, as for other civilizations around the Mediterranean, men and women were fundamentally different by nature (*phusis*). Aristotle, writing in the fourth century B.C.E., situates these differences in the larger context of all "living things" (*zōoi*):

In all types in which there is the male and the female, nature has differentiated in much the same way between the character of the females and that of the males.

About humans in particular, he goes on to say,

There are traces of these [differences] in nearly all animals, but they are all the more evident in those that have more character, and especially in humans. For the character of humans is the most fully-formed, and so these dispositions are also most evident in humans. Therefore a wife is more compassionate and more given to tears than her husband, and also more jealous and complaining, and more reproachful and combative. The female is also more dispirited than the male and more despondent, more shameless and more given to lying, more ready to deceive and less likely to forget, more wakeful and more hesitant, more inactive in general than the male, and takes less nourishment. (Aristotle, *Historia Animalia* 608a)

Aristotle offers here a "scientific" foundation (based on no real scientific evidence) for the assumptions about men and women that pervaded Mediterranean cultures of the ancient world.

Perhaps the most fundamental aspect of women's physical nature for the Greeks was their *wetness,* a condition noted directly by Aristotle and also Greek medical writers like Hippocrates and Galen, and implied in many ways by poets from earlier periods. The proper condition for a healthy human body, on the other hand, was considered to be moderate dryness. As Hippocrates put it:

The female flourishes more in an environment of water, from things cold and wet and soft, whether food or drink or activities. The male flourishes more in an environment of fire, from dry, hot foods and mode of life. (Hippocrates, *On Nourishment* 27)

In other words, males, being dry, warm, and hard, are healthier by nature than females, who are wet, cool, and soft.

The implications of this assumption about female physicality were extensive and influential. Because they were supposedly wetter, women were more susceptible to emotions, which were thought of as themselves being "moist." Sexual arousal was wet, and once aroused, women could become, because of their own wetness, insatiable. Thus women had to be controlled and kept from going wild because of their inherent susceptibility to lust; thus men had to exercise *aidos*, "shame," and *sōphrosynē*, "soundness of mind," to keep women from transgressing the bounds of propriety. Women's fluidity, in fact, caused them to be naturally transgressive and transgressed: they leak bodily fluids; they are penetrated. Their motility is reflected socially in the fact that they literally move when they marry, from their father's house to that of their husband. The Greeks' belief in women's innate tendency to migrate reached perhaps its most bizarre manifestation in the belief, first appearing in the sixth century B.C.E., that women's wombs wandered throughout their bodies, which caused "hysteria," from the Greek *hysteros*, meaning "lower down."

The consequences of women's wandering reached beyond societal impropriety. Connected by their fundamental liquidity to the elemental forces of nature, women were therefore part of what men had to control by the imposition of reason, as part of their responsibilities as agents of human civilization. Myths describing the origins of human civilization in ancient Mediterranean cultures often portray what we call a "Golden Age," when humans lived alongside gods, a completely carefree existence requiring no exertion, as all sustenance was generated spontaneously. Then something happened to cause an estrangement between gods and humans, with the latter group forced to fend for themselves. In response, humans developed agriculture and other ways of applying human reason to control nature in order to produce a product, civilization. The application of human intelligence and labor to produce civilization became necessary to compensate for the rupture between gods and humans. The earliest Greek version of this model of human civilization is found in the poet Hesiod, who composed the poem, *Works and Days*, in the late eighth or early seventh century B.C.E. The Old Testament story of Adam and Eve's expulsion from the Garden of Eden is another example of the same story pattern.

It is not surprising, given these assumptions, that metaphors for sexual intercourse in Greek literature and culture were often agricultural, with men as the ones plowing and seeding, women as the earthy, wet receptacles. In a famous choral ode from his play *Antigone*, Sophocles praises the civilizing skills of men:

Many are the wonders, but none
so awesome as man.

That wonder who crosses the gray
sea in the wintry wind, piercing the
the bellowing waves, and the greatest
of the gods, unwearying Earth, he wears
away, the plows going back and forth,
year after year, as he turns the soil
with the race of horses. (Sophocles, *Antigone* 332–341)

By plowing the earth with tame horses and snaring birds, fish, and beasts of all sorts, man yokes the power of nature for his own uses. Hector, the preeminent defender of Trojan civilization in the *Iliad,* has two epithets, "man-slaughtering," signaling his ferocity as a warrior, and "horse-taming," to mark his role as a civilizer. The dark side of these metaphors comes out in two remarks from Creon after the preceding choral ode. He can, he says, break the spirit of Antigone:

I've seen spirited horses broken
with a small bit. (Sophocles, *Antigone* 477–478)

The chorus asks if he would kill Antigone, his son Haemon's intended bride, and he replies:

There are other fields for him to plow. (Sophocles, *Antigone* 569)

Procreation was understood to be work for men, but sex for pleasure was "play." To be a mature man, then, was to practice sexuality as part of the larger male project of establishing and guarding human civilization. Women, on the other hand, were not permitted this form of "play." Their sex life was to be given over entirely to procreation with their husbands. Married women who had adulterous sexual relations were projecting their porous nature onto the household, letting the disruptive power of *eros* breach the boundaries that safeguarded the family. And as the state was made up of a collection of households, women out of control threatened the health of the entire city-state.

MASCULINE DEMOCRACY: AESCHYLUS'S *ORESTEIA*

The interconnected metaphors we have been tracing here are powerfully expressed in Aeschylus's trilogy of plays about the homecoming of Agamemnon from the Trojan War and its gory aftermath. The three plays were entered in the dramatic contest at the Athenian festival of Dionysus in 458 B.C.E. In the first play, *Agamemnon,* Agamemnon, king of Argos, returns triumphant from conquering Troy and recovering Helen, his brother Menelaus's wife. He brings with him Cassandra, the captured daughter of Priam, as a concubine. His wife Clytemnestra, having taken his cousin Aegisthus as a lover in his absence, makes a show of welcoming him home, then murders him and Cassandra and declares herself ruler of Argos along with Aegisthus. Her justification for killing Agamemnon is that, 10 years previously, he sacrificed their daughter Iphigenia to appease the goddess Artemis, who, angered for somewhat obscure reasons, was holding back the expedition to Troy by making the winds blow adversely. While his father has been in Troy, Orestes, the young royal prince, has been living in exile in Phocis, and his sister Electra has been kept under close guard in Argos.

The second play, *The Libation Bearers,* opens with the return to Argos of Orestes, now a teenager. He has come in disguise, accompanied by his friend Pylades, the son of the king of Phocis, to kill his mother and her lover. Apollo has told Orestes he must commit murder and matricide to claim his rightful place as male head of the royal household and king of Argos. After a joyful reunion of the royal children, the rest of the play is taken up with their plotting and the murders of Aegisthus and then Clytemnestra. The final scene shows the arrival of the Furies, divine spirits charged with avenging the shedding of kindred blood, to hound Orestes.

The final play, *The Eumenides,* opens with Orestes having fled to the temple of Apollo in Delphi, where he is besieged by the Furies. Apollo puts the avenging creatures to sleep, allowing Orestes to escape to Athens, where he will be given the chance to defend himself in the first state murder trial, to be held on the Areopagus, or "Hill of Ares." The Furies are to be the prosecutors and Apollo the defense attorney. Athena, as the patron goddess of Athens, summons a jury of citizens and serves as judge. After the arguments on both sides, Athena breaks a tie by voting for Orestes, assuring his acquittal. Athena eventually appeases the Furies, and they change from spirits of vengeance into fertility deities who have their shrine under the Acropolis in Athens. The trilogy ends with the Furies leading a torchlight parade out of the theater.

Such a brief description cannot do justice to this extraordinarily rich work of art. Although it was customary, at least until the 450s, for playwrights to submit three thematically interconnected plays for the dramatic contest at the Dionysiac festival, the *Oresteia* is the only trilogy to survive intact from antiquity. Aeschylus creates a complex series of images that span all three plays, and tracking their development helps us to see how the playwright mapped contemporary, fifth-century political and social issues onto the old story.

Underlying all the plays is a set of polarities, around which the action is organized:

Male	Female
Light	Dark
Sky	Earth
New	Old
Reason	Emotion
Political ties	Blood ties
Olympian deities	Earth deities

Athenians in the fifth century B.C.E. would assume that, in a healthy world, the left-hand side should dominate the right-hand side. That is, males should control females, light should conquer dark, new Olympian deities should rule over old earth deities, and so forth. By playing against these expectations, Aeschylus creates dramatic tension, which is resolved only in the finale of the third play.

One of the most prominent sources of tension in the two plays is generated by the distortion of what would be considered proper gender roles. The chorus of the *Agamemnon,* made up of old men, having heard Clytemnestra's response to the news of Troy's fall, exclaim that she speaks wisely, "like a man." All through the play, admiration for the Queen's air of command is mixed with an air of unease prompted by her adopting the authority usually reserved for the king. Agamemnon, the proper agent of male authority and control, has been missing, and, as in Homer's Ithaka, the result has been unhealthy disorder.

Clytemnestra's desire to command continues after Agamemnon has returned, suggesting that he is in danger of being feminized. When Clytemnestra is urging him to climb down from his chariot and walk into the palace on rich tapestries, he protests:

Do not treat me delicately, in the way of a woman. (Aeschylus, *Agamemnon* 918–919)

The subsequent exchange between the royal couple underscores the distortion of regular gender roles:

Agamemnon: Surely it is not for a woman to desire conflict.
Clytemnestra: Yet it is seemly even for the victor to be conquered.
Agamemnon: So this is the kind of victory in conflict that you want?
Clytemnestra: Yield! Willingly give away power to me.
                 (Aeschylus, *Agamemnon* 940–943)

The king's death, soon to follow, confirms his fears of being emasculated by Clytemnestra. He is penetrated by an axe while in the bath full of water, the woman's medium. Cassandra, in a lyrical exchange with the chorus, says of the murder of Agamemnon by Clytemnestra, which is occurring as she speaks:

Oh see! Oh see! Drag the bull from the cow!
She has snared him in her robes
and gores him with her tricky horn. (Aeschylus, *Agamemnon* 1125–1128)

Just who is the bull and who the cow is not entirely clear. When the bodies of Agamemnon and Cassandra are displayed onstage at the end of the play, the old men in the chorus are outraged and denounce Aegisthus as a "woman," who avoided the war and let a woman do his killing for him. The Queen intervenes, and it is clear that she is the one who rules Argos.

The pattern continues in the next play, *The Libation Bearers.* Orestes has arrived in disguise and unbeknownst to Clytemnestra and Aegisthus. After his joyous reunion with his sister Electra, the two siblings have a long, lyrical exchange with the chorus over the grave of Agamemnon. Orestes is back to claim his rightful place as male head of the royal household, which is presently ruled, as Orestes says, by "a pair of women." Aegisthus, a usurper, can no more wield legitimate male authority than can Clytemnestra. The next 300 or so lines are the heart of the play, where Orestes, Electra, and the chorus call on the spirit of the dead king to empower them to set things right.

The plot then proceeds, as Orestes, still disguised as a visitor from Phocis, raps on the door of the palace:

Announce my arrival to the masters of the house;
I've come to them bearing fresh news.
Hurry, since the chariot of night brings on
darkness, and it is the time for travelers to
drop anchor in houses hospitable to strangers.
Let the one with authority in the household come,
the woman in charge, or more appropriately,
the man. For then reticence in speaking does not
make the words obscure. A man speaks to a man
boldly, making his meaning clear. (Aeschylus, *The Libation Bearers* 658–667)

The door opens to reveal Clytemnestra, who orders her servants to prepare "warm baths" for her guests.

Orestes and Pylades enter the palace and kill Aegisthus. Clytemnestra appears again at the central doors, anxious about the screams coming from another part of the palace:

Oh me! I have grasped the meaning of the riddles.
We will be destroyed by trickery, just as we have killed.
Someone give me a man's axe, as quickly as possible.
Let us see if we triumph or are vanquished.
We have arrived even at this evil. (Aeschylus, *The Libation Bearers* 887–891)

Facing death, Clytemnestra wields the man's weapon. When Orestes has killed her, he begins to see visions of the Furies, female spirits who avenge crimes against kindred blood. The play ends with his fleeing the stage with the Furies in pursuit. The absence of male authority continues to be felt.

The distortion of "natural" gender roles in the first two plays has a ripple effect. Images of perverted nature signal the fundamental disorder occasioned by the absence of proper male leadership. The sea "blooms" with corpses when Greek ships sink in a storm on the way back from Troy. The chorus compares Helen to a lion cub, which, once born, proceeds to slaughter those living in its own house. Agamemnon, newly returned from Troy, hails Cassandra, who is an added goad to Clytemnestra's fury, as the "choicest flower" of his spoils from Troy.

The most spectacular of these images comes in the triumphant speech given by Clytemnestra after she has murdered both Cassandra and Agamemnon. She describes his death this way:

Fallen thus, he gasped out his life,
and spewing out quick bursts of blood,
struck me with dark drops of bloody dew,
as I rejoiced no less than the sown earth is
gladdened by Zeus's bright rain when the
flower buds are born. (Aeschylus, *Agamemnon* 1388–1392)

Although the queen thinks that her vengeance will end the cycle, it only brings a fresh round. The idea that blood spilled brings vengeance into bloom is central to the first two plays of the trilogy. And not only is blood the seed of vengeance, but once it is spilled, its effects are irrevocable:

What redemption is there for blood fallen on the earth?
(Aeschylus, *The Libation Bearers* 48)

Because of the blood drunk by the nourishing earth
vengeful blood lies clotted and will not flow away.
(Aeschylus, *The Libation Bearers* 66–67)

Yet it is the unchanging rule that drops of blood
fallen on the ground call forth more blood.
(Aeschylus, *The Libation Bearers* 400–401)

The grotesque insemination that Clytemnestra describes at the end of the *Agamemnon* comes to fruition in the central scene of *The Libation Bearers*. As we have seen, the children of Agamemnon join the chorus in calling on powers from under the earth—deities understood by the Greeks to be older than the Olympian gods who lived on Mount Olympus—to bring forth vengeance and help them to kill the queen and her consort. The appearance at the end of the second play of the Furies, ancient female agents of vengeance for crimes against the shedding of familial blood, whom Aeschylus calls "Daughters of Night," signals that the proper order of things (as the Greeks understood it) continues to be distorted. Female forces have been in the ascendance over male, with Clytemnestra killing Agamemnon and ruling Argos in his place; the older deities of the earth, associated with darkness and the vengeful dead, have more leverage than the younger Olympian gods, fueling the revenge of Orestes and Electra, hounding Orestes off the stage at the end of *The Libation Bearers;* ties of blood have been honored over political alliances, as those intent on avenging the murders of Iphigenia and of Clytemnestra—both crimes against blood relatives—continue to dominate those who are avenging the murder of Agamemnon.

All of these distortions are resolved by the end of *The Eumenides.* The acquittal of Orestes signals the final triumph of Apollo over the Furies. Athena, the judge of the trial, announces her vote first, before the jurors' votes are counted:

It is my job to make the final judgment:

I will cast this vote for Orestes,
for no mother gave birth to me,
and I honor the male in all things, except marriage,
with all my heart; I am my father's child.
Thus I will not privilege the death of a woman
who has killed her husband, guardian of the house.
Orestes wins, even if the votes are equal. (Aeschylus, *Eumenides* 734–741)

The judgment carries, as we have seen, heavy symbolic significance. Athena was born from the head of her father Zeus and so had, as she says, no mother, making her represent, in herself, a kind of compromise: her preference for the male reasserts the proper distribution of power, while suggesting a weighted blend of male and female prerogatives. As an Olympian goddess, her role as judge also reasserts the dominance of younger gods over older. But the fact that Athena is able, after the verdict, to appease the Furies and effect their transformation from spirits of vengeance (*Erinyes,* "Furies") to fertility deities (*Eumenides,* "Kindly Ones") in Athens suggests another compromise: their preoccupation with blood ties is changed from a negative, punitive role to a positive one, promoting the production of more Athenian sons.

The trilogy ends with Athena leading the chorus of Furies, who are carrying torches, out of the theater. The *Agamemnon* began with a watchman looking for the flash of beacons in the night, signaling the fall of Troy—waiting, as he says, in darkness for the light. In the event, the fire from Troy symbolized in that first play not only the victory of the Greeks but destruction falling on the palace of Agamemnon. Now that symbolism is reversed, with the acquittal of Orestes and all it entails bringing fertility and health to Athens.

There is one more dimension to this thematic synthesis. The *Oresteia* trilogy was first produced in 458 B.C.E., at the height of Athenian pride and confidence in the newly emerging democracy. That system of government, never seen before in Western civilization, came into being in the half-century preceding Aeschylus's play. In 508 B.C.E., Cleisthenes, the last Athenian tyrant, instituted a crucial set of innovations in the way political power was distributed in Athens and the surrounding territory called Attica. The oligarchic governments of the previous two centuries or so had been articulated through alliances between a few powerful aristocratic clans, related by blood. In an attempt to break the hold of those alliances, Cleisthenes reorganized the population for political purposes into units determined by geographical location rather than family affiliation. This innovation, along with the thrilling success of the Greeks in defeating the Persians, which depended in large part on the sailors who manned the Athenian navy, led to a wider distribution of political power in Athens.

In 461 B.C.E., Ephialtes, a friend and ally of Pericles, the general and politician who served as the leader of Athenian democracy more or less continuously from 460–430 B.C.E., instituted a second series of reforms. The details of these changes are lost to us, but we know that the court of the Areopagus, which had served as an important venue for murder trials and other crimes against the Athenian state, as well as an informal council advising archons, the leaders of the Athenian state, was considerably reduced in power. It remained a murder court but lost many other functions that had made it a powerful body. The membership of the court was made up of former archons and would have been a center of power for aristocratic families. The courts established to replace it in the judicial system would have juries filled by lot from the citizenry of Athens, a much wider demographic pool.

Viewed in the context of these events, the contemporary (to Aeschylus) political significance of the *Oresteia* is clear. Aeschylus himself served in the

infantry at the Battle of Marathon in 490 B.C.E., where the Greek forces re-
pelled the Persians, and his pride in the Athenian achievements of the early
and middle fifth century comes through strongly in his trilogy. The seemingly endless cycle of vengeance and reprisal represented in the first two
plays dramatizes the inherent weakness of a civilization in which the admin-
istration of justice is a private affair between families. The establishment by
Athena of the first state murder court on the Areopagus at Athens creates, for
the first time, a third party, at least potentially neutral, outside the feuding
families, which can administer justice according to principles of law.

The creation in mythic time of the court reflects, on the one hand, the
reforms of Cleisthenes, undermining the power of blood ties in favor of
political ties established by the city-state of Athens, and on the other—
somewhat ironically—the disempowering by Ephialtes of the old court of
the Areopagus, a bastion of aristocratic power, in favor of courts with wider
citizen participation. From this perspective, democracy becomes the vehicle
for peace and justice. By co-opting the dangerous power of female forces associated with blood and the family, represented by the Furies, the new male-
dominated Olympian regime, represented by Apollo and Athena, preserves
civic and societal order while safeguarding the fertility of the populace and
providing more sons for the democracy. All of this grand evolution comes to
flower in Athenian democracy of 458 B.C.E.

Stepping back from Aeschylus's rich synthesis of ideas, we can see that his
picture of what is needed for a healthy civilization is consistent with what we
have seen both in earlier works of art and, to some extent, in the later ideas of
Aristotle and the medical writers. That is, the male must dominate the female
for the forces of nature to be successfully harnessed in the service of human
civilization. At the same time, the healthiest condition for a society is a blend
of masculine and feminine elements. For the earth to flourish, Persephone
must spend some part of the year with her mother and some with Hades; the
masculine imperative for separation must be balanced by the feminine need
for connection; the heavenly Olympian regime of light and reason must be
nourished by the energy of the old earth deities.

We have seen the same striving for balance within the patriarchal model
of the world in the relationships of Gilgamesh and Enkidu and Achilles and
Patroclus. In both stories, the dominant male's masculine arrogance and refusal to accept normal human limits on his power leads to the death of his
"second self," in each case a figure representing in some way a more feminine response to the world. Enkidu has long hair "like a woman" and begins
by being fully integrated into the world of nature, running with the animals.
Patroclus is driven not by the competitive masculine desire to separate
himself from others, but by the feminine desire for connection to his fellow Greeks. In both stories, the loss of his second self plunges the hero into
grief, which accentuates his isolation for a time, until some acceptance of
limits signals his reintegration of the feminine qualities carried by his second
self. That the feminine element is carried in the earlier stories by a man and
not a woman may indicate some recognition in the authors that men must

incorporate a wider range of responses to the world than the hypermasculine, patriarchal perspectives of later writers like Aristotle require. Or, conversely, the confining of the entire speculation to male characters might be seen as a more extreme patriarchal perspective: it is truly all about men.

A HARSHER WORLD: EURIPIDES'S *MEDEA*

The integration of masculine and feminine elements we observe in earlier works gives way to a less harmonious relationship in the plays produced later in the fifth century B.C.E. This change may reflect in part the artistic temperament of individual playwrights, but the strains in Athenian democratic society brought on by protracted war with Sparta must also have been a factor. Eurpides's *Medea,* produced in 431 B.C.E., the first year of the Peloponnesian War, dramatizes the gender antagonism we have been tracing here in a particularly vivid way. Medea, the play's protagonist, contains within herself contradictory impulses that recall Aeschylus's Clytemnestra, but unlike the earlier trilogy, Euripides's somber masterpiece offers no hope for resolution.

The play covers part of the aftermath of the voyage of Jason and the Argonauts, who were understood by the Greeks to be a generation older than the heroes of the Trojan War, to recover the Golden Fleece. In the earlier part of the story, Medea, the daughter of the king of Colchis, a wild place on the shores of the Black Sea, falls in love with Jason when he comes to retrieve the magical golden lamb's fleece from her father. Medea has an illustrious (and somewhat ominous) lineage: her grandfather is Helios, the sun god, and her aunt is Circe, the witch who kept Odysseus with her for a year of reveling on his way back to Ithaka. Medea herself is a witch, and she uses her powers in various frightening ways to help her beloved secure the fleece and return home to Corinth. When Euripides's play opens, Medea has been living as Jason's wife in Corinth long enough to have given birth to two small children. As a foreigner, a witch, and a woman, she is thrice marginalized in the society of Jason's city.

The play begins with a monologue from an old nurse in Jason's household, recounting grim recent events. Jason is sleeping with the daughter of the king, Creon, a betrayal to which Medea has, reasonably enough, reacted badly. She keeps to her bed, refuses friendly advice, and has turned away from her children. The nurse fears that she is planning something. Medea is frightening

Her heart is violent, and she will not bear
suffering well. I know her, and I fear she
will thrust a sharp sword into her liver,
sneaking silently into the house, where the bed is made,
or even kill the king and the new bridegroom,
and then she will meet some greater misfortune.
For she is uncanny and powerful. (Euripides, *Medea* 38–44)

Events will show the old nurse's fears to have been justified. Creon decides that Medea and the children must be banished immediately from Corinth, fearing that she may do some harm to his daughter or to Jason. Medea begs him to allow her one more day, and he agrees. Jason then appears, and in the course of a bitter exchange with Medea, delivers two famously odious and self-serving speeches. The exile is her own fault, he says, for speaking badly of the king. Even so, he, Jason, will help her to support herself and the children in exile. Even if she hates him, he cannot think badly of her. After she angrily rejects his aid, calling him a cowardly ingrate for breaking his oath to her after all she has done for him, he answers with more arrogant self-justification. He considers that it was Aphrodite, not Medea, who saved him in Colchis. She is clever enough, to be sure, but it was *eros* that compelled her to do what she did. In any event, she ought to be thanking him for allowing her to live in a Greek city, instead of among barbarians. He did not leave Medea because he was tired of the sex with her, but because he was looking out for the best interests of their children, who will now be related to royalty. He ends with a spectacular crescendo of misogyny:

Now haven't I planned well?
You would say so, if the sex issue weren't gnawing at you.
You women have gotten to the point of thinking that
if things are going well in bed, then you have everything,
but if there should be some mishap there,
you consider most hateful the things most
desirable and beautiful. Men ought to have gotten their
children from some other place, and women ought
not to have existed. That way there would have been
no evil for men. (Euripides, *Medea* 567–575)

Jason leaves and, after a choral ode, Aegeus, the king of Athens, enters. He is passing through on his way from Delphi, where he has consulted Apollo's oracle about how to overcome his inability to father children. Medea tells him of Jason's misdeeds and her unfortunate state, and he responds with sympathy: how could a man act that way? Medea, seizing her chance, offers to give him magic drugs that will ensure his having children if he will, in return, give her refuge in Athens. He swears an oath to that effect and leaves for Athens. Medea now plans her revenge: she will summon Jason and pretend to have seen the error of her ways. She will feign gratitude for his generosity and agree to go quietly into exile, asking only that their children be allowed to stay in Corinth. She will then kill the new bride, sending her own children with a gift, a dress and diadem, both coated with poison that will bring the princess an agonizing death once she touches them. (In the event, she kills the king, too, as he tries to save his daughter.) Once that murder is done, she will then kill her own children and flee to avoid punishment.

Medea certainly presents a frightening package of traits for a patriarchal culture. As a woman and a witch, not only is she a part of nature, but she also possesses special power over its forces. Immune to most of the usual limits set for women in Greek culture, she is a free agent, a nightmare in the male imagination. It is no accident that Jason locates the problem with women in their obsession (as he sees it) with sex. As we have seen, Greeks believed that women were especially vulnerable to lust, because of their cool, wet nature. Sophocles's Antigone is dangerous because of her defiance of male control, but Medea, like Clytemnestra, is even more threatening because, unlike the virgin Antigone, she is a sexually mature woman.

This much we could say about Medea, based on other myths about her, even if the play never existed. As it is, Euripides creates an even more vivid character by combining within her a loving mother and an angry masculine hero. The volatile combination first surfaces in Medea's angry response to those who think that by avoiding combat women have it easier than men:

I would sooner take my stand three times in battle
than give birth once. (Euripides, *Medea* 250–251)

Later, as she contemplates her revenge against Jason, the masculine hero begins to emerge:

Oh Zeus, his daughter Justice, and light of the Sun,
now, now my friends, we will triumph over my enemies!
Our foot is on the road. (Euripides, *Medea* 763–765)

And at the end of the same speech:

Let no one think me weak, worthless,
a pampered housewife, but just the opposite,
one who harms her enemies and helps her friends.
For this sort of life is most glorious. (Euripides, *Medea* 807–810)

The injunction to harm one's enemies and help one's friends was one of the most fundamental tenets of proper heroic behavior. Likewise, in Greek culture heroic acts are always aimed at winning glory and renown among one's fellows.

As Medea approaches the murder of her children, the tension grows:

Oh, oh, why do you stare at me, my children?
Why are you laughing for the last time?
Alas! What will I do? My courage has left me,
friends, as I see the bright eyes of my children.
I could not do it. I renounce the plans I made
before. I will take the children into exile with me.
Hurting their father with their pain, why should I suffer
twice as many pains? No, I cannot. I renounce my plans.
But wait, what is the matter with me? Do I want to
let my enemies go unpunished and be laughed at?
No, I must do it. I am a coward even to let these
soft thoughts enter my mind. (Euripides, *Medea* 1040–1052)

We see the struggle here between two extremes, the love of a mother for her children and the angry male hero's dread of being shamed by his enemies. By framing Medea's indecision as he does, Euripides creates the obverse of a character like Patroclus, a man with a feminine side. That Medea is terrifying while Patroclus is sympathetic reflects the patriarchal bias of the culture. Men who transgress on the territory of women may be dismissed or even condemned, but women who elude male control threaten the very fabric of civilization.

A character like Patroclus or Enkidu, because he is not a threat to male control, can offer the chance for us to think about the normal boundaries of masculine experience. But Medea represents something much darker. At the beginning of the play, the nurse called her "uncanny." The Greek word, *deinē*, which is regularly used to describe heroes in Greek literature, has a somewhat wider connotation than "uncanny," encompassing any thing or person that inspires awe or fear. Certainly she has demonstrated that quality in abundance. At the end of the play, she appears in a chariot on the *mēchanē*, or "mechanism," above the stage, about to fly away with the bodies of her murdered children. Jason, utterly destroyed by the loss of his new bride, his royal father-in-law, and his children, begs for the bodies, so he may at least bury them. Medea refuses: she will bury them herself. He should go into the palace and bury his bride. Being sent inside, the private realm of women, is for Jason one more sign of his emasculation. Medea, meanwhile, hovers above and beyond, transcending the boundaries of male and female, human and divine, good and evil, the ultimate nightmare for men.

THE LIMITS OF LOVE: HECTOR AND ANDROMACHE; ODYSSEUS AND PENELOPE

Given the fundamental estrangement of the sexes we see reflected in these stories, it is hard to imagine how artists in Greek culture might portray a love relationship between a mature man and woman. We have, in fact, two such portraits, of Hector and Andromache in Homer's *Iliad,* and Odysseus and Penelope in Homer's *Odyssey.* In each case, we will see that Homer struggles against the received categories of male and female experience to create as intimate a relationship as the culture will allow.

Hector in Troy

Hector, the principal hero of the Trojans, is one of the most sympathetic characters in ancient literature. Unlike his main antagonist Achilles, he is conspicuous for both his fighting strength and his solicitude for others. In him we see little of Achilles's solipsistic self-involvement, arrogance, or yearning for immortality. Troy stands in the *Iliad* for human civilization, always at risk in the face of the raging masculine self-assertion that characterizes warriors, and Hector is its exemplary champion. In book 6 of the poem, Hector leaves the battlefield and returns to Troy for a brief time, where he encounters three women, each of whom is central to his life in one way or another: his mother Hecuba, wife of Priam and queen of Troy; Helen, his brother Paris's wife; and finally Andromache, his own wife. Each of these exchanges dramatizes from a different angle the heavy responsibilities weighing on the Trojan prince and the tensions arising from them. Hector is unique in the *Iliad* in that his character is determined so thoroughly by his interactions with women.

The first encounter is with his mother Hecuba. As we have seen, the role of the hero's mother in ancient epic poetry is to offer unqualified nurture and support to her son, no matter how misguided his behavior might be. Hecuba does not disappoint here, worrying over whether Hector is getting too tired to fight. She offers to fetch some wine for him, so he can sacrifice to Zeus and ask for help, and then drink some himself to bolster his strength. His answer is telling:

Do not bring me honey-sweet wine, dear mother,
lest you sap my strength, and I forget my fighting spirit.
I would not pour out ruddy wine as a tribute to Zeus
with unwashed hands. For there is no way for a man stained
with blood and gore to pray to the dark-robed son of Kronos.
(Homer, *Iliad* 6. 264–268)

Hector cannot let his mother take care of him, because if he accepts the comforts of civilization, he might lose his will to fight. Nor can he participate in any religious ceremonies while inside the city, because he is stained with the blood of war. The gore of battle marks Hector as fundamentally alienated from those who love him and from the civilized life of the city.

This separation persists throughout his stay in Troy. His next stop is the house of his brother Paris and the latter's wife, Helen. He finds the couple in their bedroom, Helen and her maids doing womanly work, Paris shining his armor. To enter such a seductive venue could be dangerous for Hector's fighting spirit, to be sure, and Homer has him proceed with caution:

There Hector, dear to Zeus, entered, and in his hand
he held a spear, eleven cubits long, and the bronze tip
gleamed, surrounded by a gold ring. (Homer, *Iliad* 6. 318–320)

Just what the spear means here could be a matter of dispute, but certainly the fundamental divide between the war and civilization remains intact. The contrast between Hector, covered in blood, exhausted from battle, and Paris, luxuriating in his boudoir, could hardly be stronger. Hector's weapon has been killing Greeks, whereas Paris shines his armor like a work of art.

Hector cannot understand his brother:

Strange man, it is not good to keep this coldness in your heart.
Men are dying, fighting around the city and its steep walls.
Because of you the battle and its din surround the city.
But you yourself would fight with another warrior,
whom you would see hanging back from the harsh battle.
Up now, lest the city be burned by the blazing fire. (Homer, *Iliad* 6. 326–331)

The Greek word translated "strange" here, *daimonie*, has a special resonance. An adjective from the same root as the noun *daimōn*, meaning "supernatural being," it connotes the fundamental divide between human and divine existence in Greek culture. Gods were thought of as completely unknowable, their purposes and motives unavailable to mortals. Moments when gods reveal themselves suddenly to mortals in Greek literature are always charged with electricity and potential danger: who knew what a god might do? Although *daimonie* is often used, as we will see, by mortals in what seems a tone of affectionate bemusement, the base meaning is also present and suggests a fundamental estrangement: "You are behaving as strangely as a god." Hector may love his brother, but he cannot understand him.

Paris responds in a typically offhand way, failing to catch (or refusing to acknowledge) the tone of his brother's scolding. You're right, old man, he says, Helen was just urging me to go back out to battle, and I'll do it. Just let me get dressed and I'll catch up with you. Helen speaks next, and Hector is not yet out of danger:

Then Helen spoke to him with soft words,
"Brother-in-law of mine, nasty scheming bitch that I am,
oh that snatching me up an evil gust of wind would have
taken me to the mountains or wave of the booming sea,
on that day when my mother bore me; there the surge
would have born me off before these evils came to be.
But since the gods have so contrived these evils,
I wish that I had been the wife of a better man than this one,
one who knew the meaning of disgrace and shame for men.
This man's wits are not sound, nor will they be,
and I think he will reap the fruits of it.
But come in now, and sit down on this chair,
my brother, since hard work has beset your heart
on account of my blind folly and that of Paris,
on whom Zeus put an evil fate, so that afterward
we would be the subject of song for men in the future." (Homer, *Iliad* 6. 343–354)

Helen is the most desirable (and thus dangerous) woman in the world, and it is not hard to sense an undertone of flirting here. Paris is shameless and she is a nasty bitch, but Hector is noble, having worn himself out protecting Troy. Why not relax for a little while? Hector, sensing another threat to his fighting spirit, resists her overture.

But Helen's offer and Hector's wary refusal carry a resonance beyond submerged sexuality. As we have seen, the offer of a seat and a drink carries symbolic significance in early Greek poetry. Such gestures, when made to someone who is grieving the loss of a loved one, are meant to urge the grieving person to accept the death of the one lost and to reenter the ordinary human world of death and change. We have seen that both Achilles and Gilgamesh grieve, and that each must be coaxed to let go of the dead and return to the living. Here the use of this motif is more subtle and understated. Hecuba's offer of a drink and Helen's of a seat combine to complete the motif. But Hector is not grieving for anyone in this scene. Rather, the motif is used to suggest Hector's resistance to the loss that he and we know is coming, of his wife and son, of Trojan civilization. If he lets go of his persona as warrior, if he allows himself to be comforted, he is giving in to the fact of human mortality. Hero that he is, he holds out a little longer.

Next comes the scene toward which Homer has been building for hundreds of lines. Hector goes to his own house in search of Andromache, only to be told by a serving maid that she has gone to the city walls, "like a mad woman," because she has heard that the Trojans were losing the battle. He hurries on and right at the great city gates that open onto the battlefield he finds Andromache and a serving woman who holds his son, Astyanx. Here begins one of the most famous scenes in Greek literature.

Everything about the encounter is rich in significance, for the characterization of Hector, for the portrait of a great civilization being dismantled by war, and for the poignant struggle of a man and woman to express their love for each other while other forces in their culture work to pull them apart. They meet precisely on the boundary between civilization and war, and their exchange becomes a negotiation across that crucial divide. Andromache speaks first:

Strange man, your own strength will destroy you, nor do you pity
your infant child and me, all ill-fated, I who will soon
become a widow. For quickly the Achaeans will kill you,
all of them swarming over you. But it would be better for me
when I lose you, to go under the earth. For there will be
no other comfort, once you meet with your destruction,
only pain. (Homer, *Iliad* 6. 407–413)

She goes on to say that not only will she lose him as a husband and the father of their child, but also as her father, mother, and brother. Both of her parents are dead, her father killed by Achilles, her mother by old age; all of her seven brothers have died in the war. He is, simply, all she has:

Hector, you are father to me, and beloved mother;
you are my brother too, and my young husband. (Homer, *Iliad* 6. 429–430)

Andromache's utter dependence on Hector is poignantly clear. But by invoking all of these different relationships here, Homer also attempts to widen and deepen the conventional model for the marital bond between a man and woman. This relationship goes beyond forming a household and filling it with children to include deep loyalty, reverence, and mutual respect.

And yet, extraordinary as their connection is, Hector is still "strange," *daimonie*, to Andromache. She cannot understand how it is that, given his love for her and his son, he must go back into the battle. Why not bring his troops back inside the walls and concentrate them at the place in the walls where the Greeks attacked before? Perhaps the most difficult thing about her husband for her to accept is what she sees as his self-destructive qualities: his own strength will destroy him. His next words provide an answer, if not one that will satisfy her.

All these things are a care to me too, my wife. But I would be
bitterly ashamed before the Trojan men and long-robed Trojan women,
if like a coward I were to shrink from battle.
Nor does my heart urge me to do so, since I have learned to be brave,

always fighting alongside the foremost Trojans in battle,
winning great glory for my father and myself. (Homer, *Iliad* 6. 441–446)

As strong as his love is for her and their child, shame, the fear of being seen as inadequate by others, is stronger. This particular scale of values is entirely typical of Greek heroes. Achilles feels he has been shamed before his fellow warriors by Agamemnon, when the king takes away Briseis. Ajax commits suicide rather than live with the shame of not being chosen to receive the armor of Achilles after the latter's death.

Hector's response to Andromache, although not unexpected in his culture, is particularly poignant because Homer has made sure that we feel the full weight of what the hero's masculinity is costing him. This becomes yet more clear as Hector's reply to her continues. He knows, he says, that the day will come when Troy and its people will fall to the Greeks. The hardest part of this knowledge for him is not the loss of the city, nor his father and mother, nor his many brothers, but rather, the certainty that Andromache herself will be made a slave in some Greek household, weaving at the loom, carrying water, and—worst of all—a "harsh necessity" will be upon her, a euphemism for sexual slavery. He imagines her abduction vividly:

And then sometime, someone, seeing you weeping, would say,
"There is the wife of Hector, who used to be the best fighter
Of all the horse-taming Trojans, when they battled around Ilion."
So they will say. And for you there will be fresh pain,
being without a husband to ward off your day of slavery.
But let the poured earth cover me over, a dead man,
before ever I hear you calling out as you are dragged away. (Homer, *Iliad* 6. 459–465)

Hector's love for Andromache and pain at the thought of her being defenseless are palpable here. The reciprocity of their devotion comes through in echoes of her earlier words, her vision of Astyanax's abandonment answered by his imagining of her enslavement, her wish to "go under the earth," rather than be without him returns in his desire for "the earth to cover (him) over" before he should see her enslaved. But finally, he cannot sustain a vision of losing Andromache without circling back to his own horror at being seen by others as inadequate: "Someone . . . will say . . . " Her enslavement is his shame.

We should not jump to the conclusion that Hector's shame means that finally, it is "all about him," but the tension between his love for his wife and his need to understand himself as a man is at the heart of this scene. The attachment he feels to his wife and child is always going to conflict with his masculine desire to become himself through separating from others. Because he must be "in the forefront" of battle, winning glory for himself and his father, in order to be a man he cannot take Andromache's otherwise sensible suggestion that he protect the city from inside the walls.

Hector now reaches for his infant son, who is terrified by the helmet his father wears. It is, on the surface, a light moment and both parents laugh. Hector takes off the helmet and Astyanax is apparently reassured, because he accepts his father's affection without further complaint. On another level, the helmet is a concrete symbol of the firm divide between the battlefield and civilized life in Troy, between Hector the warrior and Hector the father. These latter two versions of the hero come together briefly in the prayer that Hector now makes for his son:

> Zeus and you other immortals, allow this my son
> to become, as I am, distinguished among the Trojans,
> in force and courage, and to rule strongly over Ilion.
> Then sometime let someone say of him as he returns from battle,
> "This young man is much better than his father," and let him kill
> his enemy, bearing bloody armor, and let his mother's heart rejoice.
> (Homer, *Iliad* 6. 476–481)

Hector tries here to bring his son into the world of war, praying for a different future than the one he and Andromache have just envisioned in their fear. Once again we are made to feel how Hector's masculinity separates him from those he loves. In his vision of Astyanax's triumph, he imagines Andromache delighted at seeing her son coming back from battle, covered as Hector now is, with blood. In that moment, he pulls Astyanax away from his mother, leaving her completely alone.

Hector returns his son to Andromache, who receives him smiling through her tears. The mix of emotions fits the uneasy negotiations that have just taken place, as Hector and Andromache stand on the boundary between war and civilization, public and private, masculine and feminine, and hand their son back and forth across the divide like currency. Nor are we surprised to find Hector's next words to his wife beginning with "Strange woman," (*daimoniē*). She should not grieve too much in her heart, he says, for no man ever dies before his fated time. Instead, she should go back inside their house and tend to her duties as a wife. War, he says, is the business of men. He puts his helmet back on, effectively sealing himself off again from his wife, family, and city, and heads for the battlefield. As he leaves, Andromache returns home, turning back again and again for a last glimpse. She will not see her husband alive again. Paris, meanwhile, runs up, resplendent in his armor, and breezily apologizes for delaying his brother. Hector replies, "Strange man" (*daimonie*).

In this powerful interlude, Homer shows us Hector being pulled in two directions, by his love and solicitude for his city and family, and by his need to affirm his existence as a man in the forefront of battle. The conflict between the two worlds is left unresolved, and Hector is finally alienated from everyone he meets in Troy—his mother, his brother, and most movingly, his wife. In each encounter, we have seen how the strains brought on by the war widen the already existing gulf between Hector's understanding of himself as a man and his fierce love for his family. The war makes everything more urgent, but the conflicts are in the culture anyway. Homer works within the limitations of conventional gender roles to produce a portrait of unusual intimacy between a man and woman, but finally they must be "strange" to each other.

Odysseus Meets His Match

The other prominent example of intimacy between a man and a woman in Greek literature is the relationship between Odysseus and Penelope in the *Odyssey*. Indeed, that enduring bond is probably the best known of any in ancient literature, what many would call the first "love story." We will see that although there is much to be said for that view, the relationship between Odysseus and Penelope is both less romantic (in our modern sense) and more complicated than its reputation would suggest.

We have seen that Homer borrows from other kinds of relationships, parent-child and sibling, in an attempt to capture the richness of the bond between Hector and Andromache. In the *Odyssey*, Odysseus himself defines what will be the standard against which love relationships between men and women in the poem are to be judged. At the beginning of book 6, still far from home, he has washed up on the shore of an island called Scheria, home of the Phaeacians, a highly evolved and—from the Greeks' perspective—somewhat effete civilization. He is naked and exhausted from enduring several days in the ocean by himself after Poseidon destroyed his boat. He meets Nausicaa, the daughter of the king of the Phaeacians, who is at the shore with some girlfriends, washing clothes and playing catch. Attempting to win her over in the hope of getting help returning home, he delivers a masterful speech, playing on Nausicaa's adolescent interest in men. Is she a goddess, he asks, or a mortal? If the former, he likens her to Artemis, virgin goddess of the hunt. If she is human, then thrice-blessed are her parents, for having such an awesome daughter. He goes on for almost 40 lines, laying it on thick. At the very end, he says:

May the gods give you everything you desire in your heart,
a husband and a home, and bestow on you sweet agreement too.
For nothing is stronger and better, than when a man and woman
thinking just alike, keep a home together.
Much pain they give to their enemies, and pleasure to their
friends. Their fame reaches far. (Homer, *Odyssey* 6. 180–185)

The speech works. Nausicaa forms a crush on the handsome stranger and takes him home to her parents, who eventually give him a ride home on one of their ships. For our purposes, the key words are *homophosune,* a noun, translated here as "agreement," and *homophroneonte,* a participle, "thinking just alike." In both cases, the Greek root, *phron-,* denoting thought, thinking, understanding, is combined with the prefix *homo-,* meaning "together, in the same way." Given that Greek men usually considered women to be incapable of "male" reasoning, Odysseus seems to be envisioning something quite unusual within the context of Homer's patriarchal society, a man and woman who "think in the same way." Odysseus holds this kind of bond as an ideal, something that any girl would wish for, and we should take it seriously, in spite of the wily purposes that guide the speech as a whole. We might conclude that the concept of "thinking alike" is meant to be understood in a limited way here, meaning something like "getting along." But as we will see,

Homer in fact creates in Penelope an unusual Greek woman, whose "thinking" is enough like Odysseus's thinking to make her a match for him in the trickery and manipulation for which he is famous.

For most of the *Odyssey*, Odysseus and Penelope are separated. He has been making his weary way home from Troy for 10 years when the poem opens. She, meanwhile, has been waiting patiently for him, while fending off the attentions of the suitors in Ithaka. That Penelope will always be faithful to Odysseus is one of those things that "everybody knows." She is the model of the faithful wife. He, meanwhile, is somewhat less exclusive in his attentions, forming liaisons of various kinds on his way home, with Circe, an alluring witch, and with Calypso, a nymph who compels him to stay with her for seven years before Zeus sends Hermes with orders for her to let him go. The choice to stay with Circe seems to be entirely voluntary; the situation with Calypso is somewhat less clear. Although she is said to keep him by the force of her magic, Homer says at one point that Calypso finds him weeping and looking out at the ocean, for the nymph was no longer "pleasing" to him, suggesting that once she was "pleasing."

However we interpret this passage, it is clear that a double standard, typical of patriarchal cultures all over the world, is at work in the poem. Odysseus's dalliance with Circe is acceptable "play," but Penelope's faithfulness to Odysseus excludes sex with other men. As we have seen, the story of Clytemnestra, the "bad wife," is an important paradigm in the *Odyssey*, modeling the consequences of a wife's giving in to her natural tendency to lust. Penelope is frequently compared, implicitly or explicitly, to Clytemnestra, and one reason for urgency in getting Odysseus back to Ithaka is the increasing possibility that she will give in to the suitors. The first two-thirds of the poem follows Telemachus and Odysseus on their respective journeys. Books 18–23 shift our attention to Ithaka and especially to Penelope.

While Odysseus, disguised as an old beggar, is plotting with Athena to kill the suitors, Penelope is left in the dark. Her willingness to hold out against them in case her husband is still alive seems to be waning. Although she has been told by Theoclymenus, a seer traveling with Telemachus, and by Odysseus in his disguise as a beggar, that Odysseus is alive and will soon return to reek vengeance on the suitors, she is skeptical. We hear from the suitors themselves that she held them at bay for some time by saying that she would marry one of them once she had finished weaving a shroud for Laertes, Odysseus's father who is an old man. She managed to fool them by unraveling at night what she had woven during the day, but eventually one of the faithless maids who was sleeping with the suitors gave away her secret. Although that ploy seems to be aimed clearly at putting off marriage, her appearance before the suitors in book 18 is more ambiguous. She tells them that before leaving for Troy, Odysseus gave her explicit instructions: if he was not back by the time Telemachus had a man's beard, she should assume he had died and marry whomever she pleased. This news causes great excitement among the suitors, for Telemachus has returned from his journey and is asserting himself in a manly way.

Clearly, we are at a crucial point in the story. Penelope seems to be on the verge of abandoning her bond to Odysseus to take another husband, a move that, as we have seen, would threaten the health of the royal household in a fundamental way. Odysseus himself is in the room when his wife tells the suitors that the time is approaching for her to remarry, so the urgency of his mission is abundantly clear. Still, not trusting her to keep his plans secret, he does not tell her that it is he behind the disguise. She is, for the moment, on her own. As we will see, she manages to maneuver with great intelligence and tact, influencing events in such a way that Odysseus and Telemachus, with Athena's help, are able to surprise the suitors and kill them, restoring the male head of the household to his proper place and thus returning the household to its proper order.

Part of the power and charm of the *Odyssey*'s final books comes from the way various agents, all working independently, arrive at the right place at the right time. Will Odysseus get back in time? Can he and his few trusted retainers defeat the mob of suitors? And if these things work out, will Penelope still be there for him to win? We have here the first cliffhanger. Adding to the fun is the fact that, whereas Odysseus's and Athena's motives are made clear to us as they plot, Penelope's true desires are more veiled. We can in fact understand her actions in more than one way. We may see her as remaining completely faithful to her husband, in which case the appearance before the suitors becomes another manipulation. She coyly mentions that men who come courting usually bring gifts and provokes an avalanche of goodies. Homer tells us, in fact, that Odysseus observes this ploy with pleasure. We may go further and say, as some have wanted to do, that Penelope actually communicates in a kind of code with her disguised husband when she meets him, still in his disguise as beggar, after dinner one night. She tells him of her dreams and of her decision to hold the contest of the bow. In this version, he gets the message and interprets the dreams in an encouraging way. When she offers the bow to anyone who can string it, he makes sure he's ready.

Finally, and most tantalizingly, we can interpret Penelope's actions as showing that a part of her, at least, is moving toward remarriage. Her appearance before the suitors becomes a preliminary flirtation, and her dreams betray an interest in the suitors that is threatening to Odysseus. In this version, we have the most exciting climax for the story. Penelope gives up and decides to stage a contest to choose a new husband. Odysseus, ever the master of good timing, maneuvers himself into position to be chosen. After the slaughter of the suitors in book 22, which Penelope has not seen, having been sent to her bedroom beforehand by Telemachus, Odysseus begins the process of revealing himself to his wife. At first, she is resistant: there have been many travelers who claimed to be her husband, and all so far have been frauds. Why should she believe this one? Telemachus is angry with his mother, calling her "harsh," but she tells him that she and Odysseus have their own ways of recognizing each other:

If truly
this is Odysseus, and he has returned home, we two

will easily recognize each other. For we have signs,
hidden and secret from others, which we two alone would know.
(Homer, *Odyssey* 23. 107–110)

Now, we think, the great moment has finally arrived, when Odysseus and Penelope will be reunited. Homer, in typical fashion, makes us wait a little longer. Odysseus reassures Telemachus: his mother can test him and will soon come to see him for who he really is. Meanwhile, he needs to bathe, covered as he is with the gore of the battle—we are reminded of Hector in Troy. Telemachus is to arrange for a feast that will make those living outside the palace think that a marriage feast is underway. This last detail is richly evocative. The fake festivities are practical, in that they will give Odysseus and Telemachus cover, hiding the deaths of the suitors for a while. They can plan their defense against the families of the suitors in the interim. But of course Odysseus also hopes that he will be "remarrying" Penelope, if he can convince her of his identity.

The ruse apparently works, and Odysseus is not only bathed but also made especially beautiful by Athena:

A maidservant, Eurynome, bathed great-hearted Odysseus
and anointed him with oil in his own home, throwing
around his shoulders a beautiful tunic and robe.
But Athena poured great splendor over him from head to toe,
making him seem bigger and stronger. From his head
she made to grow thick curls, like blooming hyacinth.
As when some skilled craftsman pours gold over silver,
he whom Hephaestos and Pallas Athena have taught
in every art, and he fashions exquisite works,
thus she poured beauty over his head and shoulders. (Homer, *Odyssey* 23. 153–162)

Athena's intervention here repeats exactly a passage in book 6, when the goddess enhances the hero's looks after he has emerged from the sea onto the island of the Phaeacians, beaten up by his ordeal at sea. In both places, Odysseus faces a crucial test, to be given by a woman, which will determine whether he succeeds in returning to his former glory as king, husband, father, and son in Ithaka. The extra beauty works on Nausicaa, as we have seen, and we wonder how he will fare this time.

Looking "like a god," he approaches Penelope and tries again:

Strange woman, the gods on Olympus gave
you a heart harder than other fragile women's.
No other wife, with a stubborn heart like yours,
would resist her husband, who had suffered so much
and then come home to his own land in the twentieth year.
But come, nurse, make up a bed so that I may
Sleep. For this woman has a heart of iron. (Homer, *Odyssey* 23. 166–172)

Penelope answers:

Strange man, I am not proud, nor do I condemn,
nor am I much confused, for I know well what you

looked like when you left Ithaka in your long-oared ship.
But come now, make up a firm bed for him, Eurykleia,
outside the well-built bedroom, that bed he himself made.
Put that firm bed outside, and throw over it
fleecy blankets and warm covers. (Homer, *Odyssey* 23. 174–180)

We are not surprised, perhaps, to find the two addressing each other as
daimonie/ē. Like Hector and Andromache, their love for each other is always
in the context of the fundamental estrangement we have seen between the
sexes in Greek culture. But what comes next is indeed a surprise. Penelope's
instructions to the maid bring an angry response from her husband:

What you've said is painful, woman!
Who moved my bed? It would be hard,
even for someone skilled, unless he were a
god, easily to put it elsewhere, even though he wished to.
No living man, not even a young strong one,
could lightly budge it, since there is a special feature
of this curiously wrought bed. I made it myself, no one else.
(Homer, *Odyssey* 23. 183–189)

He goes on to say that his house is built around the trunk of an olive tree, still
rooted in the ground, and that the trunk forms one of the bed posts. No one
could move it without tearing down the house itself.

Now, for the first time in the story, Odysseus loses his self-control. His
indignation at the possibility that anyone could tamper with what is the
foundation of his house and, symbolically, of his very existence, as the olive
is sacred to his divine protector, Athena, has completely unnerved him. With
her ruse, Penelope gets her husband to reveal himself involuntarily, something he never does anywhere else in the story. Her own self-control has been
a match for his. She has held out against the suitors, and also against her
own passionate desire to see her husband again, until she could be sure he
is back. She now gives in to him, and they have the reunion that they—and
we—have been waiting for so long. Although a woman, Penelope has proven
herself a match for Odysseus in cunning and self-control. Now we see what
Odysseus—and Homer—meant by *homophrosunē*.

As in the case of Hector and Andromache, so here Homer works against
the conventional assumptions in Greek culture about the nature of men
and women. Although Odysseus and Penelope, like their counterparts in
book 6 of the *Iliad*, are "strange" to each other, they are portrayed as having
a deep bond in spite of their differences. In the case of Hector and Andromache, Homer borrows from other relationships, sibling and parental, to
represent the exceptional richness of the connection between them. In the
Odyssey, the unusual strength of the bond between Odysseus and Penelope
is dramatized more as a contest—always welcome to Greeks—between
husband and wife. Penelope can hold Odysseus not only because she waits
faithfully (if we take that view of her actions), but because she is a match
for him.

CONCLUSION

The patriarchal cultures of the ancient Mediterranean, and particularly Greek culture, which we can know best, saw the world in such a way that the nature of men and women seemed to them to reflect what was "natural." Women were by nature wetter, cooler, and softer than men. Thus because it was considered healthier by nature to be warm, dry, and hard, women were biologically inferior to men. At the same time, women, because of their basic nature, were thought to be more susceptible to strong emotion and thus less able to think rationally. Because human civilization was the product of the application of rational intelligence to control the powerful forces of nature, men were more suited by nature than women to be the agents and guardians of civilization. Beginning from these assumptions, which may now seem quaint and dubious to us, we can see how men explained the need for women to be subservient to men, to be confined to the house and kept out of the public sphere of politics.

At the same time, we have seen examples of male Greek authors struggling to imagine how a man and woman might overcome their fundamental differences and achieve a strong bond, based not on dominance and submission but on love and mutual respect. From these latter relationships, so fraught with contradictions, we turn now to the arena that men in the cultures of the ancient Mediterranean would have felt was most "natural" to them and most alien to women—war.

Four

Men and War

War is the work of men.

—Homer, *Iliad* 6. 492

To write about men and war would seem to be the easiest job I have in this book. After all, the civilizations around the Mediterranean were, as far as we can tell, constantly at war with each other in the first millennium B.C.E. ranging from raids on each other's cattle to major campaigns for the control of whole civilizations. They maneuvered large forces across land and sea, and they dueled hand-to-hand. They summoned citizen armies, and they hired mercenaries. Yet it is precisely the universality of war in the ancient world that makes it so challenging to discuss how it was practiced within individual cultures. The variety of modes of warfare and their changes over time also make generalization difficult. What we can do, relying on the relatively limited sources available to us, is attempt to see how some men might have imagined the experience of war as a part of the model for masculine behavior we have been building here. Why was war such a fundamental venue for expressing masculinity? Why were men suited to fighting in war and women not? These questions have taken on a new relevance in the last 50 years or so in countries where women have begun serving as soldiers. But even if that were not so, we would want to look at how ancient civilizations represented the experience of men in war, for the role of warrior seemed to them to exemplify something quintessentially masculine.

The Greeks, like most Western cultures until the late twentieth century, believed that combat was naturally and appropriately an exclusively male activity. (The mythical Amazons were an object of fascination precisely because they behaved "unnaturally.") We have seen that Greek intellectuals rationalized this belief in various ways: war requires physical strength, and men are naturally stronger than women; because they are naturally drier than women, men are simply healthier in general, and thus more reliable in combat; soldiers must depend on each other when they risk their lives to defend their communities, and women are by nature more prone to lying

and untrustworthy behavior; discipline is necessary for a smoothly functioning army, and women are more reproachful and combative than men.
Most of these assumptions were based, as we have seen, on what now seem
like extremely dubious pseudo-scientific theories. But Greek ideas about
war as a venue for expressing masculinity went well beyond what they
thought of as the natural differences between men and women. In their
perspective, war becomes a powerful vehicle for articulating and exploring the paradoxical nature of human beings, as creatures who can create
civilization as a refuge from the very forces within themselves that would
destroy it.

WAR AND DEATH IN THE *ILIAD*

In book 12 of the *Iliad*, Sarpedon, an ally of the Trojans, pauses in the
midst of furious fighting to talk to his fellow warrior Glaucus:

Glaucus, why are the two of us honored so,
with the best seats, with the best meat and full cups
in Lycia, and all look on us as gods,
and we rule great estates beside the banks of the Xanthos,
rich in vineyards and grain-bearing fields?
Therefore now we must take our stand among
the front ranks of the Lycians, and enter the raging battle,
so that someone of the close-armored Lycians might say,
"Not without glory are these kings of ours
who rule over Lycia, eating fat sheep and
drinking the choice, honey-sweet wine. No,
their strength is great, since they fight among the foremost Lycians."
Oh friend, if fleeing this battle we could be
ageless and immortal, I myself would not
fight in the forefront, nor urge you into the battle where men win glory.
But now, seeing that the spirits of death stand close by
in their thousands, whom no man can flee or escape,
let us go forward, winning glory for ourselves or yielding it to another.
(Homer, *Iliad* 12. 310–328)

This speech is often cited as the definitive representation of the hero's life
in Homeric epic. Sarpedon begins by asking, "why are we two heroes?" His
answer is that they are honored by their community because they fight in the
front lines to protect their fellow citizens. The warriors in the *Iliad* come from
small, individual states, ruled by *basileis*, "kings." Sarpedon and Glaucus
come from Lycia, an area south of Troy, which has allied itself with Priam's
kingdom to repel the Greek invaders. Although some stories and characters
in the *Iliad* are as old as 1200 B.C.E., the social and political arrangements of
Homeric societies mainly reflect the period from 900–700 B.C.E., when warring between small kingdoms was constant. In this kind of world, the warrior
who can defend his city becomes the man on whom all of the other communal arrangements depend.

The first part of the speech thus envisions a kind of bargain, high status in return for fighting on behalf of one's city. We hear a certain degree of self-satisfaction here: they are conspicuously famous and they deserve it. Then at line 323, the speech takes a somewhat surprising turn, as Sarpedon imagines what conditions would cause him to avoid fighting. If, he says, they were immortal, he would neither fight nor urge Glaucus to do so. But because the "spirits of death" surround them, they should either seek glory by killing their enemies or die trying. In these last lines, Homer embeds a fundamental truth about the world as he—and his heroes—see it: only the fact of mortality produces the necessity for humans to have virtues. If men were immortal, then nothing they did would finally matter. The Greeks had no developed sense of an afterlife as reward or punishment for one's behavior in this life. The Underworld, as it appears in Greek literature and religion, is a shadowy place. The souls there exist in an insubstantial, impotent kind of oblivion, hardly an alluring destination worth exerting oneself to achieve. The only real hedge against nothingness in this model of the world is fame that lives on after someone dies. So Sarpedon briefly contemplates the existence he would have as a god, but then discards it: because he must die, glory must be won. We return here to the definitive quality of a masculine life as the Greeks understood it—mortality. As Sarpedon's speech emphasizes, if the nearness of death clarifies meaning in a man's life, then war, especially as Homer portrays it, is the foremost crucible of masculinity.

Although fully one-third of the *Iliad* is devoted to scenes of battle, the poem's representation of fighting is in fact confined to a fairly narrow range of experience. Virtually all combat described in any detail is individual duels. There are some descriptions of group movements, but none of large-scale strategy. Within the duels, the range of events is also restricted. There are no lengthy battles or lingering deaths. Two warriors confront each other. One is either killed quickly or wounded. If wounded, he is quickly healed and sent back into battle. This concentration of focus brings us, again and again, to a man facing death. In that definitive moment, Homer often pauses to mark what will be forever lost:

Meriones killed Phereklos, son of the carpenter
Harmonides, who knew how to make beautiful things
with his hands, for Pallas Athena loved him above all others.
This man built balanced ships for Paris,
carriers of evil, which brought death for other Trojans
and for him, since he knew nothing of the gods' plans.
This man Meriones struck, when he caught him in the chase,
in the right buttock, and the spear's sharp point
went straight through his bladder, under the bone.
He fell to his knees, and death covered him over.
Then Meges slew Pedaios, the son of Antenor,
a bastard, and yet shining Theano nursed him,
as she did her own children, to please her husband.
The son of Phyles, famous for his spear, approached this man,
and struck him in the back of the head with his sharp spear.

The blade cut under his tongue and through his teeth,
and he fell in the dust, and bit the cold bronze with his teeth.
Eurypylos, son of Euaimon, killed bright Hypsenor,
the son of high-hearted Dolopion, who was made priest of
Skamandros, and was honored like a god in his country.
Eurypylos, the glorious son of Euaimon, struck this man
On the shoulder, running him down as he fled,
leaping with his sword, and cut off his heavy arm,
and the bloody arm fell on the ground. Over both eyes
purple death and strong fate took hold. (Homer, *Iliad* 5. 59–83)

Although Homer's battle descriptions are subtly varied and seldom repetitious, these lines are fairly representative. None of these figures—Meriones, Phereklos, Meges, Pedaios, Eurypylos, or Hypsenor—appear elsewhere in the poem. They and many, many others flash by us in a moment, their sole function to triumph or disappear in death. In a poem that devotes more than 5,000 lines to battle scenes, we might expect some glorification of winners, and there are in fact many gloating speeches by victors in the poem. The death that awaits a warrior in battle is doubly emasculating: he is defeated by another man in the ultimate competition, and his death is nearly always brought about by his being penetrated, and thus losing his bodily integrity. Nevertheless, Homer's own voice as impersonal narrator never lingers to praise the winners, only to memorialize the losers. Although the *Iliad* is the first and most famous poem about war, it does not finally invite us to share the thrill of exerting power over others. Rather, its real subject is the fact of death as a part of human life.

The *Iliad*'s best warriors, Achilles and Hector, are both in fact problematic forces within their own societies. Hector, as we have seen, is walled off by his status as warrior from those he loves within the city of Troy. The blood on his hands keeps him from sacrificing at the temple. His helmet frightens his son. Achilles, the greatest of all warriors, is completely alienated from his fellow Greeks by that very greatness and the pride it engenders. When he acts to preserve his status, he causes death and suffering for those he is supposed to be protecting. To win honor from their fellows, both of these warriors must excel, must be "in the forefront of battle." Being there, they are alienated from those they love. This paradoxical tension is characteristic, in fact, of all Greek heroes. If their heroic will is aimed at goals that benefit their fellows, they can be saviors; if not, they can destroy everything and everyone they love.

AJAX IN THE *ILIAD:* THE SOLDIER'S SOLDIER

The least problematic of all the warriors in the *Iliad* is Ajax. Physically powerful and fiercely dedicated to his comrades, taciturn and formidable in his single-minded attention to duty, he is the only major warrior in the poem who receives no special attention or help from the gods. He is characterized by his massive and immovable bulk. Whereas Achilles is swift and mercurial, Ajax is steady and absolutely unshakeable. When all of the other major fighters on the Greek side have had to leave the battlefield because of wounds, Ajax begins a long, slow retreat, holding off the Trojans for hours while his comrades recover. His courage and strength are commemorated in a rare double simile. Ajax has just rescued Odysseus from a Trojan ambush and now finds himself hemmed in by the enemy:

He stood there at a loss, and threw the seven-layered shield
behind him; glancing at the attackers, he bristled, like a wild beast,
turning this way and that, moving his knees only slightly.
As when farmers with their dogs chase a tawny lion
from the cattle-yard, and they will not allow him
to strip the fat from the cattle, keeping guard all night.
He, craving flesh, attacks, but cannot get what he wants.
For the javelins fly at him thick and fast from
their bold hands, and also blazing torches.
Of these he is afraid, for all his fury,
and he retreats in the morning, hungry in his heart.
So Ajax, disappointed in his heart, drew back
unwillingly from the Trojans, since he feared for the Achaean ships.
As when a donkey, stubbornly resisting some boys, goes
into the fields, and many sticks are shattered against him,
but he keeps on eating the rich crops. And the boys keep
hitting him with sticks, but their strength is too infantile.
Finally they drive him out, when he has had his fill.
So it was for great Ajax, the son of Telamon,
when the high-hearted Trojans and their allies
stabbing his big shield with spears kept harrying him. (Homer, *Iliad* 11. 545–565)

Strong as a lion, stubborn as a donkey, Ajax is a vivid presence in the poem. When the Trojans try in book 17 to drag off the corpse of Patroclus to desecrate it, Ajax holds them off in a desperate struggle. Earlier in the story, he and Hector are chosen by their respective sides to fight a duel. They begin, and it appears that Ajax is definitely winning, when the herald Idaios urges them to suspend fighting, as darkness is coming on. Ajax answers with characteristic bluntness: Ask Hector, he says. He is the one who challenged me. If he wants to quit, that's fine with me.

Later the next day, Ajax is part of the three-man embassy sent by Agamemnon to urge Achilles to return to the fighting when the Trojans threaten to overwhelm the Greeks. Odysseus leads off with a long and rhetorically sophisticated plea for Achilles to accept Agamemnon's offer of compensation for the insults inflicted on him in the quarrel of book 1. Achilles replies with a passionate defense of his refusal, his most famous speech in the poem. Next comes Phoenix, an aged retainer, who once held the infant Achilles on his knee. The old man appeals to Achilles's affection for him and tells a long cautionary tale about another warrior, Meleager, who held out from fighting as a matter of honor, refusing lavish gifts. But in the end, Meleager had to return to battle without compensation, the implication of the story being that Achilles ought to take the gifts while he can, as he will have to return eventually anyway. This argument, too, falls on deaf ears. Finally, Ajax has his turn:

Zeus-born son of Laertes, clever Odysseus,
let us go. For I do not think anything will be
accomplished with words on this mission.
We ought to tell the outcome, bad though it is,
to the Danaans, who I suppose sit waiting for us.
For Achilles has made savage the great spirit in his heart,
harsh man, nor does he heed the affection of his friends,
by which we honor him above all others by the ships.
He is pitiless. Another man accepts recompense
from the murderer of his brother or his dead child,
and the killer stays in his homeland, having paid a heavy price.
And the other restrains his heart and manly spirit
when he has received payment. But in your chest, Achilles,
the gods put an unrelenting and evil heart on account of one girl
alone. Now we have offered you seven women, by far the best,
and many other things besides. Adopt a kindly spirit
and respect your house; for we are under the same roof,
out of the whole host of Greeks, and we yearn to be dearest
to you and most honored out of all the Greeks. (Homer, *Iliad* 9. 624–642)

This is the shortest speech by far and, unlike the other two, calls only on two qualities in Achilles, friendship and honor. It is the appeal of the soldier's soldier, the man's man.

Although Ajax appears in relatively few passages, he is one of Homer's most vivid creations. He makes an equally memorable cameo appearance in the *Odyssey,* when Odysseus travels to the Underworld in search of knowledge about his homecoming. Having spoken at length with the ghosts of Agamemnon and Achilles, he sees Ajax standing silently in the distance. The two of them competed at Troy after Achilles's death for the right to have his armor, and Odysseus won. (The nature of the contest is not revealed.) Now Odysseus wants to patch things up and makes a conciliatory speech. Ajax strides away, refusing to have anything to do with him. This story of the contest for Achilles's armor in turn became the background for Sophocles's play, *Ajax,* produced sometime in 440 B.C.E.

SOPHOCLES'S AJAX: WARRIOR AS THROWBACK

Because the warrior lives in the shadow of death, he exemplifies heroism as the Greeks understood it with particular intensity. He stands, we might say, on the boundary between nature and culture, drawing on elemental forces to fight—thus the frequent use of animal similes to describe the warrior's ferocity in Homeric epic—but working most of the time on behalf of culture. This marginal, or "liminal" status becomes yet more complex in Athenian tragedy, where the Homeric warrior is problematic in two ways, as a warrior and as a representative of an older, aristocratic society, out of tune with the newer communal values of the emerging democracy. Ajax, in Sophocles's play, exemplifies this disjunction with particular force.

The play, from beginning to end, focuses on Ajax. This concentration on a single heroic figure is characteristic of Sophoclean drama in general, but in no other play does one character so completely dominate our attention and that of the actors on stage. Ajax speaks with passion and acts decisively, brooking no opposition. These qualities make him an object of awe for others in the play, powerfully present but at the same time remote, austere. He represents, in his attitudes toward himself and others, an anachronistic figure for the Athenian audience of the 440s B.C.E., a Homeric warrior in the midst of the new democratic society.

The play is set on the shore near Troy, with the central doors of the structure behind the *skene* representing the entrance to Ajax's tent. As the play opens, Athena is standing above the building, perhaps on the *mechane* or on the top of the central building. Odysseus enters and moves across the stage, as if tracking footprints. Athena speaks to him, asking what he is up to. He replies that he is tracking Ajax, his enemy, who sometime the night before attacked and slaughtered herds of sheep and cattle—plus the men guarding them—belonging to the Greeks. Ajax was sighted carrying a bloody sword near the slaughter, and the tracks from the field lead to his tent. Although he hates Ajax, Odysseus cannot understand the attack: why kill animals? Athena replies that Ajax thought he was killing the leaders of the Greek army, Agamemnon and Menelaus, whom he hates, blaming them for depriving him of the honor that Achilles's armor would bring. He had, she says, set out to murder the Greek leaders and had reached their tent when she sent a delusional madness on him, making him think the flocks were his human targets. After killing many animals, he tied up a few more and dragged them to his tent, where he tortured them, thinking he was avenging himself on the Greek leaders.

At this point, Athena calls Ajax out of the tent. Odysseus is alarmed, afraid what his enemy will do, but Athena assures him that Ajax is still under her control and that he will not see Odysseus. There follows a poignant and somewhat nasty interlude, as Athena goads Ajax into boasting of the conquests he has made. His delusional satisfaction at the suffering of his enemies is a sad spectacle, the once-great warrior humiliated for the amusement of the goddess and Odysseus. The scene emphasizes vividly Ajax's isolation, as Athena stages a play within a play, a private performance for Odysseus, with Ajax as her unwilling actor. Odysseus finds the experience unsettling, but Athena sees nothing wrong with this spectacle. After all, she says, isn't it good to laugh at your enemies?

The actors leave the stage, and the chorus, made up of sailors from Salamis loyal to Ajax, now march in and sing their first song. The subject is their dependence on Ajax. Great men always draw attention:

Aiming at great men,
one would not miss. But if
he should speak such slander against me

no one would believe it.
Envy stalks those who have power.
Lesser men, without the great, are
a feeble prop for a fortress.
The humble man had best depend
On the great, and the great should
Be supported by the lesser. (Sophocles, *Ajax* 154–161)

The chorus's words remind us of Sarpedon's speech: great men must stand out from the general run of people. The community depends on them and must in turn, the loyal sailors affirm, support them, not indulge in envious attacks. Here we return to the problem with heroes: lesser people must depend on them, but in doing so they risk disaster if the hero's will and pride lead him to destructive and self-destructive acts. As we have noted, the warrior represents this ambiguity in its purest from. Ajax fought for and protected the same men whom his angry pride now leads him to try to destroy.

At the end of the choral song, the door to the tent opens, and Tecmessa, Ajax's concubine, steps out. He has won her as a war prize at Troy, and they have a son, Eurysaces. We now see further evidence of the suffering that great men can visit on those under their protection. Tecmessa describes how Ajax left the tent in the night and then returned with his "captives," how he slowly came out of his madness, and his subsequent horror and self-loathing. As she points out, she has suffered grief twice over, once in response to Ajax's delusions, then again when witnessing his subsequent pain. At least when he was still mad, Ajax could delight in the suffering of his enemies. She had no such luxury.

As her exchange with the chorus continues, Ajax begins to groan and shriek from inside the tent. He calls for Eurysaces and for Teucer, his half-brother. Tecmessa opens the doors to the tent, and we now see the ruined warrior sitting amidst the slaughtered animals, covered with their blood. The chorus is horrified as Ajax calls to them to help him die. He would rather end his life than endure the shame of his humiliating failure to avenge himself on his enemies. Homeric heroes live in what we call a "shame culture," in which a man's status is determined by how others view and judge him, based on basically external qualities, beauty, strength, possessions. Those commodities can in turn be gotten only through victory in various kinds of competition, of which there is no lack in Greek culture. Ajax expresses the Homeric warrior's shame at being perceived to have failed. Unlike Sarpedon, he is not seen to be "first," "in front." Rather, he has lost a public contest with another man, the prize for which was to inherit the armor that would have marked him as the best warrior. And now, even worse, his enemies, and especially Odysseus, are laughing at him.

The exchanges between Ajax, Tecmessa, and the chorus in the next 200 or so lines take us back to book 6 of the *Iliad*, an echo that is surely deliberate on Sophocles's part. In both works, the warrior expresses his fear of, and distaste for, the shame that accompanies being perceived to fail in the eyes of other warriors. Those who depend on him, meanwhile, beg him not to leave them defenseless. The parallels are sometimes explicit. After Ajax ponders how best to respond to his humiliation, ending with what seems to be a decision to commit suicide, Tecmessa responds with a long speech. She was, she says, born to a free father, but since being captured, she has given herself entirely to Ajax. She begs him not to let the voices of his enemies cause him to desert her and their infant son. If he does so, her fate is sealed:

If you die and having died desert me,
know that on that day I will be carried off
by force by the Argives along with
your son, to lead the life of slaves.
Then some one of the rulers will spit
out bitter words, a nasty speech,
"See the bedmate of Ajax, who was
the strongest man in the army,
leading a slave's life, she who once was so grand."
So they will say, and my fate will drive me on,
a shameful thing for you and your family. (Sophocles, *Ajax* 496–504)

She goes on to remind him that he has utterly destroyed her own country and that her parents are dead. He is all she has left, her only protection.

The echoes of Andromache's speeches to Hector are clear. But whereas Homer's hero responded to his wife's abject pleading with great sympathy, Ajax gives Tecmessa little in return. He will consider her plight if she does as he says, which is to bring his son to him. Eurysaces has been hidden away, for fear that Ajax would harm him in his madness. He is brought forth, and Hector's prayer for his son in *Iliad* 6 echoes through the speech that follows:

Lift him, lift him up. He won't be afraid
seeing all this freshly-splattered gore,
if he is truly his father's son.
But break him in right away to his
father's harsh ways, train him
to have his father's nature.
Oh my son, be luckier than your father,
but like him in all other things,
and you will not be base.
Indeed, I even envy you this,
that you know nothing of these evils.
The sweetest life is ignorant,
for ignorance is a painless evil,
until you learn to rejoice or suffer.
And whenever you come to that knowledge,
you will have to show what kind of son,
of what kind of father, you were raised to be.
Until then, enjoy the soft breezes, sporting
your young life, a delight to your mother. (Sophocles, *Ajax* 545–559)

Eurysaces is to be a warrior-hero like his father, tough and eager for killing. And like Hector's son, he is to be a "delight for his mother." Ajax, like Hector, shows no awareness that his son's mother might not be happy to see her baby grow up to be a ruthless fighter like his father. The speech continues, as Ajax orders his men to entrust Eurysaces to Telamon, Ajax's own father, and bequeaths the boy his famous shield. The rest of his armor is not to be the prize of any contest after his death: it must be buried with him. The chorus and Tecmessa are alarmed at what sounds like preparations by Ajax for his own death. He brushes aside her questions about his plans, demanding that she obey in silence. He goes back into his tent and closes the entrance, leaving Tecmessa outside.

After the chorus sings a mournful lament for the ruin of Ajax, their once proud leader, he reappears and delivers a long and powerful speech. His theme is the inexorable forces beyond human control, to which all must bend:

Great and measureless time gives birth
to light from darkness, then covers it again.
Nothing is so unexpected that it cannot come to pass;
the dreadful oath and the unbending will can be conquered.
Even I, who was so rigid just now,
like iron when it is dipped, am growing soft,
speaking like a woman for my wife's sake.
I pity her and my son, left a widow and orphan
among my enemies. (Sophocles, *Ajax* 646–654)

He will now go, he says, to the seashore, to cleanse himself of Athena's heavy anger. He'll then hide his sword, a gift from Hector, in the ground, so that no one may see it. It is, he says, the most hateful of weapons, proving the old saying that "gifts from enemies never bring profit." Therefore he will be different from now on, yielding to the gods' will, learning to respect Agamemnon and Menelaus, his former enemies. This new wisdom is true to nature's laws:

Indeed the most awesome and powerful things
yield to deference. Winter's snowy footprints
give way to fruitful summer; the wearying circle of
night makes way for the white steeds of day to shine;
the blast of dreadful gales dies down and soothes
the ocean's moaning; all-conquering sleep at last
relents, releasing its captives' fetters.
Shall I not learn wisdom? (Sophocles, *Ajax* 669–677)

The tone of Ajax's words has prompted much discussion among classical scholars, but his intent seems clear enough. Since Tecmessa is on stage and presumably within hearing, the speech is in one sense deliberately deceptive. Ajax is indeed on his way to the seashore, where he will "bury" the sword, but with the blade pointed up, so he may fall on it and end his humiliation. By deceiving his wife and friends, he can carry out his plans without interference. At the same time, Ajax's comment about becoming softer is not entirely false. His brusque dismissal of Tecmessa's wishes earlier might have led us to expect a blunt, soldierly exit, with no attempt to spare the feelings of his family. The beauty of the poetry here gives greater weight to Ajax's words, adding some hint of compassion for those who love and depend on him.

Ajax, Tecmessa, and Eurysaces exit the stage, and the chorus sings again, this time a short but ecstatic song, expressing relief that Ajax, their leader, will not be abandoning them. Again, we see and hear how much others depend on Ajax. As it turns out, their joy will be short-lived. A messenger enters and tells the chorus that Calchas, a prophet, has prophesied to Teucer, Ajax's half-brother, that if Ajax leaves his tent he will die. Tecmessa is summoned, and we see her panicky realization that all is lost. The hunt for Ajax begins, but they are too late. The setting now shifts—a relatively rare thing in Athenian tragedy—to the seashore, where we see Ajax kneeling over his sword. He gives one final speech, asking the gods for a swift death and saying farewell to the sun, a traditional prelude to the tragic hero's death. He then falls on his sword, again a rare sight in Athenian tragedy, in which death almost never occurs on stage.

The chorus, which exited the stage when the scene shifted, returns, looking frantically and unsuccessfully for Ajax. Tecmessa then returns and finds the body. Yet again, we see the devastating effects on her of Ajax's death. She foresees slavery for herself and Eurysaces and imagines Ajax's enemies exulting at his death. She calls for Teucer, her only family now, and covers the corpse. Teucer enters, bringing with him a fresh wave of grief and fear: Eurysaces must be found immediately, as some enemy of Ajax may kill him. In a long lament over the corpse, Teucer foresees that Telamon, the father to him and Ajax (his mother was a captive war-prize, like Tecmessa), will hate him for coming home without his brother. He, like everyone else we have seen so far, both loved and admired Ajax; and like everyone else, he will suffer because Ajax is gone.

The echoes of Hector continue in Teucer's speech, as he reflects ruefully that the two warriors, fighting on opposite sides in the Trojan War, gave to each other deadly "gifts." Hector was bound to Achilles's chariot with Ajax's belt, which strangled him (an alternate version of the story we find in the *Iliad*, where Hector is already dead when Achilles ties him to the chariot). Now, Hector's sword, which came to Ajax after the latter's death, has become the instrument of his destruction. As we have seen, Sophocles has been intent on having us remember Hector when we think of Ajax, in the exchange with Tecmessa, in the prayer for Eurysaces, and now in his suicide. By reminding us of these connections here, the playwright prepares for the second part of his story, when the legacy of Ajax, as a warrior, a husband, a friend, and a man, comes under intense scrutiny.

THE WARRIOR'S BURIAL

Tecmessa finds Ajax's body at line 891 of the play. He has dominated the actions and thoughts of all the other characters, but now he is dead and we expect the focus to shift. Not so: the corpse remains onstage, covered by Tecmessa's cloak, and for another 500 lines or so, everything continues to revolve around its disposition. Menelaus enters and gives orders that, because Ajax tried to attack him and his brother Agamemnon, no one is to bury the body. It is to be left out for scavenger birds to tear and devour. Both the chorus and Teucer are appalled at this demand and argue for a warrior's burial, in recognition of all that Ajax has done for his fellow Greeks.

The question with which the play began remains: what to do about Ajax? Now he is no longer an active participant in the debate, but his presence is still powerful. Sophocles updates here a familiar theme from the *Iliad*, the struggle over an unburied corpse. A series of scenes, of increasing scope and intensity, forms the backbone for the plot of the Homeric poem in books 16 through 24. In book 16, Patroclus kills Sarpedon, the Trojan ally we have heard speaking to his friend Glaucus about the nature of heroism. Sarpedon is a son of Zeus by a mortal woman, and his impending death causes Zeus to consider changing fate, a drastic step:

Seeing them, the son of crafty Kronos felt pity,
and spoke to Hera, his wife and sister:
"Alas for me, that Sarpedon, dearest of men,
is doomed to die at the hands of Menoitios' son
Patroklos. My heart within me ponders two ways:
should I gather him up from the tearful battle while
he lives, and set him down in the fertile land of Lycia,
or destroy him at the hands of Menoitios' son?"
Ox-eyed mistress Hera answered him then,
"Most terrible son of Kronos, what are you saying?
A mortal man, long destined for his fate, him
you wish to release from ill-echoing death?
Do it, then. But none of us other gods shall praise you.
I will say another thing, and you store it in your heart:
If you should send Sarpedon home alive,
take care, lest then some other of the gods should wish
to send his own dear son away from the fierce battle.
For around the great city of Priam fight many sons
of gods. In them you will rouse up a bitter grudge.
No, though he is dear to you, and your heart laments,
still let him be destroyed in the harsh battle
at the hands of Patroklos, Menoitios's son.
But when the soul and years of life desert him,
send Death and gentle Sleep to carry him
until they come to fields of wide Lycia
where his brothers and friends shall bury him
with funeral mound and marker;
this is the gift of honor for the dead."
So she spoke, nor did the father of gods and mortals
disobey her; yet he wept tears of blood upon the ground
honoring his dear son, whom Patroklos was about
to kill, in fertile Troy, far from his fatherland. (Homer, *Iliad* 16. 429–461)

This speech is often cited as evidence for the relationship between the will of the gods and fate (about which it says, in fact, nothing definitive), but its real function is to introduce the theme of the hero's burial. For the soul of a warrior to pass into Hades, the body must be properly buried. If the corpse is left unburied, the man's soul wanders restlessly on the boundaries of the Underworld, an even bleaker existence than that of a ghost in Hades. The threat of the dead warrior being left unburied, prey for birds and animals, is ever-present in the *Iliad,* although never realized for a major character until the end of the poem.

Patroclus is the next prominent victim. He is killed by Hector in a memorable scene at the end of book 16, and then all of book 17, 761 lines, is devoted to the struggle over his dead body, the Trojans eager to steal it and then leave it unburied as carrion, the Greeks fighting furiously to preserve the corpse for burial. Ajax and Menelaus eventually prevail, and the body is returned to Achilles at the beginning of book 18. He keeps it close to him, and Thetis preserves it from corruption with ambrosia. Finally, at the beginning of book 23, the ghost of Patroclus comes to Achilles in his sleep:

You sleep, Achilles, and have forgotten me.
You were not careless of me while I lived, only in death.
Bury me as quickly as possible, so I can pass through the gates of Hades.
The souls keep me at bay, images of the dead,
nor do they ever let me mingle with them across the river,
but I wander, just as I am, around the wide gates of Hades.
Give me your hand, as I am wretched, for never
will I leave Hades, once I have been given to the funeral fire.
(Homer, *Iliad* 23. 69–76)

Achilles now gives his friend an elaborate funeral, followed by athletic contests that take up the rest of book 23. By this time, he controls another corpse, that of Hector, whom he has killed in a particularly brutal way at the end of book 22.

After killing Hector in book 22, Achilles ties the dead body to the back of his chariot and drags it around the battlefield. This desecration continues at the beginning of book 24, after the interlude of Patroclus's funeral, until Zeus intervenes and prompts the eventually ransoming of the corpse by Priam, Hector's father. The poem comes to a serene close with the funeral of Hector:

But when Dawn appeared, rosy-fingered, early-born,
then the people gathered at the pyre of famous Hector.
And when they were all assembled close around
first they quenched the fire with gleaming wine,
all of it, as far as the flame's force held. And then
his brothers and friends gathered up the white bones,
so many in their mourning, and their cheeks were wet with tears.
Then lifting up the bones, they set them in a golden casket,
wrapping them first in soft robes of purple.
Right away they laid it in a hollow grave, then
piled up stones, packed tightly over the top. Quickly
they poured over all a funeral mound, and guards stood watch
everywhere, for fear the Achaeans would attack too soon.
Once the mound was poured, the people returned to the city,
and came together there for a glorious feast

in the home of Priam, king nourished by Zeus.
Such was the burial of Hector, tamer of horses. (Homer, *Iliad* 24. 788–804)

The gentle melancholy of these lines echoes the picture of Sleep and Death
carrying Sarpedon back to Lycia for burial, forming a frame around the violence and pain that comes in between.

The unburied corpse lies squarely on the boundary between life and
death. By focusing on this succession of unburied heroes, Homer keeps our
attention on that divide and, by extension, on the fact of mortality as the definitive quality of human life. As we have already seen, limits create meaning
for us as humans. Focusing on the limit of mortality prompts, then, consideration of the meaning of human life. This is the rich context Sophocles taps
by keeping our attention on the disposition of Ajax's unburied corpse. But
the play dramatizes a dimension of meaning beyond Homer's epic. Ajax's
unburied corpse is on the margin of heroic life and death, as are all his pre-
decessors in the *Iliad*. He is also, like Hector in *Iliad* 6, a warrior who has not
been able to reintegrate himself into his community, in this case the Greek
army. But Sophocles's character is, as we have said, alienated in one more
sense: he is an anachronistic, old-fashioned aristocratic warrior in the midst
of fifth-century B.C.E. Athens. The struggle over his burial represents in this
sense an argument about how—or whether—the warrior fits into the new
democratic community.

The role of hierarchical status as a guide for evaluating a man's worth
surfaces immediately in the argument between Menelaus and Teucer. The
Greek leader attacks Ajax as a traitor but also as a "common soldier," who
should obey without question his superiors. He goes on to draw a telling
analogy:

For neither will the laws be preserved in a city
where fear is not firmly in place,
nor will an army be led wisely,
if there is no bulwark of fear or awe. (Sophocles, *Ajax* 1073–1076)

Menelaus's language has an obvious relevance in the context of the emerging Athenian democracy, with its emphasis on a wider and more egalitarian
distribution of political power. Teucer answers by urging Menelaus to think
about Ajax's actions, what he did for his fellow soldiers at Troy, not his status.
He has earned, says his brother, a hero's burial. Menelaus exits, reiterating
his order not to bury Ajax.

Issues of status persist in the next angry exchange, between Teucer and
Agamemnon, who dismisses Ajax's brother as the son of a slave. Teucer is
"nothing," arguing for another nobody. It is disgraceful for the leaders of the
expedition to have to listen to slaves. These remarks bear a contemporary
relevance in Athens of the 440s B.C.E., for a new definition of citizenship had
been legislated in 451 under Pericles: to qualify for citizenship, one had to
prove that both parents were citizens, whereas before only the father had to
be a citizen. Reference to the status of Teucer's mother seems to point insistently to this law.

Both Menelaus and Agamemnon seem definitely to be cast as villains here, arrogant and bullying. This impression is confirmed with the appearance of Odysseus, who joins Agamemnon onstage and urges that Ajax's transgressions be forgiven and that he be buried honorably:

Hear me, now. By the gods, do not let
this man's body be cruelly thrown out, unburied.
Do not allow force to drive you to hate
such a man, so that you trample on justice.
He was ever the most hateful of all the warriors to me,
from the time I won from him Achilles' armor,
but nevertheless, I could not dishonor such a man,
nor refuse to acknowledge him as the best of all
the Argives, as many as came to Troy, after Achilles.
Just so, he could not in justice be dishonored by you.
For doing so, you would harm not this man,
but the laws of the gods. It is unjust to harm
a brave man, should he die, even if you hate him. (Sophocles, *Ajax* 1332–1345)

Odysseus stakes out a new position here, one that demands flexibility and compromise instead of implacable hatred. His words seem in fact to reject what was, as we have seen, a traditional moral standard in the fifth century B.C.E., that one ought to help one's friends and harm one's enemies. That principle clearly informs the attitudes of Menelaus and Agamemnon, but it also seems to lie behind Athena's urging Odysseus to laugh at his enemy, Ajax.

Agamemnon grudgingly yields to Odysseus, and the play ends with the body of Ajax being carried off to a hero's burial. The problem of what to do with Ajax has been resolved in a way that seems to point beyond the traditional, aristocratic warrior ethic toward a more flexible approach, involving the compromise between two positions, one more suited to democracy. Behind the specific negotiations over Ajax lie others, with wider implications for fifth-century Athens: How do traditional values associated with aristocratic warriors fit into the new society? Ajax's body, lying on the stage, represents in one sense the warrior—who will be just as necessary to the new state as to the old—on the margins of civilized community. Can he be reintegrated with a citizen's rights in the democracy?

We usually date Sophocles's *Ajax* to sometime in the 440s, perhaps a little before *Antigone,* which is usually dated around 442–41 B.C.E. The latter play also centers on the disposition of a soldier's corpse, in this case that of Polynices, the brother of Antigone, who had raised an army and attacked Thebes, in an attempt to take over the kingship from his brother, Eteocles. The brothers kill each other, leaving the kingship to their uncle, Creon, who orders that Eteocles's body be given a hero's burial, but that Polynices's body be thrown out of the city unburied, to be eaten by scavenger birds. Polynices does not dominate the action of *Antigone* as Ajax does in the earlier play. The emphasis is instead on Antigone's defiance of Creon's order and the disastrous consequences of the ensuing conflict. Still, it would seem that Sophocles was preoccupied to some extent in the 440s—if our dating of the plays is right—with the question of how the soldier fits into Athenian society.

That decade in Athens seems to have been a time when the great confidence inspired by the defeat of the Persians and consequent ascendancy of Athens on the mainland of Greece was beginning to be undermined by various disputes with other cities, especially Sparta. After Athens made an alliance in 460 B.C.E. with Argos, Sparta's enemy in the Peloponnesus, the two cities had been in a conflict over the leadership of Greece, which would culminate in the outbreak of the Peloponnesian War in 431 B.C.E. In 447 B.C.E., the Boeotians defeated Athens at the Battle of Coroneia, a blow to Athens's control over the cities in northern Greece. Then in 446 B.C.E., the island of Euboea, east and north of Athens, revolted from the Delian League. When Pericles took an army to quell the revolt, Megara, a city on the Gulf of Corinth, took the opportunity to massacre the garrison of Athenian soldiers stationed there. At the same time, Pleistoanax, the Spartan king, invaded Attica by land. This may have been to prevent Athens from intervening at Megara, and once that was done, the Spartans withdrew again. Nevertheless, Athenian ascendancy in Greece was clearly on the wane, and this must have caused considerable anxiety in Athens. Perhaps the question of the soldier's place in Athenian society became a popular topic as a result, although we do not have enough contemporary evidence apart from Sophocles's plays to know for sure.

PERICLES'S FUNERAL ORATION

The disposition of the unburied corpses of warriors fallen in battle was clearly, from at least the time of Homer's *Iliad*, 750 B.C.E., a highly charged event in the imagination of Greek poets. As it happens, Thucydides preserves in his *Histories*, published sometime after 411 B.C.E., a version of the oration given by Pericles at the public funeral of Athenian warriors who had died in the first year of the Peloponnesian War in 431–430 B.C.E. The relationship of what the speeches in Thucydides's *Histories* say to what might actually have been said is a hotly debated problem, and, for our purposes, insoluble. The historian himself says that he records what was demanded of each speaker by the circumstances at the time, while holding as closely as possible to the general sense of what was truly said. We will never know, barring the unlikely discovery of a contemporary transcript, what Pericles said verbatim. But we can learn from Thucydides's version what probably would have sounded to an Athenian citizen like a reasonable facsimile. In it, we will find many of the same themes that appear in the poetry we have been looking at in this chapter.

Thucydides begins with a description of the arrangements for the funeral. Three days before the funeral, the bones of the fallen were laid out in a tent in the agora, and relatives brought various offerings for the dead. The remains were then placed in coffins, according to their tribe, and carried—along with an empty bier in the procession for the "unknown soldiers"—to the Potters Quarter in the city, where they were interred in a special grave. After the burials, a man chosen by the city, who was known for wisdom and a good reputation, delivered a fitting tribute to the dead warriors, and everyone departed. By 431 B.C.E., Pericles was definitely the most powerful and eminent politician and general of the new democracy, and the obvious choice to give the oration.

Pericles begins by lowering expectations: he would have thought that the greatness of the fallen warriors was sufficiently marked by the state funeral itself, and had no need of speeches. In any event, entrusting the reputation of these brave men to the persuasive powers of one person is perilous—what if the feelings of others toward the speaker cause them to mistrust what he says? Nevertheless, he will do his best. He then passes on to praise of the ancestors of those present, who secured through their bravery and determination the present Athenian empire and system of government. Their military exploits in the past are too well known to be repeated. Instead, he will turn now to the present:

> From what sort of practices we came to our present state of affairs, and with what sort of system of government and out of what habits our greatness grew, these things will be my first subject, before I turn to the praise of these men, thinking as I do that in the present circumstances it is fitting for these things to be said and for all those now here, citizens and foreigners, to hear them. (Thucydides, *Histories* 2. 36)

What follows is a proud description of what makes Athens unique among all other Greek cities, politically, socially, and militarily. Although the richness of the thought—and the difficulty of Thucydides's Greek!—make paraphrase difficult, we can discern some recurring themes. The new democratic political system allows Athenians freedom of action and expression. Although this freedom might in other places lead to lawlessness, Athenians freely choose self-restraint and respect each other's privacy. Athenians celebrate their freedom in various festivals and games, thinking that refreshing their spirits makes them all the better as participants in public affairs. Militarily, Athens depends on the courage that comes from the character of its citizens, rather than on enforced discipline—a dig at Sparta here, which had a rigid system of compulsory military training beginning in youth. The city of Athens—again, unlike Sparta, where foreigners were kept out—is open to all, which some might think risky because enemies could learn about its society. But Athenians choose to rely less on systems and policies and more on the character of the citizens.

The uniqueness of Athenian society is nowhere more evident, he says, than in artistic and intellectual achievements: "We cultivate beauty without excess, and we love wisdom without effeminacy" (Thucydides, *Histories* 2. 40). Pericles here celebrates of course Athens's most famous legacy—along with the creation of the first democracy—to succeeding generations of the Western world. The art and literature of Athens, especially in the fifth century B.C.E., remain one of the great glories of Western civilization. Pericles does not say explicitly that Athenian artistic and intellectual achievements are a product of democracy, although the implication seems clear enough.

At the same time, Pericles argues that the particular character of Athenians is the source of greatness for the Athenian state:

In sum, I say that the whole city of Athens is a school for Greece, and that it seems to me that each one of the citizens of the city is able to show himself to be, in all the aspects of life, self-sufficiently autonomous, and to do so with versatility and grace. And that this is no boast produced for the occasion, but is indeed the plain truth in fact, is shown by the power of the city, which is acquired from these ways of living. (Thucydides, *Histories* 2. 41)

There is, Pericles says, a reciprocal relationship between the freedom that comes with democratic government and the character of the citizens of that democracy, and both are finally the source of Athenian greatness. So far, the encomium of warriors who have fallen in defense of the city has been in fact a speech in praise of the city itself and its citizens. He does go on to praise the bravery of the soldiers themselves, who chose to sacrifice their lives for the city. But the predominant message of the speech is that the unique greatness of Athens produces the kind of citizen warriors whom they have gathered to honor. On the one hand, he offers solace to those grieving in the assertion that their sacrifice was warranted by the worth of what they died to protect. But beyond that, we can discern in the form of the speech an echo of the mini-biographies given to the losers in the *Iliad*. Nearness to death prompts reflection on the meaning and value of life. Reflecting on the deaths of Athenian warriors leads Pericles to evaluate the essence of their existence as human beings, which turns out to be encompassed by the collective achievement that is Athens in 431 B.C.E.

We see Pericles—and perhaps Thucydides—struggling in this speech with the question raised by Sophocles in the *Ajax:* how does the individual strength and bravery of the warrior fit into the new democratic society, with its increased emphasis on collective wielding of power? Pericles suggests that the warrior's strength, which is put in the service of the city, is itself the product of that city. By making this assertion, he offers an escape from the perilous bargain represented by the traditional model of the relationship between the hero/warrior and his community. The imperious will of the individual hero, so dangerous to his community, in this case both contributes to and dissolves into the collective greatness of that community.

Before leaving Pericles, we should pause to acknowledge his telling remarks on the topic of Athenian women:

If it is necessary for me to mention something, to those of you who will not be widows, about the excellence of women, I will do so in a brief exhortation. A great reputation for you will consist in your not being worse than your inherent nature, and the greatest glory for women is to be least talked of by men, either in praise or blame. (Thucydides, *Histories* 2. 45)

The Greek word here for "glory," *kleos,* has as its most basic meaning, simply "report," what is known. Pericles, in his struggle to find a way to talk about women as a separate class of human being from men, creates what might be charitably called a piece of deliberate irony. Men win glory when their excellent acts are known by others: they must be visibly in the forefront. By nature, women are best when they are silent and invisible. Perhaps nowhere in all of Greek literature is there such a bald statement of what it means for women to live in a patriarchal culture. Pericles has been at pains to articulate a vision of Athenian greatness that captures the reciprocal relationship between the unique "character," *arete*, of Athenians on the one hand, and the greatness of the Athenian political, social, and military systems on the other. The city is the product of the collective excellence of the citizens, which in turn provides the freedom of expression that brings that excellence to light for the admiration of others. Women are not citizens, and their collective excellence consists in being entirely unknown in the arena where *kleos* may be won.

CONCLUSION

War is the crucible, full of risks and opportunities, where masculinity is forged and expressed most vividly in Greek culture. The warrior risks losing control of his body when he goes into combat, of being penetrated and thus losing his bodily integrity. On the other hand, war is a primary arena for winning *kleos*, the most important hedge against oblivion for the Greeks. By confronting death directly, the warrior is an agent for the creation and contemplation of meaning in life. Sarpedon's musings about why some men are honored more than others come in the midst of battle, with enemies all around. Contemplating his own death, Ajax, normally a taciturn figure, reflects on the place of human striving in the larger context of nature and divine will.

The warrior's position on the boundary between human civilization and more elemental forces, which he shares with animals and on which he must draw to defend civilization, makes him a problematic figure in Greek culture. His fellow citizens depend on his strength for the preservation of their community. At the same time, that strength, turned against the community, can destroy it. This paradox is present in many of the heroes of Greek epic and drama, Achilles in the *Iliad* being a prime example. Sophocles's exploration of the story of Ajax after Achilles's death adds a further complexity, which is particular to Athenian culture. The aristocratic values that govern expectations of the warrior hero in Homeric epic reflect the political and social conditions of Greek societies from 750–500 B.C.E. These values came under scrutiny in Athens after the advent of democracy, a new system for distributing political power with significant implications for how human worth in general was to be determined. The double-edged nature of the warrior's power within the community is yet more challenging in a society where old ideas about human excellence are no longer taken for granted. The question that dominates Sophocles's play, of what to do about Ajax, takes on a much wider significance in this perspective: what to do about the old-fashioned warrior in the new world of democracy?

We may end our consideration of the warrior as exemplar of masculinity with a somewhat surprising case. In Plato's dialogue, *The Symposium,* set in 416 B.C.E., Alcibiades, one of the most glamorous—and notorious—figures in late fifth century Athens, recalls his attempts to seduce Socrates. It seems that Alcibiades, by all accounts a handsome man well known for his fondness for chariot racing and drinking parties, developed a passion for Socrates, a decidedly unhandsome figure. The younger man unleashes all of his charms but to no avail: Socrates will not give in, thus displaying the crucial masculine traits of self-control and preservation of bodily integrity. This amazing fortitude—it is clear that Alcibiades is not used to being turned down—is further on display as Alcibiades recalls Socrates's behavior as a soldier. His physical endurance, it seems, was outstanding: he could go without food for much longer than other soldiers, and when supplies were abundant, he could drink any man under the table. He went barefoot in winter, with no extra cloak. Ruminating on a problem, he stood in one place for an entire day and night. During the battle of Potidaea in 432 B.C.E., on the eve of the Peloponnesian War, when Alcibiades won a commendation for valor, it was Socrates who saved the younger man, staying by him when he was wounded, rescuing him and keeping the enemy from stealing his armor. The generals insisted on giving the award to Alcibiades, because of his social standing, but it was Socrates who truly deserved it. During the Athenian army's retreat at Delium in 424 B.C.E., Socrates displayed exemplary courage and unflappable composure.

Plato was hardly a supporter of Athenian democracy. The dialogue, although set during the Peloponnesian War, was in fact composed sometime around 387 B.C.E., well after Athens's defeat and the end of the city's ascendancy in Greek affairs. His dialogues represent a further stage in the examination of human morality and values, beyond the model of the democratic citizen-soldier of the fifth century B.C.E. His use of traditional masculine ideals, however ironic, as a foil for his unlikely hero Socrates is a testament to their enduring strength in Greek culture.

Five

Men, Gods, and Fate

Man is the measure of all things.

—Protagoras

We began with a series of questions, one implying another: "what kind of man am I?" leading to "who am I?" pointing further to "where do I fit in the larger order of things?" We turn now to that last question and all that it suggests about the meaning of a masculine life. Greek thought is distinguished particularly by its insistent focus on what it means to be human as opposed to divine or animal. In that perspective, divine forces were part of a larger context within which human life could be understood. In this chapter, we focus on how the Greeks' attitudes toward and relationships with transcendent forces reflect their understanding of where men fit in the cosmic order and what this position implies about the nature of a masculine life. As usual, we look closely at a few representative works of art. By way of introduction, we will need to explore some of the Greeks' fundamental beliefs about the gods. The varieties of religious experience in ancient Greek culture were many, and we will not be attempting a comprehensive survey, but some preliminary distinctions will be helpful.

GREEK RELIGION: PERILS AND OPPORTUNITIES

As in the case of warfare, generalizing about ancient Greek religious beliefs can be challenging. First of all, we face the usual problem of relatively scanty and uneven sources for what we know. Divine beings of all sorts figure prominently in most Greek literature and art, and we rely on these portraits for most of what follows in this chapter. But the Olympian gods and goddesses we encounter in literature to some extent represent a blending of cult beliefs from all over the Greek-speaking world. The characteristics of, say, Athena in Homeric epic and the plays of Aeschylus are more uniform than the variations in local cult practice might suggest. At the same time, it seems that local worshippers also tended to adopt ideas from Homeric epic or the *Theogony* of Hesiod, two particularly important literary sources for the representation of Greek gods and goddesses. Herodotus, writing in the 440s B.C.E., describes the role of Homeric and Hesiodic poetry in the development of Greek religious belief this way:

Hesiod and Homer lived, I think, not more than four hundred years earlier than I. It was they who made a theogony ["geneaology of the gods"] for the Greeks, giving them names, recounting their offices and their crafts, and describing their outward appearance. (Herodotus, *Histories* 2. 53)

Herodotus probably overstates the originality of the contribution of the two poets. We know from earlier non-Greek sources, for instance, that Hesiod's ideas about Greek deities often reflect common stories from other Near Eastern cultures around the Mediterranean. Still, the Greeks themselves seem to have accorded a certain canonical status to the portraits of the gods in Homeric and Hesiodic poetry, and if they reflect old and widespread patterns of belief beyond Greek culture, so much the better for our purposes.

The poetic sources we will be using, then, present a more homogenized view of the attributes of various deities than we find in local cults. There is no evidence, on the other hand, that any Greek poet or dramatist offers a view of the beliefs surrounding any particular god or goddess that is fundamentally different from what archaeology tells us about worship at different shrines. In any event, we must depend on literature if we are to explore ideas about the interplay of human and divine held by the Greeks, as they are the only source for that kind of speculation. Archaeological finds can tell us what shrines looked like or what religious artifacts were used, but not much about what people thought about their gods.

Apart from its sources, the actual form of Greek religion offers some additional challenges when viewed from the perspective of most modern religious practice. Polytheistic, lacking any specific creed, and, for the most part, attached to no system of ethics, Greek religious practice played a rather different role in the spiritual life of its adherents than do most modern religions. Whereas Christians, for instance, look to their God for guidance about right behavior toward their fellow humans, Greek deities are in themselves neither models of ethical behavior—quite the reverse in many ways—nor are they seen as the sources of advice about such matters. When the gods are described as guardians of human behavior, it is almost always in very general terms, as when Odysseus tells one of the suitors that the gods walk the earth watching the attitudes and intentions of mortals. Zeus in the *Odyssey* is portrayed as protecting guests from mistreatment by their hosts, but specific rules for hospitality are not ascribed to him. Later, in the plays of Aeschylus, we hear that Zeus works to protect *dikē*, "justice," but there is no definitive explanation of what exactly constitutes justice. In *Iliad* 24, as we have seen previously, Zeus is represented as the source for good and evil in every man's life:

Two jars sit on the threshold of Zeus;
one contains evil gifts, the other good.
He to whom Zeus who loves thunder gives a mixture,

meets evil one time, good the next.
The man to whom he gives only from the jar of miseries,
he makes wretched, and evil hunger drives him across
the bright earth; he wanders, honored by neither gods nor men.
(Homer, *Iliad* 24. 527–533)

Again, there is no sign here of what ethical code might inform these decisions, only that the reasons for prosperity or suffering in a man's life are beyond his comprehension.

Greek deities are rarely cited as a source for correct human behavior because they are defined not by their exceptional goodness or wisdom, but because they are all-knowing, all-powerful (with some exceptions), and—most important—because they are immortal. There are many gods and goddesses, each with his or her own area of influence. They often disagree with one another, and their treatment of mortals reflects no discernible code of ethics, beyond helping their personal favorites and punishing others for what appear to be petty or frivolous reasons.

From our perspective, these deities may present a disquietingly amoral existence—if the gods do not enforce moral and ethical norms, who will? Where is the source of order in the cosmos? The usual portrait of the Olympian gods does represent them as a family, with Zeus and Hera as the parents, others as siblings or children of gods. But although Zeus asserts himself from time to time, he still encounters all of the frustrations and difficulties with establishing control over his often rebellious family that modern parents would recognize. His power sometimes seems far from absolute, again undermining one's confidence in the stability of the universe.

At the same time, polytheism offers some relief from particular kinds of moral dilemmas that we encounter in a monotheistic universe. If things go wrong, it could be the operation of one of the gods or goddesses. Perhaps we can get some relief from another deity. If my behavior seems to be condemned by one god, it may still be supported by another. The troubling question often arising in a monotheistic universe—"How could God allow such a thing to happen?"—becomes less mysterious in the perspective offered by Greek polytheism, as there is no expectation that the gods will agree in the first place.

Perhaps not surprisingly, the Greeks' beliefs about the nature of their deities reflect, in a more extreme form, characteristics we observe in Greek culture generally. Deities are conspicuous for their competitive virtues such as strength, knowledge, and beauty and have little interest in cooperative virtues such as honesty, compassion, and selfless generosity. They help their friends and hurt their enemies, just as Greek aristocrats exhorted each other to do. Their favorites are almost exclusively those who succeed in competitive venues. Thus to please these powerful beings, mortals are required first of all to do what the culture valorizes already: win. Beyond that, Homeric deities demand that mortals offer sacrifices at their shrines, a recognition of the need for divine favor in an otherwise harsh universe.

In *Iliad* 24, as the gods look down on Achilles savagely abusing Hector's corpse, a characteristic disagreement breaks out among the Olympians as to whether they should intervene. Should they have Hermes steal the corpse? Athena and Poseidon hate the Trojans, the former because Paris chose Aphrodite over her and Hera in the famous beauty contest that led to Paris's abduction of Helen, the latter for equally personal reasons. Apollo, meanwhile, hates the Greeks, in part because Agamemnon dishonored his (Apollo's) priest by refusing to return his daughter. Hera—herself an enemy of the Trojans because Paris did not choose her—disagrees with Apollo, offering the following argument:

Angry with him, white-armed Hera spoke forth:
What you say would be true, silver-bowed god,
if you accord the same honor to Achilles and Hector.
Hector was mortal, and suckled at a woman's breast.
But Achilles is the child of a goddess, whom I myself
nurtured and raised and offered to a mortal man as his wife,
Peleus, who was very dear to the hearts of the immortals.
All of you gods and goddesses were at the wedding, even you,
with your lyre, dined among us, companion of evils, always faithless.
(Homer, *Iliad* 24. 55–63)

Nothing here about Achilles's deserving behavior, just his lineage, which trumps all other considerations. Zeus then settles the matter:

Answering her, cloud-gathering Zeus spoke forth:
Hera, do not be too angry at the gods,
for the same honor will not be given to all. Still, Hector
was the dearest to the gods of mortals who live in wide Troy.
So he was to me, since he never failed to deliver precious gifts.
Not ever has my altar lacked a worthy sacrifice,
of libations or the savor of burning fat. For that is our gift of honor.
(Homer, *Iliad* 24. 64–70)

Here at least there is some attention to actions taken, but still the favor of the gods comes not according to any moral or ethical criteria, but for loyal subservience.

The case of Orestes, caught between the demands of Apollo and the Furies, represents of course a serious—and perilous—disadvantage for mortals in Greek polytheism. Relations between mortals and deities, seen from the point of view of mortals, are characterized by human fear and uncertainty. Mortals can never know the intentions of gods or goddesses. They might, like Philoctetes, inadvertently stumble into a divine sanctuary and be punished for life. They might, like Agamemnon, unknowingly offend Artemis in some way and be required to kill their own child. Because the gods are so powerful and because they are completely unaffected by time and change, they can wreak terrible damage in the mortal world for what seem like the most trivial reasons. Within their own unchanging world on Olympus, by contrast, their actions are, as we have seen, inevitably comic, for nothing they do there matters.

THE GODS AND MASCULINE AGENCY

The dynamic between mortals and gods that we have been sketching here presents challenges for the Greek ideals of masculinity. If control over others and self-control, physical and otherwise, are measures of successful masculine agency, then sharing the universe with the gods of Greek religion would be unnerving. We have already seen how, in the case of Gilgamesh and Achilles, the simple fact of human mortality, an imperative of nature, eventually forces a reassessment of one's place in the universe. That the gods were also amoral and capricious would only make things more difficult. Those in authority, whose masculinity would be otherwise marked by their status, would always be vulnerable to the possibility of sudden and catastrophic reversals brought on by divine intervention in human affairs.

We arrive at the phenomenon of envy, an inevitable result of the intensely competitive nature of Greek masculinity. The high stakes in winning and losing in such a social system breed envy and resentment in those less successful. The danger of reprisal, of revolution from below, would add yet another element of uncertainty to the already precarious situation of those in authority. But envy can come not just from those below. The danger of great success in human affairs breeding envy in the gods was also present for the Greeks. The operation of divine envy offers one explanation for sudden reversals of fortune. If a man is too successful, if his life appears too blessed, the gods may strike him down. Thus we observe two apparently contradictory imperatives at work in Greek culture. On the one hand, success in competitions of all kinds is the primary measure of worth. At the same time, warnings about excess are common: the great man is especially vulnerable to disaster. Too much success can be dangerous. We often see this tension reflected in the words of the chorus in Athenian tragedy. They admire and defer to the conspicuous glory of the hero but shy away from that status themselves, as the danger of divine envy is too great.

We can see this dynamic at work in the chorus of Aeschylus's *Agamemnon*. As they proudly recount the heroic deeds of Agamemnon and the Greek army at Troy, a note of anxiety keeps creeping into their songs. In destroying the city of Troy and its holy shrines, did they go too far, overreach in their power?

There is no defense
for the man who insolently
kicks the great altar
of Zeus into nothingness.
Persuasion, the persistent,
unbearable child of fore-thinking Ruin,
overpowers him.

All remedy fails. It is not hidden,
but shines forth, burning bitter destruction. (Aeschylus, *Agamemnon* 381–389)

The dangers envisioned here come to life in the pivotal scene of the *Agamemnon*, when the king arrives onstage in his chariot. Clytemnestra, intending to murder her husband, rolls out lavish tapestries for him to walk on as he enters the palace:

Clytemnestra:	Serving women, why delay? You have been
	ordered to spread out tapestries in his path.
	Let a dark red way be made straight
	that Justice might lead him into the home
	he never hoped for.
	All the rest my thought, never conquered
	by sleep, will arrange, justly and according to fate.
Agamemnon:	Child of Leda, guardian of my home,
	you have spoken appropriately for my long absence,
	since you stretched out your speech. Praise, though fitting,
	is an honor that should come from others.
	As for the rest, do not treat me delicately, in the way of a woman,
	nor grovel gaping, as if before some Asian potentate.
	Do not draw envy with tapestries strewn in my path.
	Such worship is fitting for gods.
	Never without fear could I, a mortal,
	tread on intricate brocades.
	I should be honored like a man, not a god.
	My glory sounds forth without these
	delicate draperies. Thinking rightly is
	the gods' greatest gift. Call no man
	blessed until his life has ended in sweet felicity.
	If I should do all this, I would have hope.
	(Aeschylus, *Agamemnon* 908–930)

We see here, in Aeschylus's characteristically economical symbolism, all that the chorus feared: persuasion leading to excess, ending in ruin. Agamemnon, persuaded in spite of his fear by Clytemnestra's flattery, walks on the tapestries, symbolically playing the part of an arrogant monarch. The red tapestries prefigure his blood, soon to be spilled in the bath.

Agamemnon is portrayed as caught between the cultural imperative to win glory and the angry reprisal by his wife that his sacrifice of his daughter provokes. The chorus's fears about the dangers of overstepping the limits of human action seem to have been realized here. His masculine desire for glory causes him to undervalue his blood tie to his daughter, and Clytemnestra becomes the agent for retribution. On another level, we see the king caught between Artemis and the Furies, the latter being ancient earth deities devoted to avenging crimes against blood. The association of Clytemnestra with the Furies only becomes explicit when they appear at the end of the second play of the trilogy, *The Libation Bearers,* to chase Orestes off stage after he murders the queen. Along with his father's status as head male of the household, Orestes also inherits from Agamemnon the dilemma of being caught between two sources of divine power, in his case Apollo and the Furies.

FATE

If nature and divine will work against masculine agency, the challenge is compounded by the Greeks' ideas about fate. Incontrovertible and mysterious, this force was understood to operate in many ways like divine will, although separate from it. In the Homeric epics, fate, which is described with words in Greek that mean "portion," as in one's "lot," is confined to the time at which a man is destined to die. The image often used elsewhere in early Greek poetry is of the *Moirai*, "Fates," as three semipersonified sisters, who are spinning wool to make yarn. A man's life is fated to take up a certain length of yarn. *Moira*, the most common word translated as "fate," is a noun from the verb "to cut:" when a man's time is up, the sisters cut the thread. In later Greek literature of the classical period, and particularly Athenian tragedy, fate sometimes seems to govern a wider range of human experience, as we will see.

If both divine will and fate were always fulfilled, then we might ask how the Greeks believed them to be related. In the passage from the *Iliad* quoted in Chapter 4, we saw Zeus contemplating the idea of changing the fated death of his son, Sarpedon. Here, it would seem, Homer is prepared to settle the question of the relationship between divine will and fate. As we have seen, however, the issues are not presented in a way that settles anything. Hera tells Zeus that, although he *could* change Sarpedon's fate, if he did so, "none of us other gods shall praise you." Zeus gives in to this rather muted threat, once again yielding to a kind of familial blackmail. Homer declines to decide the issue.

We could survey many more examples of fate working in the lives of mortals, but we would be no closer to understanding exactly how Greeks saw this mysterious force fitting into the larger universe. About fate as the Greeks saw it we can say the following: it is incontrovertible—no one escapes his or her fate; it seems to operate independently of divine will; the fate of any human is established at birth. The English word "fate" comes from the Latin *fatum*, meaning that which "has been said." Perhaps the best way for us to proceed is to use this definition as our guide. We do not know *who or what* said it, only that it was not an Olympian god, and it cannot be unsaid. It seems clear that the Greeks—as far as we can tell from written sources—were not concerned to work out a detailed, systematic description of the nature of fate. What was important was that a mortal could not escape his or her fate, no matter how hard he or she tried. Finally, we should also recognize that storytellers like Homer would not necessarily be interested in achieving clarity about the nature of fate. As students of Greek thought, we are curious to know as much as we can about the subject, but from the storyteller's point of view, mystery is often a plus, heightening suspense and drawing the audience more deeply into the story.

OEDIPUS AND THE TRAGEDY OF FATE

The preceding survey points us once again toward the question of what it means to be human as opposed to divine or animal. Seen from this perspective, the differences between divine will and fate are less compelling than the quality they share in relationship to human life, *transcendence.* To these two forces we may add the imperatives of nature, represented most often by death. Because masculine agency demands control over oneself and other beings, animals and humans alike, it is not surprising that the most characteristic model in Greek culture for thinking about the meaning of a man's life is the opposition between human intelligence and will, and the transcendent forces that constrain it. The most thoughtful and compelling explorations of this dynamic in Greek culture are found in Athenian tragedy. These plays, along with Shakespearean tragedy, offer the richest portraits in Western art of powerful men in the grip of inalterable forces. We begin with perhaps the best known of all tragedies, Sophocles's *Oedipus Rex.*

The story of Oedipus, who killed his father and married his mother, was already very old by the time Sophocles wrote his play. The first allusion to the myth in Greek literature appears in the *Odyssey,* some 250 years before *Oedipus Rex* was produced. During his trip to the Underworld, Odysseus sees a ghostly parade of famous (or infamous) women. Among them is Epikaste, mother of Oedipus:

I saw the mother of Oedipus, the beautiful Epikaste,
who, in all innocence, committed a terrible deed,
having married her own son. He killed his own father
and married her. Yet the gods brought all these things to light.
But he ruled over the Kadmeians in lovely Thebes,
suffering pains through the gods' dreadful plans.
She went into the house of powerful Hades, the gate-closer,
having hung herself from a high beam in a noose,
strangled in her grief. And to him she left all
the pains brought on by a mother's Furies. (Homer, *Odyssey* 11. 271–280)

The basic events of Sophocles's play are already here. Epikaste becomes Iokaste (or Jocasta, in the more familiar form) in the later version; but Oedipus's patricide and incest, and Jocasta's suicide, are all present. It is what Sophocles does with this material, the masterful timing of his plot and the subtlety of his understanding of human motivation, that make it a rich exploration of the collision of masculine will and the mysterious forces of fate and divine will.

Oedipus Rex was probably first produced in 427 B.C.E., right after the beginning of the Peloponnesian War in 431 B.C.E. A terrible plague had swept through Athens in 429 B.C.E., killing many Athenians, including Pericles. In these circumstances, the old story of Oedipus would have considerable power. Because the play opens with Thebes in the grip of a mysterious plague, it is hard not to think of Pericles—heroic leader of the Athenian state for 30 years, killed by a plague—when watching the downfall of the glorious king of Thebes. In the opening scene, a group of suppliants approaches Oedipus, who is standing near an altar to Apollo, seeking help against the plague. Oedipus speaks first:

Oh my children, new offspring of ancient Cadmus,
why do you sit here praying to me at this altar,
wreathed in suppliant boughs?
The city everywhere reeks of the incense,
filled with prayers to the Healer and groans for the dead.
I judged it wrong to hear these things from strangers,
and so, my children, I have come to you myself.
I am called Oedipus, known to all. (Sophocles, *Oedipus Rex* 1–13)

Oedipus presents himself here in several roles, king, priest—even god?—parent. The suppliants approach him as if he were a god, something he does not discourage. As we now discover, the group includes children, young men, and also old men, so that Oedipus's use of *tekna,* "children," is striking: here is a ruler so comfortable in his authority that even men older than he can qualify as his "children."

A priest of Zeus answers for the group. The city, he says, is dying, the crops withering, cattle dropping in the fields, women dying in labor as they give birth to stillborn children. The "fire-bearing god" hurls fevers on the people, emptying the city. They pray to Oedipus, knowing he is not himself a god but the "first among men," in the misfortunes of life and the encounters with gods. The priest recalls the first such crisis Oedipus resolved when he freed the city from the clutches of the Sphinx, "the harsh singer," to whom they were paying tribute. He did this without any help from the people, although it is said he had a god to support him as he "made straight" the lives of the citizens. He "stood (them) up," only to have them "fall down" again.

Oedipus now invokes yet another model for his status in the city:

Oh pitiable children, you come to me,
and I already know what you long for.
For well I know that you are all sick,
but sick as you are, no one is as sick as I.
Your pain comes for each alone, confined
within him, no other. But my soul groans at once
for myself, for you, and for the city, so that
you have not awakened me from sleep.
Know that I have wept through many nights,
wandered down many roads of thought.
Searching hard, I have found one cure,
and I have done what I must, sent Creon,
child of Menoikeos, my wife's brother, to Delphi,
the shrine of Apollo, that he might learn what we
must do or say to save the city. (Sophocles, *Oedipus Rex* 58–72)

The good doctor who stays up all night worrying about his city, Oedipus has taken action to effect a cure.

In this first exchange, Sophocles puts the focus squarely on the issues we have been exploring here. The city of Thebes has been set upon by a destructive force, for which they know neither the origins nor the cure. They suspect the hand of some deity is at work, but the purposes of the gods cannot be known by mortals, and so they suffer in fearful uncertainty. Their famous king has saved them once before, and they approach him again, trusting in his special powers: he is not exactly a god, but he seems to have the support of a god and has conquered mysterious forces before. Oedipus, meanwhile, seems entirely confident in his ability to protect his "children," positioning himself in various roles that project authority.

Creon, Jocasta's brother, now arrives on stage, having just returned from Delphi. He brings troubling news: the plague will not abate until the Thebans drive the "corruption," *miasma,* from the land. The murderers of Laius, the king of Thebes before Oedipus, must be punished, either with banishment or death. The perpetrators are still in Thebes, the oracle says. Oedipus remembers hearing about the king's death—as we learn later, right before he arrived in Thebes, conquered the Sphinx, and was awarded the kingship and Jocasta—but nothing more, and he presses Creon for more details. The king, he is told, was killed by the band of thieves on his way back from consulting the oracle at Apollo's shrine in Delphi. Why, Oedipus asks, did they not hunt down the murderers then? The Sphinx diverted them:

Creon: The Sphinx, with her riddling songs, led us to let go of mystery and focus on what lay at our feet. (Sophocles, *Oedipus Rex* 130–131)

This news drives Oedipus into action, his preferred mode. Apollo is right, and Creon too: they must hunt down the murderers. Oedipus will be the people's champion and the god's as well. They are to summon the people and tell them that he will do everything. The murderer may be after *him* now, and so by avenging Laius, he will help himself.

Mysterious transcendent forces are arrayed against Oedipus here. Although Apollo's oracle seems to know *why* the plague has attacked Thebes, *where* it came from, who or what sent it, remain unclear. That the "corruption" has settled on the entire city as a result of Laius's murderer going unpunished is also somewhat unusual. Murderers were thought by the Greeks in this period to be stained with a ritual pollution, which must be cleansed in some way by higher powers. When Orestes kills his mother, he is "polluted," and must be cleansed by Apollo. Here, however, the stain has spread from the murderer to the entire city. There is in fact a parallel to this situation, in the first book of the *Iliad,* where Apollo sends a plague on the Greek army at Troy because Agamemnon refuses to give up the daughter of Apollo's priest. We, the audience of the play, can see that in both cases the community is suffering as a result of the king's misdeeds. Those on stage, of course, have no such perspective.

Then there is the Sphinx. The story of the strange three-part creature, part woman, part lion, part bird, must have been well known at the time of the play, as Sophocles can invoke it with brief references. The Sphinx asks travelers who pass her a riddle, and if they fail to answer correctly, they die. (*Sphinksō* in Greek means "I will throttle.") The creature itself is very old, dating back to as early as 3000 B.C.E. in Mesopotamian and Egyptian art. Literary references are confined to Greek, with the earliest being Hesiod in the late eighth to early seventh centuries B.C.E. The substance of the Sphinx's riddle is not in Sophocles's play, appearing first in print about 100 years afterward. The riddle went this way: what creature walks on four feet, two feet, then three feet? Answer: humans. It is tempting to think that Sophocles would expect the audience to know this riddle, as it fits with the rest of the play so well.

In particular, the focus on "feet" is significant. Creon's reference to the Sphinx impelling the Thebans to focus on what was "before their feet" may hint at the riddle. Oedipus's name was believed by the Greeks to mean "swollen foot" (*oidaō*, "I swell," plus *pous*, "foot"), an apparent reference to the fact that his ankles were pierced when he was exposed as an infant. There is another possible etymology, however: *oida*, "I know," plus *pous*. If the Sphinx's riddle about feet is meant to be in the audience's mind, then Oedipus's name has a double reference, to the helpless infant son of Laius and Jocasta, exposed at birth, and to the heroic conqueror of the Sphinx, who "knows feet," and solves the riddle.

Whether or not the substance of the riddle is supposed to be part of the play's meaning, the Sphinx provides Oedipus with a telling opponent. Part woman, part animal, she represents vividly what must be controlled by the masculine hero. Indeed, by doing so, Oedipus certifies what being a male human means. But there is another dimension to his triumph. Although apparently a strong fighter, Oedipus is most famous for his intelligence. He defeats the creature and frees the city from her grasp by solving the riddle. The entire play revolves around what Oedipus knows and when he knows it. If we remember the Greek model for civilization, imposing limits on the power of nature to channel it for human use, Oedipus's intellectual prowess is typically masculine: he imposes structure, that is, limit, on the riddle and extracts meaning from it, thereby controlling the unruly monster. Odysseus is the first intellectual hero in Western culture, surviving in a hostile world through his intelligence: knowledge for him is power. Oedipus draws on the same kind of power to control the world, but his story emphasizes more strongly the dark side of the masculine desire to control what is ultimately uncontrollable.

Oedipus Rex derives much of its power from dramatic irony, the discrepancy between what the characters on stage know and what the audience knows. When Oedipus declares that he will hunt down the murderer of Laius and rid the city of the plague, we know that he will be training his powers unwittingly on his own destruction. As the plot unfolds, details from the past come out, making his downfall more and more certain. Like the group of suppliants in the first scene, the chorus, made up of Theban citizens, looks to the gods and to Oedipus for salvation. Their first song abjectly calls on Zeus,

Apollo, Athena, Artemis, and Dionysus for aid. When they finish, Oedipus is the first to speak:

You ask for help. If you would listen to me
and do what the plague requires of you,
you will find salvation and relief from your troubles.
A stranger to the story and to the crime, I
will speak out. If I had been here then, I would have
had no long hunt without any clue.
Now, since I am counted as a Theban citizen,
I will proclaim this to all you children of Cadmus:
Whoever of you knows who killed
this Laius, son of Labdacus,
I urge him to reveal all of it to me;
even if he is afraid to accuse himself,
he should speak up and remove the charge.
For he will be punished with nothing more
harsh than exile from this land.
If someone knows of another, from another land,
who is the murderer, let him not keep silent.
For I will pay him a reward, and be grateful to him.
But if you keep silent, if anyone tries in fear to hide
himself or someone dear to him, and rejects my offer,
then hear what I will do:
I command all of you, citizens of this state I control,
where I hold power, to neither receive this man nor
speak to him, nor invite him to join in prayers
and sacrifices, nor include him in purification.
Drive him out from your homes, all of you.
For he is the corruption of our land, as
the oracle at Delphi has just told me.
Such a fighter for the murdered man and for the god am I.
I curse the man who did this, whether he acted alone
or as one of many; may he struggle to drag out his hateful life;
I curse him, if he should turn out to share my hearth,
living with me with my full knowledge,
to suffer all that I have just now called down upon him!
(Sophocles, *Oedipus Rex* 216–251)

It is all here: Oedipus's pride, standing in for the gods in answer to the chorus's prayer, his supreme self-confidence, and his blindness to his own fate.

Next to appear onstage is Tiresias, the blind prophet of Apollo, whom Oedipus has summoned from Delphi. In the scene that follows, we see the clash of two men with fundamentally different views of their place in the universe. The result is definitive for our understanding of Oedipus as a man. The chorus is the first to see Tiresias being led on stage by a boy and some other attendants:

Here is the one who will convict the murderer, for they
are leading him here right now, a holy seer, in whom,
alone among men, lives the truth. (Sophocles, *Oedipus Rex* 297–299)

The chorus's word for "lives . . . in" is *empephuken,* from the verb *phuo,* meaning "to bring forth," "produce," but also "to beget." The Greek text suggests that truth has been planted inside Tiresias, is there by nature. The model is strikingly feminine, as if Apollo had impregnated the prophet with his wisdom, and Tiresias in turn gives birth to it. The source of Tiresias's power, which is considerable, as we will see, comes from without, passes through him, and hits its target, which is outside of him.

This way of experiencing and wielding power is quite different from the usual masculine model, of which Oedipus is a prime example. The masculine agent trains his power, which he experiences as originating with himself, fueled by his will, out onto the world, exerting control. Oedipus is famous for his power to know, and thus understand, and thus control, the world outside him. His name, as we have seen, could be understood as "know-foot." The Greek *oida,* which forms the first part of his name in this version, comes from a verb that can mean both "I know," and "I see." This overlapping set of meanings suggests that the knowledge that is gained results from the knower actively "seeing" what he comes to know, training his sights on something outside himself. This way of acquiring knowledge is obviously different from the rather more passive way Tiresias comes to wisdom, which cannot involve seeing, as he is blind. When the play begins, Oedipus and others assume that the following equation represents how the world is:

sight : knowing :: blindness : ignorance

By the end of the story, this understanding will have been shown to be inadequate.

Things go awry immediately after the prophet arrives. Oedipus hails him as the potential savior of the city. He is the master of life's mysteries and even though blind, he "understands" (*phronein*) the sickness that has fallen on the city. Tiresias demurs:

Alas, how dreadful it is to know (*phronein*) when
there is no profit to the one who knows.
I knew all these things, but forgot them,
or else I would never have come. (Sophocles, *Oedipus Rex* 316–318)

Oedipus doesn't understand: why so faint-hearted now? Tiresias will not say more but asks to be sent back to Thebes. Oedipus becomes increasingly agitated and soon loses his temper, calling Tiresias "the worst of the worst," who would drive a stone to anger. The seer hints that Oedipus attacks him out of ignorance: if he knew whom he lived with . . . Oedipus replies that anyone would be angry in this situation, and then accuses Tiresias of dishonoring his own city. To which the seer replies that his words will have no effect on what is to be. The exchange continues, growing more heated and intemperate on both sides. Oedipus accuses Tiresias of lying because he himself was part of the plot to kill Laius. This charge pushes the prophet to blurt out the truth he has within himself:

Is that so? I charge you then to abide by
the decree you've just uttered: starting today,
speak to no one, neither these people nor me,
since you yourself are the unholy plague upon this land!
(Sophocles, *Oedipus Rex* 350–353)

Oedipus cannot even consider this charge. Does Tiresias think he can lie to the king and get away with it? This attack brings from Tiresias another image of the prophet as mother:

I already have, for I nurture a strong truth inside myself.
(Sophocles, *Oedipus Rex* 356)

Pushed relentlessly by Oedipus, Tiresias again names the king explicitly as the murderer, but again this truth falls on deaf ears. To the charge that he lives with his family "shamefully," Oedipus replies that, being blind, the prophet can never have any power:

Nourished by night alone, you can never harm
me or anyone who sees the light. (Sophocles, *Oedipus Rex* 374–375)

He goes on to say that envy, not truth, lives inside Tiresias, that he has been hired by Creon to help steal the kingship. He knows nothing compared to Oedipus, who conquered the Sphinx, not with help from birds, but when his own intelligence hit the mark. Tiresias's response to this challenge picks up the theme of blindness and sight, then alludes more explicitly to incest:

I will speak out, since you have mocked my blindness:

You look around, but do not see the evil you inhabit,
nor where you live, nor with whom you are living.
Do you know who your parents are? In your ignorance
you are loathsome to your own, both above and below the earth.
The double lash of your mother and father
will drive you, oh dreaded-foot, from this land.
Now you can see, but soon you'll live in darkness.
What harbor will not echo your screams?
What rock on Mount Cithaeron will not re-echo them,
whenever you understand your wedding day,
that harbor of no refuge, into which you sailed,
finding a fair voyage, and when you learn
the full load of other horrors, that bring you
to yourself and level with your own children? (Sophocles, *Oedipus Rex* 413–425)

Oedipus orders Tiresias to leave and he does so, but not without flinging a last blast of truth over his shoulder. The murderer of Laius is in Thebes, he says, one who is thought to be a stranger but is a native. He who now has eyes will soon be blind, tapping his way into exile with a blind man's cane, revealed at last to be both brother and father to his children, son and husband to his wife. He slept with his father's wife, spilled his father's blood. Many editors assume that Oedipus has left the stage before this last set of revelations, for they seem to have no effect on the king. That may be right, but given the angry denial that Oedipus displays earlier, it is not impossible that he could hear these charges but simply refuses to consider them.

The rest of the play flows from this crucial confrontation. To Oedipus's masculine model for understanding himself and the world, Sophocles has opposed a starkly different perspective. Oedipus understands himself as powerful insofar as he can act out into the world and shape it with his will. He "sees," *oida,* and also "knows," people and things outside of himself, and by doing so imagines himself as controlling them. To use a modern metaphor, he "wraps his mind around" things, imposes shape on them, and so extracts meaning. His idea of who he is follows from this understanding. He creates himself through action, what we now call an existential view of the world. This model for understanding the self, as we will see, has a particular relevance to Oedipus, for he has been consciously remaking himself in defiance of a frightening prophecy he heard years before. Notice too, the connection between exerting power and becoming himself: the more Oedipus seems to succeed in imposing his will on the world outside himself, the more he thinks he is creating himself through this action.

Tiresias could hardly be more different from Oedipus. His role in the wielding of power is to be the conduit, the vehicle for delivering the decrees of Apollo's oracle, which always come true, no matter what mortals may do to stop or avoid them. He is not powerful because he imposes his will on the world outside himself, but rather because he is one part of a larger order, which includes nature and the transcendent powers of the universe. Whereas Oedipus tries to re-create himself in defiance of the gods' will or fate—it is never clear which—Tiresias is powerful only insofar as he conforms himself to Apollo's will, as expressed by the oracle. Whereas Oedipus is hypermasculine, Tiresias has what the Greeks thought of as a feminine mode of existence. The truth is inside him by nature, and he "nourishes" it. The verb used for this act is *trephō,* the word for a mother nurturing a child. When Tiresias refutes Oedipus's charge that he is ignorant because he is blind, he describes the king in a particularly telling way:

You look around, but do not see the evil you inhabit. (Sophocles, *Oedipus Rex* 413)

The verb for "look around" is *derkomai,* which has the meaning "cast a glance at," as if the one looking were directing a beam of light out of his eyes onto the thing he sees. Tiresias emphasizes the masculine, active seeking in Oedipus's sight, but then says that he fails to perceive (*blepō,* "to look at," but in a less instrumental sense) the evil of which he is a part. He trains his gaze on things outside himself but cannot see the larger context in which he exists.

It becomes clear as the play progresses that the truth Tiresias nurtures inside himself is not only who the murderer is, but who Oedipus really is. By staging the confrontation between Oedipus and Tiresias, Sophocles emphasizes as strongly as possible the *masculine* nature both of Oedipus's actions and of his understanding of himself. As the full story of Oedipus's life gradually comes out, that strongly *gendered* view of self-knowledge will be undermined.

We also learn from Oedipus's confrontation with Tiresias that he is quick to anger when he does not get his way. The picture he presents of himself in the first few scenes of the play, as a kindly, selfless father-figure, is blown away as soon as Tiresias refuses to tell him what he wants to know. He blusters, threatens, and lodges wild accusations. When Tiresias answers his tirades with explicit information about Laius's killer, he cannot even begin to accept what the prophet says, because it clashes with his idea of who he is. This behavior brings us to an important set of issues for our inquiry. *Oedipus Rex* is often described as a "tragedy of fate." As we have seen, it is not easy to say exactly what "fate" meant to the Greeks, but it is clear in any event that Oedipus's struggle with mysterious transcendent forces is the focal point of Sophocles's drama. When thinking about that struggle, we soon come to the question of Oedipus's responsibility for the horrendous events that dominate his life. The innocence and/or guilt of Oedipus have been discussed endlessly by students of Athenian tragedy. We will try to avoid getting too tangled up in these latter categories, both potentially slippery, but some consideration is necessary if we are to understand how the play represents the interaction of divine will or fate on the one hand and human choice on the other. In the second half of the play, from the departure of Tiresias to the death of Jocasta, Sophocles draws our attention to these issues insistently, by gradually filling in the background to Oedipus's actions in the play, his childhood and the frightening prophecy he receives at Delphi.

Oedipus's willful and imperious behavior continues after Tiresias leaves the stage, in conflicts with Creon, and to some extent, with Jocasta. The former he accuses of plotting with Tiresias to grab the throne of Thebes. Creon is a thorough villain in some other plays, but here he is presented as basically decent, trying to be helpful to his brother-in-law. At first, he patiently refutes Oedipus's charges—why should he want the responsibilities of kingship when, as the queen's brother, he already has the perks? Oedipus will not back down, however, and the argument descends into a nasty fight, which is finally broken up by the return of Jocasta:

What is this foolishness, you miserable men,
why start a quarrel in public? Are you not ashamed
to air your private grievances when the city is so sick?
Oedipus, go inside, and you, Creon, to your own house.
Why make a big fuss over nothing? (Sophocles, *Oedipus Rex* 634–638)

The tone of Jocasta's rebuke is uncomfortably maternal here, reminding us that she is, after all, Oedipus's mother, even if she and her son/husband do not yet know it. After more name-calling, Creon exits, and Jocasta begins to question Oedipus about the quarrel. Learning that Oedipus has been accused by Tiresias of killing Laius, and that the oracle has said that the plague will lift when the murderer is found, she tells him to cease worrying. Prophets, she says, are notoriously unreliable. Take for example, she says, the prophecy that she and Laius were told in Delphi, that their son would kill Laius. That was obviously wrong, as they exposed their son when he was only three days old, and Laius was killed by a band of thieves where three roads meet.

Oedipus is nervous now: what three roads? At Phocis, she replies, where the roads from Delphi, Daulis, and Thebes meet. Now Oedipus becomes quite agitated, asking when the murder occurred. Just before you arrived in Thebes, she says. Oedipus reveals that he remembers killing a man and his retinue at that very spot at that time. Jocasta is still sanguine: the lone survivor said that "thieves" attacked, not a single man, so obviously Oedipus was not the murderer. Sophocles never resolves this discrepancy. We never hear why the survivor reported that there was more than one attacker, although there are hints that the man realized the new king was Laius's murderer, and that is why he begged Jocasta to be allowed to live in the hills as a shepherd. To modify his report slightly would only be prudent in these circumstances.

Oedipus sends for the shepherd and then tells Jocasta, apparently for the first time, the story of his childhood. He is the son, he says, of the king and queen of Corinth. One night at a dinner party when he was a teenager, a drunken guest said that Polybus was not Oedipus's father. Despite his parents' attempts to discredit the story, he could not let it rest and went to Delphi to consult the oracle. He got no information on the question of his paternity, but instead heard the terrible prophecy that he would kill his father and beget children with his mother. He resolved to avoid the prophecy coming to pass by never returning to Corinth. Instead, he headed for Thebes, where he had a nasty encounter on the road.

We, the audience, now begin to see the full horror of Oedipus's past come inexorably to light. Oedipus leaves the stage, Jocasta remains, and the chorus sings a song in which they proclaim themselves skeptical of prophets if they are accusing Oedipus, their king. But if prophecies are not reliable, then what is? They have pinned their hopes on the king, but the bargain begins to look perilous: either he is guilty of hideous crimes, or the world does not make sense. Next, a messenger from Corinth arrives with good news: the king Polybus has died, and the citizens are asking Oedipus to be king. Oedipus returns and presses the man: how did he die? Hearing that it was a peaceful death from old age, Oedipus rejoices in denouncing prophets. Obviously they are worthless!

He soon becomes anxious again: what about Merope? Is she alive? Jocasta breaks in here:

What should a man fear, whose life is ruled
by chance? There is no clear foreknowledge of anything.
Best to live at random, however one is able.
You must not fear a marriage with your mother.
Many men before now in their dreams
have shared their mother's bed. But such things
are not real. Live without care! (Sophocles, *Oedipus Rex* 977–984)

Our attention is drawn to the lines made famous—or infamous—by Freud, but the most important part of this speech is Jocasta's claim that men should live *eikē*, "without purpose," for no one can know what will happen in the future. As the prophecies seem to be catching up with Oedipus, everyone—Jocasta, the chorus, the king himself—begins to look for ways to escape. In their desperation, they hope to take comfort in a world ruled by random chance, something quite alien to the Greeks of this period.

The messenger, always eager to deliver good news, now breaks in again. Why worry about Merope? She is not Oedipus's mother anyway. He himself brought Oedipus to Merope, who was unable to have her own children, when he was a little baby. Oedipus presses on: where did the messenger find him? He was a gift from a shepherd the messenger knew. Where was this shepherd from? He said he was a servant of Laius. At this point, Jocasta realizes everything, and we imagine her stiffening. Oedipus wants to find this shepherd, and the chorus leader helpfully says he thinks it's the same man he has already summoned to report on the death of Laius. Jocasta now begs Oedipus to give up the search. Let it go, she pleads, but he is relentless, and she leaves the stage wailing.

This part of the play contains some of the most brilliant dramaturgy in all of Western literature, as Oedipus energetically pursues his own doom. As we watch, it seems clear that Oedipus did not want to kill his father or sleep with his mother. Quite the reverse: he has dedicated his entire life after hearing the dread prophecy to *not* fulfilling it. There are various ways to assess Oedipus's responsibility in this situation. Legally, he might well be thought of as "guilty" of the acts he committed, in Sophocles's time and perhaps in our own. Ignorance is no excuse, we might say. But moving into the more slippery area of moral responsibility, which involves intent and foreknowledge, we encounter a murkier picture. It seems that Oedipus's decisions, acting on what appear to be good motives, the desire to avoid killing and incest, all produce exactly the results he was hoping to avoid. Sophocles never gives us any explanation for why Oedipus should suffer such a horrible fate, no mention of past misdeeds or offenses against a god. The prophecy comes out of nowhere, as does the earlier prophecy to Laius, that his own son would kill him.

At this point it might be useful to make the distinction between what Oedipus did before the time when the play opens, killing his father and marrying his mother, and what he does in response to the immediate crisis of the plague. In the earlier period, the role of divine will or fate seems more prominent, and we can understand Oedipus as the victim of forces beyond his control (although the killing of Laius, a rather strong response to a dispute over right-of-way, does remind us of the imperious king). Later, Oedipus's acts seem to flow more from his own pride, arrogance, and quick temper, conscious choices not directly influenced by higher powers.

This approach allows us to absolve Oedipus of any conscious wrongdoing in regard to the main elements of the prophecy—no mortal can know his or her own fate; that is reserved for the gods. Oedipus seems to have done his best to avoid committing the horrible acts the oracle predicts. At the same time, his willful insistence on his own ability to save Thebes, set against the background of exorable transcendent forces at work, does not cast him in a favorable light. Finally, Sophocles does not offer a clear picture of why Oedipus is singled out for terrible disaster, or whether there would have been some other, better way to respond to events. Like Homer, Sophocles is less interested in working out in detail the reasons for human suffering than in presenting a vivid picture of how a gifted man with characteristic human limitations responds to the world as it is.

The remainder of the play is familiar to most students of Western literature, Jocasta's suicide, Oedipus blinding himself, the poignant spectacle of a great man brought low. As he is led back on stage, his eyes streaming blood, Oedipus still insists on his own agency:

Apollo it was, friends, Apollo
who brought all these evils piled on evils, these my sufferings.
But I alone and no one else struck my eyes.
For why should I have sight, when there is
nothing sweet to see? (Sophocles, *Oedipus Rex* 1329–1335)

These words reflect the larger dynamic that informs the play, transcendent powers acting to bring pain to mortals, and mortals responding by inflicting yet more pain on themselves. Oedipus suggests that he has blinded himself because he does not want to see what he has done, certainly an understandable reaction to what has happened. But we could also say that by blinding himself, the king has also chosen (he insists that this is his choice, not Apollo's) to become more like Tiresias, the antithesis of Oedipus's hyper-masculine persona. Unable to go on with the life he has pursued through masculine agency, he now chooses the more feminine existence modeled by the old prophet. Looking inward, he might learn to understand himself not as a self-created man but as part of a larger whole, over which he has little control. As we will see, Sophocles returns to his famous hero in his last play, to explore the end of a life lived through this new perspective.

Oedipus Rex presents to us, in a highly compressed and powerful form, a typically masculine life as the Greeks understood it. Oedipus attempts to re-create himself as a different person in order to avoid the future predicted for him. The results display vividly the consequences of living in a culture that on the one hand honors self-control and control over other people and things, while at the same time believing in a universe ultimately ruled by transcendent forces whose motives and intentions are mysterious and often appear capricious. Oedipus, confronted with a set of imperatives that are believed to be unchangeable, decides simply not to be the person who will live that life. He thinks that by imposing his will on the world outside himself, avoiding Corinth, defeating the Sphinx, saving Thebes from the plague, he will become a different man, a glorious masculine hero, rather than the helpless victim of divine will or fate, symbolized in the story by the infant left to die on a hillside. These two lives are symbolized by the two possible meanings of Oedipus's name, "swollen foot" and "know foot."

The downfall of Oedipus seems to acknowledge that finally, mortals' attempts at self-creation are doomed to fail in the face of overwhelming forces beyond human control. Thus it is best not to be too successful, lest the gods decide to strike you down. Yet the implications of Oedipus's self-blinding offer some hope of escape from the dead-end to which masculine self-assertion seems to lead. To be the instrument of divine will, rather than defying it, might open up new ways of understanding one's life. At the end of his own long life, Sophocles will return to this question in his last play.

NO ESCAPE: EURIPIDES'S *THE BACCHAE*

The collision of masculine will and divine power is at the center of Euripides's late masterpiece, *The Bacchae*. Produced in 399 B.C.E., seven years after the playwright's death and five years after the defeat of Athens by Sparta, the story of Dionysus's return to Thebes and subsequent clash with his cousin Pentheus is even darker in tone than *Oedipus Rex*. Whereas Sophocles's play focuses on a strong but flawed protagonist confronting transcendent powers whose purposes remain opaque, in Euripides's play the god Dionysus is on stage for most of the play, interacting freely with mortal characters. Pentheus, his main human antagonist, is a young, inexperienced man, vain, proud, and no match for the cruel and wily god. His destruction at the end of the play is a frightening demonstration of the potential for divine cruelty in the Greeks' conception of the gods.

The play opens with a prologue, spoken by Dionysus, who establishes his ascendancy from the outset:

I am Dionysus, child of Zeus, come
back to this land of the Cadmeans. Semele,
daughter of Cadmus, gave birth to me,
midwifed by the lightning's fire.
Having changed my appearance from god
to mortal, I have arrived at Dirce's stream
and the waters of Ismenus. I see my mother's grave,
marked by lightning, near the ruins of her house,
the smoldering flame of Zeus still alive,
the deathless violence of Hera against my mother.
But I praise Cadmus, who has made this place sacred,
a tomb for my mother. I have wreathed it with
the clustering green vine of grapes. (Euripides, *The Bacchae* 1–12)

He has come from Asia, he says, westward through the Greek cities on the coast of what is now Turkey, on to the mainland of Greece, and finally to Thebes, his birthplace. He bears a grudge against his mother's sisters, who have spread a slanderous lie. The sisters claimed that to hide the shame of Semele being pregnant out of wedlock, Cadmus made up the story that Zeus begat Dionysus, when in fact the father was a mortal. To punish the sisters, Dionysus has enchanted all the women of Thebes, driving them up onto

Mount Cithaeron, dressed in fawn skins, to celebrate his rites. Cadmus has abdicated the throne to his grandson Pentheus, who has refused to celebrate Dionysus in Thebes and is attempting to force the Theban women off the mountain and back to Thebes.

Euripides assumes his audience knows the rest of the mythic background: Hera, angered that Zeus had impregnated Semele, manipulated him into striking the mortal woman with lightning. Before Semele died, however, Zeus snatched the baby Dionysus from her body and sewed it into his own thigh, from which he was then born. The baby was taken away to grow up in Asia. Now that he has grown up, he has returned to wreak vengeance on the Thebans and introduce his rites into the cities of mainland Greece. We see reflected here the Greeks' belief that Dionysus' worship must have originated in Asia, which would explain the god's androgynous nature and association with unrestrained, eruptive force of nature, with all the emotions this releases.

By the late fifth century B.C.E., the wilder aspects of Dionysiac ritual, orgies and symbolic eating of the god in order to be possessed by him, had been replaced by a more rationalized worship. Dionysus was now a part of the Olympian pantheon and patron of the Athenian festival where dramatic contests were held. He was essentially the patron deity of Athenian comedy and tragedy, a safer venue for expressing powerful emotions. A century later, Aristotle canonized this idea, in his famous theory of *catharsis,* where the audience of drama cleanses itself of potentially damaging emotions by vicarious engagement with the characters on stage. But Euripides is not interested in a denatured version of the god. Although Dionysus initially presents himself as a mysterious but relatively passive figure, the devastating, primal force of the emotions he can release eventually washes over everyone on the stage.

The chorus, made up of female devotees of the god who have come with Dionysus from Asia, now enter and sing their first song, ecstatically praising the god and his rites, with a brief recap of the myth of Dionysus's birth from the thigh of Zeus. We note that the familiar dynamic found in many other plays, of the chorus playing the role of normal citizens as a foil to the protagonist's edgier persona, is missing here. Dionysus is not so much edgy as totally other, a frightening being with the power to destroy the city and its people at will. The chorus will offer no resistance to his plans, for they are completely devoted to him. As the play progresses, this new configuration will serve to emphasize the increasing isolation of Pentheus.

Next come Cadmus and Tiresias, two old men incongruously dressed in fawn skins and carrying the *thyrsus,* a wand wreathed with ivy and grapes leaves with a pine cone at the top. They dance around feebly on their way to Cithaeron, declaring their allegiance to the god and his new rites. They are, apparently, the only men in Thebes who have joined the worship:

Cadmus: Are we the only men of this city who dance for Dionysus?
Tiresias: Yes, for only we can understand. The rest cannot see.
            (Euripides, *The Bacchae* 195–196)

That the only men who will give themselves over to Dionysus are old raises some interesting questions to which we return in the next chapter. But we should be cautious about giving too much weight to the apparent devotion of the old men to Dionysus and his rites. First of all, the portrait here is meant to be demeaning to the characters, who seem comic and perhaps a little pathetic in their geriatric friskiness. More important, as we will soon see, neither is ecstatically possessed as much as shrewdly calculating: Cadmus wants to stay on the good side of a god who is in his family, and Tiresias wants to get in early on what looks like the next important cult.

Their cynical adherence to the cult makes the old men an effective foil for Pentheus, who now makes his entrance. He has heard of this new god, Dionysus, and of Theban women deserting their families to join the rites, to become Maenads, "mad women," as Dionysus's female devotees are called. He believes the rumors that these "rites" are really an excuse for drinking wine and illicit sex, and he has already imprisoned some of these women and will go after the rest, including his own mother, Agave, and her sisters, Ino and Autonoë. He has also heard about a foreigner who has come to Thebes:

They say that some foreigner has arrived in the city,
a fake wizard from the land of Lydia,
with perfumed yellow curls,
face flushed with wine and Aphrodite's charms,
who mingles day and night with girls,
dangling before them the joys of his rites.
If I catch him inside this palace,
I'll stop his pounding of the wand and
shaking his curls. I'll cut off his head!
He says that Dionysus is a god,
and was sewn into the thigh of Zeus,
but in truth he was burned in the lightning
with his mother, because of her lie, that
she had sex with Zeus. Are these acts
not worthy of hanging, whoever this stranger is? (Euripides, *The Bacchae* 233–247)

In light of what we already know from Dionysus's prologue, Pentheus comes across as both pathetically deluded and shrill in his claims to power. Euripides has made it clear that the god will be in charge here. Pentheus's contemptuous tone when talking about the Theban women whom Dionysus has enchanted, combined with his blustering about the stranger, suggests an insecure young man, uncertain of his powers and overcompensating with hyper-masculine swagger. The old men may be insincere and silly, but Pentheus's self-delusion will be deadly.

Pentheus now turns his contempt on Tiresias and Cadmus, deriding their dress and their professed devotion to the new rites. He is embarrassed that his own grandfather could behave so foolishly. For Tiresias, he reserves stronger language, accusing him of trying to use the new religion to make money. If the prophet were not so old, he would love to imprison him along with the women in the chorus. Anytime you have wine and women in the same festival, he says, there is something unhealthy to come. Once again, the young king's response to the old men seems disproportionate, given their feeble state. Each replies in his own defense, Tiresias with a long speech about the benefits that Demeter and Dionysus bring to humans and a rather contrived alternative explanation for the story of Dionysus's birth from Zeus's thigh, Cadmus with a more overtly calculating assessment: even if Dionysus is not a god, it is good for the family if people think he is. Neither has any effect on Pentheus, who orders his attendants to destroy the shrine where Tiresias prophesies and to arrest the mysterious stranger and bring him there in chains. Tiresias denounces Pentheus as a fool and a madman, as the two old men exit.

The chorus sings another beautiful lyric in praise of Dionysus and his rites and the dangers of defying the god's wisdom. We now finally see the mysterious stranger, who is brought to Pentheus in chains. Next comes the first of three encounters between the king and his prisoner that form the heart of the play. We hear from the attendant that the stranger has come along willingly, without any struggle, smilingly offering his hands for binding. Meanwhile, the women Pentheus had thrown in prison have been magically freed, their chains simply falling off them. Pentheus's first words show that the stranger has already had an impact on him:

Untie his hands. Caught in our nets,
he is not quick enough to escape me.
Your body is not unattractive, stranger,
for chasing women at least, which explains,
I suppose, why you are here in Thebes.
Your hair is long—you're no wrestler—
the curls hanging to your chin, alluringly.
Your skin is pale and smooth, from careful attention;
no sign of sunburn, but of the night's darkness,
when you hunt for Aphrodite with your beauty.
But first tell me who you are and where from. (Euripides, *The Bacchae* 451–460)

Pentheus seems drawn to the stranger in spite of himself. We see the power of the god here, and the first hints of the unsettling relationship that will develop between the two. The exchange begins with questions from Pentheus about the new rites and opaque answers from the stranger. The king becomes frustrated by his opponent's evasions, as he sees them, and begins to alternate between bluster and sneering insinuations about the sexual content of the god's rites. Pentheus cuts off the stranger's long hair, a gesture meant to show the king's power, but carrying an uncomfortable undercurrent of intimacy. He demands the thyrsus, which the stranger hands over willingly—again, an exchange with sinister implications for the king. Now Pentheus tells his henchmen to put the chains back on, and this time the stranger resists:

Pentheus: Seize him. He insults me and Thebes.
Dionysus: I tell you, do not bind me, fools.

Pentheus: I say do it, and I am stronger than you.
Dionysus: You do not know the life you are living or what you do or who you are.
             (Euripides, *The Bacchae* 503–506)

The last charge by Dionysus recalls Tiresias in his dispute with Oedipus, which we have explored previously:

You look around, but do not see the evil you inhabit,
nor where you live, nor with whom you are living. (Sophocles, *Oedipus Rex* 413–414)

Whether this echo is deliberate by Euripides we cannot know, but it prompts some further reflection on the two scenes. As in Sophocles's play, so here we have a confrontation between a proud, assertively masculine young king and a visitor who reflects qualities that the Greeks thought of as feminine. In both scenes, the king thinks he is more powerful, but the visitor and the audience know that the reverse is true. Tiresias reflects back to Oedipus truth about himself that is unavailable to him, blocked by his arrogance and ignorance of his own nature. We might go further and say that in his inwardness and femininity, the old prophet functions as a kind of second self to the king, like Patroclus to Achilles, or Enkidu to Gilgamesh, showing him parts of himself he has denied or lost track of.

These latter two aspects of the scene in Sophocles's play are also present in the clash between Pentheus and Dionysus. Pentheus certainly lacks self-knowledge and has arrogance in abundance. And Dionysus reflects back to him the feminine parts of himself that his insecurity causes him ruthlessly to repress. His penchant for putting women and androgynous men in prison can be seen as a concrete acting out of his inner battle. That Euripides means to suggest this battle comes out strongly in the next two scenes between Pentheus and the stranger. After another choral song, the voice of Dionysus is heard, presumably from offstage, and the palace appears to burst into flames and shake, as if in an earthquake. (How these effects might have been achieved on the stage in Athens we do not know.) The stranger then reappears and describes to the chorus how he has escaped from Pentheus's prison. The chains, he says, were never really on his wrists. He only made Pentheus believe they were, and when the king went to investigate the fire, he created another illusion, of a fierce bull that Pentheus tried to fight. At this point, Pentheus reappears, angrily questioning the stranger about his escape. When the stranger says that Dionysus set him free, the young king threatens to throw the god into prison, as well, a sign that he is further losing touch with reality.

Their exchange is interrupted by a messenger, a shepherd who, along with some other herdsmen, has just encountered the enchanted Theban women on Mount Cithaeron. The women were not, as has been suspected, indulging in drunken orgies, but rather mingling freely with animals and performing miracles such as drawing wine and milk from the ground. After spying on the women for a time, the men decide to curry favor with the king by capturing Agave. This plan goes disastrously awry, as Agave sees the men and calls to her companions. The men barely escape with their lives, while the women tear their flocks to pieces with their bare hands and then proceed to attack other villages, taking children and whatever else they want. The men of the village try to fight back, but their weapons are useless against the crazed Maenads, who slaughter them and then return to their lair. Whoever this god may be, says the messenger, Pentheus should welcome him to Thebes, as he is invincible and brings wine and sexual pleasure to mortals.

Pentheus is undeterred and begins to plan an attack on the women with his army. The stranger advises against this plan, predicting utter defeat for the troops. Instead, he offers to bring the women back himself. Pentheus brushes this suggestion aside and is leaving the stage to prepare his army when the stranger asks if the king would like to see the revels of the women. At this point, the tone of the encounter shifts, as Pentheus seems to fall under the spell of the god. He responds eagerly that he would pay a large sum in gold to see them. Dionysus leads him on, suggesting that if his mission is to be successful, he will have to disguise himself as a woman, so as not to be discovered by the women. The young king resists momentarily: he would be ashamed to dress in women's clothing! He asks, nevertheless, how he would dress if he were to accept the stranger's suggestion, displaying a rather keen interest in the details. He then leaves the stage, saying that he must decide whether to attack with his army or take the stranger's advice.

After another choral song, Dionysus calls Pentheus back on stage. Now the young king is completely under the god's spell. He is dressed in the costume of a female devotee of Dionysus, complete with a blond wig. He is concerned only with whether he looks suitably dressed, like his mother or his aunt. Is his hem straight? How does a Maenad hold the thyrsus? His questions continue, showing him to be quite out of touch with reality, imagining the god has given him superhuman strength. The final exchange between the disguised god and his deluded victim is cruelly ironic, full of double meaning. Pentheus sees himself as the savior of the city, on a critical mission. Dionysus puts it this way:

You alone will suffer for this city.
Great but crucial struggles await you.
Follow me. I will lead you safely there,
and another will bring you back. (Euripides, *The Bacchae* 963–966)

We learn the truth of these words after the chorus sings. A messenger reports to them the horrors on the mountain. Pentheus was put on the top of the pine tree by the god, who then alerts the Maenads. The women, led by Agave, tear him apart, ripping the flesh from his limbs. Agave decapitates the corpse and impales the head on a thyrsus, triumphant. She believes she has the head of a lion and hurries back to Thebes to show off her trophy. The play's final scenes are somewhat uncertain because of gaps in the manuscript, but Agave's slow reemergence from the god's trance, alongside her son's mangled remains, is clear. Her moment of realization is harrowing.

Euripides's *The Bacchae* dramatizes, in a particularly stark and somber way, the implications for the relations between men and gods of certain underlying beliefs in Greek culture. As he did in his *Medea*, the playwright throws contradictions in the culture into sharp relief by embodying them in powerful characters whose conflicts seem to be fundamentally irresolvable, because they exist in different realities. Dionysus, like Medea, is a creature whose powerful nature is beyond human control. Euripides stacks the deck even more, by having the play open with the god's chilling announcement of his plans. Medea's witchery is part of the mythic background of the play, but her determination to use it to destroy Jason and his intended emerges more gradually. In *The Bacchae,* the contest is decided at the outset.

We have also seen how Euripides seems at times to echo *Oedipus Rex,* prompting comparisons between the two plays. In each, the plot hinges on the conflict between two characters who represent diametrically opposed but complementary gender characteristics. Both men eventually move toward a more feminine mode of existence, although the effect of these transformations is radically different in the two plays. In each case there is also a marked disparity in power between the two characters, the presentation of which generates strong irony. Both Oedipus and Pentheus assert what they think of as invincible claims to power and authority, in defiance of forces that the audience knows from the outset they can never control. Both men proceed from a typically masculine set of assumptions about their position in society and in the larger cosmos, and both are eventually crushed by a combination of casually malevolent higher powers and their own arrogance.

Finally, Euripides's vision is darker than that of Sophocles. The earlier play keeps the uncontrollable powers of the universe offstage, represented indirectly and somewhat mysteriously, and its protagonist is an admirable if flawed man. Euripides brings the god into direct contact with his mortal victims, embodying and thus demystifying the frightening powers he wields. Pentheus, meanwhile, is no Oedipus. He is crushed by the god so brutally that we cannot help but pity him, but his youth, ignorance, and arrogance are not tempered by any nobility. Whereas Oedipus chooses a more feminine existence with rich implications for his future, Pentheus is enchanted by the god into his new perspective, about which there is nothing ennobling.

These differences are typical of the two playwrights' approach to Greek myth and its reflection of cultural assumptions. No matter how bleak the outcome of his plays, Sophocles always urges in us a recognition of the fundamental moral seriousness of his heroes, in whose struggles we, the audience, can recognize something of our own humanity. Euripides draws our attention to the impossibility of resolving the contradictions that Sophocles's heroes struggle to surmount. His protagonists are often formidable, but not noble. Their ignorance is joined more often with less attractive qualities: vanity, cowardice, and cruelty. But beneath these differences lies the same set of assumptions about the nature of a masculine life and its inherent contradictions.

CONCLUSION

As the Greeks saw it, the quest for authority as a man led inevitably to a fundamental contradiction, as the inherent limits of human existence put an end to the male dream of control over oneself and others. We saw in our initial study of *The Epic of Gilgamesh* and the *Iliad* how the fact of mortality, enforced by the participation of humans in the natural order, influenced the meaning of a masculine life. We can now see how this perspective is further complicated and enriched when a man's life is seen within a universe shared with omnipotent and often seemingly capricious forces whose motives are unknowable to mortals. The polytheistic universe of Greek religion might seem to offer opportunities for self-aggrandizement not available in a monotheistic system, but the basically amoral existence of the all-powerful gods in that universe necessarily generated great anxiety. One could account for the fall of apparently successful men by assuming that the gods struck him down out of envy, but this conclusion is far from a substitute for a rational universe.

Sophocles's Oedipus would seem to have all the qualities necessary for success as a man. Intelligent, physically powerful, and self-confident, he exudes masculine force. Faced with an unpalatable future, he simply decides to remake himself as another person, impressing his will on the world outside himself to change from a doomed orphan to the glorious king of Thebes. This inner decision is expressed in the myth by his taking another fork in the road, away from Corinth, toward Thebes. The apparent success of his self-fashioning is in turn represented by his conquering of the Sphinx. Controlling the creature through his intellect, he thinks his way to a new self. He "knows feet" and so controls the monster, who is part bird, part lion, and part woman. The new Oedipus epitomizes the ultimate masculine dream, moving beyond self-control to self-creation.

The great power of Sophocles's play comes from the fact that Oedipus's failure to control transcendent forces is realized through his confrontation not with Apollo, but with his own true self, the helpless infant, "swollen foot." Nowhere in Greek literature is there a more economical demonstration that the dream of unlimited masculine self-assertion cannot survive the confrontation with the true nature of human life. At the same time, Oedipus's story, as Sophocles tells it, reinforces another aspect of a man's life as the Greeks understood it: it is precisely the fact of limit that creates meaning in human life. Oedipus is doomed to fail in his efforts to deny his true self and the destiny that awaits that self, but as we watch him struggle, we are forced to consider again and again what it means to be human.

The same universe is dramatized on the stage in Euripides's *The Bacchae*, but without the same focus on the meaning of a man's life as it emerges from his struggles with mysterious powers beyond his knowledge. We can see all too clearly the nature of the power wielded by Dionysus and its devastating effect on the fragile society of Thebes. As it is portrayed in this play, the collision of divine will and human choice offers no arena for exploring human nobility in the face of unconquerable power. The world of *The Bacchae* has the same makeup as that of *Oedipus Rex,* but here we are left not with any feeling of the potential for human greatness in spite of human frailty. The glimmer of hope represented by Oedipus's final choice to embrace the will of the gods by blinding himself is nowhere evident in Euripides's play. There the servants of the god are either enchanted devotees with little capacity for independent judgment or cynical, slightly pathetic old men. Whether Cadmus and Tiresias represent the full potential of a man's life as it nears its inevitable end is the focus of our last chapter.

Six

Old Men

Oukalegon and Antenor, prudent both,
elders of the people, sat by the Skaian gates,
old men fighting no more, but fine
speakers still, like cicadas, perched
in trees, sending forth delicate voices.

—Homer, *Iliad* 3. 148–152

Like children, old men lived outside the central focus of ancient Greek culture. Past their prime physically, their power to control diminished, less active sexually, those who survived into old age faced daunting challenges. In Athens during the classical period, where most of our evidence comes from, there was no support system for older people of either sex outside of the family. When young men married, they usually moved back into their father's household and took over as head male, with all the masculine prerogatives and responsibilities that position carried. Their fathers, meanwhile, entered a kind of limbo state, with no established authority or function beyond what their children might confer on them. Retirement had no real meaning in such a society. Men would work as long as they were able and then become dependent on others, not a situation that granted much authority. As we will see, Athenian tragedy is filled with portraits of feeble—and sometimes foolish—old men.

Recent comparative surveys of aging in different kinds of cultures suggest one possible exception to this dismal picture. According to these studies, old men in traditional, often preliterate societies tend to turn away from the competitiveness, agency, and independence that characterizes the ideals of masculinity for younger males. These men are more likely to be receptive to the needs of the family and to the experience of women. This receptivity extends, in the Greek literature we will be exploring, to the needs not only of the family but also of the community as a whole, however that group is defined in a particular context. Most important for our purposes, old men in traditional societies tend to cultivate a more passive affiliation with transcendent powers, which replaces the need for control and the use of authority based on their own strength. In such a culture, old men, because of their "passive mastery," as it is called in the scholarly literature, and the fact that they are closer to the mysteries of death, can be seen as intermediaries between humans and gods. Old men in traditional societies have power not because they can dominate other mortals, but because they can influence the gods. One manifestation of this influence is the tendency for old men to use curses as an exercise of power, calling on the leverage available to them as a result of their closeness to the country of the dead and therefore to the powers that police the boundaries of that country. The wise old man is valued, in these kinds of societies, not only because he has been alive longer and seen more, but also because he has access to a kind of power not available to younger men. We will return to the distinction between active and passive mastery from time to time in the course of this chapter as a guidepost for exploring the way old men were understood in relation to Greek ideals of masculinity.

OLD MEN IN HOMERIC POETRY I: THE *ILIAD*

Although democratic Athens would not qualify as a traditional society, we might expect that the *Iliad* and the *Odyssey* would be good places to look for examples of old men who are given respect and some authority as a result of their wisdom and experience. Indeed, there are several examples of such men, but as usual for these great poems, the portrait of old men in each is subtle and varied, adding nuance that repays our attention.

We learn during the embassy to Achilles in book 9 of the *Iliad*, that Achilles's childhood mentor was a man named Phoenix, who was supposed to help his young charge become "a speaker of words and a doer of deeds." This description encompasses in broad terms what the poem presents as the primary criteria for masculine effectiveness. Old men cannot fulfill the second requirement anymore, but they can exert masculine power through the first. Nestor, the aged king of Pylos, is the foremost example of such a man in the *Iliad*. He no longer fights, but he is one of the most accomplished speakers in the poem and does not hesitate to give advice. He is honored by Agamemnon as the best adviser in the Greek army, and Homer calls him,

sweet-speaking . . . the clear-voiced orator of the Pylians,
from whose tongue the sound flowed sweeter than honey. (Homer, *Iliad* 1. 248–249)

Responding to Agamemnon's praise in book 4, Nestor stakes his claim to continued influence in old age:

Son of Atreus, indeed I wish that I myself could be
as I was when I killed brilliant Ereuthalion.
But the gods do not give everything to men at once.
If I was a young man then, old age is upon me now.
Still, I will take my place among the horsemen, and
urge them on with counsel and advice. For this is the gift of honor
for old men. (Homer, *Iliad* 1. 318–323)

We first meet Nestor during the disastrous quarrel between Agamemnon and Achilles, when he tries unsuccessfully to convince the two warriors to cease fighting for the sake of the army. Two generations of men have died since he was born, we are told, and he is king over a third. Counting a generation as 30 years, this puts Nestor in his seventies at least, well beyond the usual time for Greek men to be in charge. His opening speech illustrates his character well:

Ah me, a great sadness arrives in the land of the Achaeans.
Priam and his sons would now be happy,
and the other Trojans would rejoice mightily in their hearts,
if they should find out about you two quarrelling,
you, who surpass all the Danaans in counsel and fighting skill.
But be persuaded. You are both younger than I am.
I have worked alongside better men even
than you are, and never once did they disregard me.
Never have I seen such men as they were, nor will I,
like Peirithous and Dryas, shepherd of the people,
and Kaineus and Exadios, and godlike Polyphemus,
and Theseus son of Aegeus, like a god himself.
The strongest generation of mortal men these were,
the strongest and they fought against the strongest,
the beast-men from the mountains, and destroyed them utterly.
Coming from Pylos, I mingled among these men,
far from my own fatherland, for they summoned me.
And I fought depending on myself alone, yet no one
of those now living could fight against them.
They agreed with my counsel and were persuaded by my words.
But come now, you two obey also, since it is better to be persuaded.
Agamemnon, do not take the girl from him, noble though you are,
but let her go, since the sons of the Achaeans gave her as a gift of honor.
And you, Achilles, do not wish to struggle against the king
with force, since honor equal to that of the rest is not accorded
to a scepter-bearing king, to whom Zeus grants glory. Even
though you are stronger, and goddess mother gave you birth,
yet he is greater, since he rules over more men.
Son of Atreus, stop your anger. I ask you to let go of your
against Achilles, who is the greatest bulwark against evil war for all the
Achaeans. (Homer, *Iliad* 1. 254–284)

The speech, first of all, is long (although not nearly as long as Nestor's major efforts, as we will see). Nestor rarely makes brief remarks. His tendency to long-windedness has won him the reputation among modern readers as something of a blowhard. Although he does go on, we should bear in mind that in a culture that was portrayed as primarily oral, the ability to compose long speeches would be viewed more positively than it might be in a literate culture. And in Homeric poetry, scale generally marks importance, so Nestor's speeches would command special attention. Here we see him establishing two important sources of authority at the outset. First, he is older than Agamemnon and Achilles, and so they should listen to him. Second, he has fought beside warriors from earlier generations who were better fighters than anyone now living. This latter point is one Nestor makes frequently, and none of the younger men contests it.

The structure of the speech is carefully calibrated. He opens by attempting to inspire shame in the two young men: their quarrel is hurting the Greek army, and so the Trojans would be delighted to know about it. Nestor fits the profile of the traditional old man here, invoking the claims of the greater community over the pride of individual warriors. Moving directly into his reminiscences about former generations of fighters implies that these men, who were stouter fighters than the present generation of warriors, could also look beyond their own prerogatives to the greater good. He then builds a bridge between past and present by noting that these exemplary men were happy to take his advice—so why shouldn't Agamemnon and Achilles do likewise?

The last part of the speech shows Nestor's sensitivity to the necessities of the moment. He has intervened in a dispute between two proud and touchy men, which has already descended into name-calling. One wrong step here might lead to a major explosion. He addresses each man separately in a respectful, conciliatory tone, trying to suggest a way for the virtues of the two men to be complementary rather than in direct competition for honor. Agamemnon should let Achilles have Briseis, as the entire army awarded her to him as a prize for his bravery in battle; again, Nestor brings the weight of the community to bear on the dispute. Achilles, meanwhile, must recognize that however great his own physical gifts may be, Agamemnon is the king in charge of the expedition, and Zeus honors kings.

Nestor's tactic in this last overture is subtle: Achilles's claim to primacy is based on his performance as a fighter, which the Greeks recognize as the product of his innate gifts as the son of a goddess; Agamemnon's authority rests on political considerations—he is the organizer and leader of the expedition. By invoking Zeus, Nestor suggests an extra-human source of power for Agamemnon that could be seen as parallel to Achilles's semidivine nature. At the same time, he exerts some pressure on Agamemnon to acknowledge that Achilles, too, has divine support. He concludes by circling back to Achilles's great achievements.

The speech fails to defuse the quarrel, but we should not see this outcome as a mark of Nestor's ineptitude. The main thrust of the surrounding episode is to show how pride can blind men to otherwise compelling arguments. In what is his longest and most elaborate speech, given to Patroclus in book 11 of the poem, Nestor is in fact disastrously successful. Achilles has by this time stayed out of battle for a few days, with the eventual result that the Greek army teeters on the brink of defeat. The day after the embassy to Achilles fails, some of the other major fighters on the Greek side, Diomedes, Odysseus, and Agamemnon, have been wounded and driven from the field, leaving Ajax to hold the line. Achilles steps from his tent in time to see Nestor racing by in a chariot, carrying the wounded Machaon, himself a healer.

He calls for Patroclus and tells him to go find out if the body he saw was indeed Machaon. Homer hints darkly at the importance of this seemingly minor mission:

Patroclus heard him and
rushed from the hut. This was the beginning of evil for him.
(Homer, *Iliad* 11. 603–604)

The scene now switches to Nestor's quarters, as we see him and Machaon settling down for some rest and recuperation. Next comes a wonderfully vivid dramatic episode, full of comic elements but deadly serious in its outcome. Patroclus suddenly appears, and Nestor jumps to his feet, putting out his hand and offering his guest a seat. Patroclus immediately begins to backpedal, seeing the glint in the old man's eye:

Patroclus moved backward, and spoke to him:
No chair for me, aged sir beloved by Zeus, nor will you persuade me.
Respected and quick to blame is the man who sent me to find out
who this wounded man is that you brought back. Now I myself
know, and can see it is Machaon, shepherd of the people.
I will go back with my message to tell Achilles.
You know how *he* is, aged sir, a dangerous man
who might blame another who is innocent. (Homer, *Iliad* 1. 647–654)

We can see Patroclus edging nervously toward the door. He knows Nestor and realizes that he is in for a speech. Not only will it probably be long, but it may also put him in the unenviable position of representing Achilles, whose holdout from battle is even less defensible after the embassy. He tries to distance himself from his friend, enlisting Nestor as a witness to how unreasonable Achilles can be, but to no avail.

Now, as we feel Patroclus's eagerness to be off, Nestor launches into his speech. He begins with a swipe at Achilles. Why should he be so interested in who has been wounded when he doesn't even know that Odysseus, Diomedes, and Agamemnon have already been driven from battle? Nestor knows that Patroclus will be moved by this news, even if Achilles is not, and it is Patroclus he must convince. Is Achilles just going to sit there in his hut, while all the Greeks are killed, until the Trojan fires reach his ship? If I were only still young, as I was when . . .

Next come the old stories, the young Nestor victorious over Itymoneus, the cattle he won, the 50 herds of oxen, the sheep, the goats, 150 horses! His father Neleus much impressed with a warrior so young and yet so powerful. The games to celebrate, memories of Herakles's past raids, and so on and on for nearly 50 lines. Nestor at this point seems to be winding down, and we imagine Patroclus taking another hopeful step toward the door and, "On the third day the Epeians attacked." Off we go again, the attack on Thyroessa by the Epeians, Athena's warning to Neleus and his men, Nestor forbidden because of his youth from joining the battle—another possible end point? No—although he was among the best horsemen—Nestor goes out on foot!

Next he and his comrades plan an ambush of the Epeians, still encamped around Thyroessa. First sacrifices to various gods, and then Nestor's glorious duels with several luckless opponents. He is the first to kill an Epeian; he charges on them like a black whirlwind, and so forth, for another 50 or so lines, until finally Nestor kills his last man. All are praised, Zeus among the gods, and Nestor among men:

So I was among men; it seems like a dream now. But Achilles
will enjoy his greatness alone. And I think that he
will weep afterwards, when all the army has been destroyed.
(Homer, *Iliad* 11. 762–764)

Nestor seems to have gotten carried away once again, lost in his memories for 100 lines. But all of this is for a purpose. The abrupt transition in the middle of a verse, from the youthful Nestor to Achilles, is meant to drive home a point. The old man is surrounding Patroclus with the world in which heroes fought to defend their city and their friends, when wounded pride was not a reason to avoid battle, as Achilles does. The name Achilles is meant to focus Patroclus's attention. Now Nestor plays another card, reminding him of what happened when he and Odysseus came to get him and Achilles and take them to Troy. He quotes the instructions that Patroclus's father, Menoeteus, gave him:

My son, Achilles is above you in his lineage,
but you are older. Though he has the greater strength,
you must speak wise counsel to him, advise him
and show him the way. He will be persuaded for his own good.
(Homer, *Iliad* 11. 786–789)

Patroclus is distinguished among warriors in the poem for his sense of responsibility to others. He puts the good of the army and the well-being of his friends before all else. Nestor, knowing his man, appeals to these qualities and then finally makes the fatal suggestion that we now see he has been moving toward all along. If there is some reason why Achilles still will not return to battle to save his friends, then Patroclus should borrow his armor and take the field in the hope of fooling the Trojans into thinking he is Achilles, and thus buying time. This time, Nestor succeeds and the plot of the rest of the poem unwinds from his suggestion.

Long-winded though Nestor seems to be, careful attention to his speeches shows that he rarely rambles on without a purpose. His stories can appear to be pointless boasting or wistful reminiscence, but they always play a role in his larger rhetorical plan. Conditioned by sound bites, we may think that he talks too much, but the Greeks listen to him. Here, in his longest speech, we can see that by framing his reminiscing with pointed references to Achilles, he urges Patroclus to see his friend in a different light. The very length of the old stories is partly to distance Patroclus emotionally from what he has no doubt been hearing in Achilles's quarters. The last memory of what Patroclus's father told him strikes at the heart of his dilemma: he loves his friend, but indulging him further is not only dangerous to his other friends, but—as we now discover—is in fact a betrayal of his father's trust. What might seem like an old man's comically inappropriate trip down memory lane is in fact a masterful, opportunistic manipulation of the good-hearted Patroclus.

Nestor represents clearly one avenue open to continued influence for old men in traditional societies. His society in the *Iliad* is the Greek army, which must, like other fighting forces, maintain clear lines of authority from the top down. This imperative is threatened by Achilles's walkout in book 1, and it is significant that Nestor is the one who tries to smooth over the quarrel: if the customary, or we might say "traditional," structure of authority breaks down, Nestor, as an old man, would be particularly vulnerable, unprotected in his physical decline. His stories of previous generations also stress the need to preserve traditional systems for distributing power and status. Insofar as this is the case, his own influence will remain.

Phoenix, the old man who makes a brief but vivid appearance during the embassy to Achilles, draws on a different set of influences from Nestor's. As one of the three ambassadors sent by Agamemnon to Achilles, he gives a long speech attempting to convince the young warrior to return to battle. He begins with an appeal to Achilles not to leave Troy and abandon him, a defenseless old man who depends on him. By way of explaining why he has a claim on Achilles's affections and loyalty, he then revisits his own youth—how he became estranged from his father in a dispute over the latter's mistress and left his homeland and was taken in by Achilles's father, Peleus, who treated him kindly and set him up with his own kingdom, ruling over the Dolopians. Unable to have children of his own because of his father's curse, Phoenix became a kind of nurse/mentor for Achilles, holding him on his lap and feeding him as a baby, later teaching him to be, "a speaker of words and a doer of deeds." He then accompanied Achilles on the Trojan expedition to watch over him for Peleus, essentially becoming his surrogate father.

Phoenix shifts next into a mythical paradigm about the contest for men's allegiance between the *Litai*, "Spirits of Prayer," and *Atē*, "Ruin." If a man should follow the *Litai*, then his life is full of good things. If he should give into anger, however, then the *Litai* go to Zeus and ask that the man be punished with *Atē*. Achilles should avoid anger and cultivate the *Litai*, letting go of his grudge against Agamemnon and returning to battle. To make this perspective more concrete, Phoenix next tells the story of Meleager, a young man from Aetolia in north central Greece, whose anger makes him withdraw from defending his home city of Calydon from the invading Kouretes. He goes to his bedroom and stays there with his wife, Cleopatra (no relation to the Egyptian queen), refusing the gifts that Aetolian elders and priests offered and all entreaties from his family and friends, until Cleopatra begs him to return, fearing that the city will be sacked and she will be enslaved. This last attempt works and Meleager returns to battle, but he never gets the gifts. Thus Achilles should go back now while the gifts are still available, for he will have to return eventually to defend his own ships, and by then he may miss the reward.

Phoenix, like Nestor, draws on his past actions for leverage. His long association with Achilles, his nurturing and mentoring, allows him a claim on the young man's affections. His appeal, however, is not based on his former youthful masculine prowess but rather on what the Greeks would have seen as a more feminine role in Achilles's upbringing. He does not demand that his advice be followed because greater warriors from the past have done so, but because he has always supported Achilles and deserves the same in return. It is true to his more feminine stance that the successful suppliant in his story is a woman. Cleopatra's name is in fact identical to Patroclus's, with the syllables reversed; in Greek, the resemblance is more obvious: *Kleopatrē* and *Patrokl(e)os*, a parallel that will become clearer at the end of the poem. As we will see, Priam's successful supplication of Achilles in book 24 echoes Phoenix's unsuccessful one here.

As we have seen in the Introduction, Priam journeys to see Achilles in book 24, in an attempt to effect the release of Hector's corpse. Their moving exchange becomes the vehicle for the thematic resolution that brings the poem to a close. The old king of Troy appears earlier in a few brief but memorable scenes, most notably on the walls of the city in book 3, where he questions Helen about the identity of the Greek warriors on the plain before them, and again in book 22, when he and his wife Hecuba, again standing on the city walls, beg their son Hector not to fight with Achilles, who is bearing down on the city as they speak. At the beginning of book 24, after Zeus has decided to intervene and bring about the ransom of Hector, we see Priam again, this time in the throes of his grief. Iris, sent by Zeus to get Priam going on his way to Achilles, finds him rolling in the dirt, veiled and covered with dung. His sons sit around him, weeping. The goddess delivers her message: He must go to Achilles under the cover of night, bringing lavish gifts as ransom for the body of Hector. He should take with him only one old herald to drive the mules that pull the wagon carrying the ransom. He is not to fear because Hermes will guide him safely and secretly into the Greek camp and back again.

The divine command energizes Priam, who orders his sons to prepare the wagon and carrying basket. He goes to Hecuba and asks what she thinks of the plan. She objects strenuously: How can he dare go into the presence of Achilles, who will certainly kill him? Instead, she urges him to stay with her and mourn for Hector. He brushes off her objections and selects the many gifts for Achilles. He then drives off the Trojan men who have been crowded around, calling them "disgraces" and "failures," beating them with a stick, and then turns on his own surviving sons. They, too, are failures, soft dancers, not warriors. He wishes they had all died instead of Hector. They cower before him and slink away to finish preparing the wagon. Hecuba returns and urges him to at least pray to Zeus for safe passage, which he does. Then he and the old herald set off across the plain of Troy on their perilous night mission.

In this elaborate prelude to the ransoming, we see Priam transformed from a feeble old man, weeping and covered with dung, to a vigorous leader, impatiently scolding younger men and physically driving them away in his anger at their failings as men. Zeus's command revitalizes him, and he assumes a much more regal and masculine stature. Homer's description of the journey itself invokes a significant mythical pattern: Priam travels in the darkness, crossing a river and passing a tomb. He is led by Hermes, the god who traditionally guides souls to the Underworld, gains an audience with Achilles through his special status, and returns with the corpse of his son, who he thought was lost to him forever. What we see reflected here is a story pattern with great symbolic power, the hero's trip to the Underworld and confrontation with the god of Death. Perhaps the oldest and most wide-spread heroic journey in Western literature, this exploit, insofar as it is reflected in Homer's description of Priam's mission, confers great status on the old king, implicitly equating him with heroes like Herakles and Theseus, who made similar journeys and returned to the land of the living. No other old man in Homeric poetry is invested with so much heroic and masculine force.

Priam is not actually made younger and stronger by Zeus, as Odysseus is by Athena in the *Odyssey*. When Hermes, disguised as a young man, appears from the darkness during the journey, Priam is afraid, and the hairs stand up on the back of his neck. Later, he kneels submissively before Achilles, grabs his knees and, in a gesture of inexpressible poignancy, kisses his hands, "dreadful, manslaughtering," which have killed so many of his sons. His frailty is emphasized by the extreme gentleness with which Achilles treats him. He is an old man still, but by invoking the traditional story pattern, the poet confers on Priam heroic status in spite of his diminished physical condition. Here, as nowhere else in Homeric epic, we see an old man imbued with masculine force by virtue of the courage he shows in undertaking a dangerous mission. This is a special gift conferred on the old king in two different frames of reference, inside the poem by Zeus, and in our eyes by the poet.

Priam's first overture to Achilles echoes in many ways the earlier appeal of Phoenix:

Remember your father, godlike Achilles,
aged as I am, on the threshold of old age.
His neighbors all around wear him down,
nor is there anyone to ward off death and ruin.
But that old man, hearing that you are alive,
rejoices in his heart, and hopes every day
to see his dear son, returning from Troy.
Yet I am all hapless, since I fathered great sons
in wide Troy, of whom I say not one is left to me.
Fifty there were, when the sons of the Achaeans came.
Eleven were mine from one woman,
and the others were borne to me by women in the palace.
Of many of these rushing Ares loosened the limbs.
But one alone was left to me, who guarded the city and people,
whom you have just killed while he defended his fatherland,
Hector. For his sake I have come to the Achaean ships,
to ransom him from you, and I bring boundless gifts.

But you revere the gods, Achilles, and pity me,
remembering your father. I am more pitiable than he,
since I endured what no other mortal man has,
to draw to my mouth the hand of the man who killed my son.
(Homer, *Iliad* 24. 486–506)

The structure of Priam's speech is circular, framed by his plea to Achilles to remember his father, Peleus. Priam's strategy here is clear: if Achilles thinks of Peleus when looking at him, perhaps the young warrior will show him some compassion, seeing Priam not as his enemy but as an old man who, like Peleus, misses his son. He tactfully does not mention that Achilles has also killed some of his other sons, focusing only on Hector.

Priam's appeal seems to affect Achilles, who raises him gently to his feet and then delivers the first of his two consoling speeches, about the two jars of Zeus, which we discussed in the Introduction. As we saw there, by establishing Priam as a kind of surrogate father for Achilles here, Homer invokes another widespread and telling story pattern. To achieve maturity as a man, the male hero must always move away from the sheltering nurture of his mother and reach some kind of accommodation with the world of his father. Priam thus becomes a crucial part of Achilles's movement into mature masculine adulthood, another mark of his stature in the poem.

We can also trace some significant parallels between Priam and Phoenix. Both old men urge Achilles, directly or indirectly, to think of them as surrogates for his father Peleus. Initially, Phoenix portrays himself as having been a substitute son for Peleus, the homeless young man whom Achilles's kindly father took in and loved as a father would love his own son. But later, when he had become a mentor and caretaker for the young prince, Phoenix saw the relationship differently:

So over you I have suffered much, and had many troubles,
thinking that the gods would not bring to birth any children
from me. But I made you, godlike Achilles, my own child,
so that you would ward off destruction from me one day. (Homer, *Iliad* 9. 492–495)

The last line of Phoenix's speech is echoed in Priam's dismal picture of Peleus, surrounded by unfriendly neighbors, with no one to "to ward off death and ruin."

Neither Phoenix nor Priam claims, as does Nestor, masculine authority by invoking youthful fighting prowess. Instead, both claim for themselves paternal authority through their relationship with Achilles. Although old and physically diminished, both men are able to convince the fiery young warrior to see them, based on their past roles, as figures of authority who now merit compassion. Taken together, the exchanges between Achilles and these two old men form an arc within the poem, tracing the young man's progress out of selfish pride and toward a more mature, compassionate manhood. Their role in this progress establishes a position and stature for them in the *Iliad* that widens and deepens the perspective on the sources of power for old men beyond the model exemplified by Nestor.

OLD MEN IN HOMERIC POETRY II: THE *ODYSSEY*

The *Odyssey* takes place primarily in what we might call a postwar society. For most of its characters, the Trojan War is only a memory, a source of entertaining stories that perpetuate the *kleos,* "glory," of heroes. As we have seen, Nestor appears in the poem as a wealthy king, doting father of Peisistratus, and reverent observer of religious and social customs. In his role as keeper of proper custom, Nestor models for Telemachus something of how a male in authority should behave. And his memories are important for Telemachus, to be sure, offering him some tidbits of information about Odysseus. In these ways, Nestor exemplifies the possibility of continued authority for males well into old age.

At the same time, some of his qualities appear in a less favorable light in the *Odyssey.* His speechmaking, which functions so effectively in the *Iliad,* comes across more as mere garrulity when removed from the urgencies of wartime. In spite of (or because of) his enthusiastic welcome, Telemachus tactfully tries to avoid returning to Pylos after his trip to Sparta, fearing that he will be trapped by the old king's hospitality. The links to a heroic past that Nestor uses to establish his authority in the *Iliad* carry less weight in the war's aftermath, and when Nestor claims that Odysseus and he were alike, never disagreeing in their advice to the Greeks in council, it sounds more like wistful boasting.

Menelaus, although certainly a mature man, is not portrayed as having passed his prime in the *Odyssey.* The only genuinely old man in the Spartan episode is Proteus, "the Old Man of the Sea," the sea creature who appears in Menelaus's story of his escape from Egypt. Calling Proteus a "man" might seem inappropriate, since he's clearly a magical being, but Homer's word for him is *gerōn,* "old man," so we will give ourselves permission to take a brief look at his unique qualities. His role as a source of knowledge about the lost heroes of the Trojan War parallels that of Tiresias later in book 11 of the poem. Both characters have access to special knowledge, Proteus apparently of the past, Tiresias of the future.

Proteus is also a shape-shifter, who must be bound in order to force him to release knowledge. The scene in which Menelaus and his men ambush and restrain the old man is in fact a symbolic representation of the Greeks' understanding of the nature of human civilization, which is produced when the changeable forces of nature are shaped and bounded by the imposition of human intelligence. In essence then, Proteus in the *Odyssey* is portrayed as a representation in creatural form of the raw energy in the natural world that is the source for creating human civilization. As such, he certainly embodies a crucial element in the making of human experience, but how he in himself exemplifies something human is not so clear.

We have already met Tiresias in his later appearance in Sophocles's *Oedipus Rex.* His basic role there, as blind prophet, is already in place in *Odyssey* 11. Odysseus has been told by Circe that he must travel to the Underworld to find out from Tiresias how to get home safely. The prophet does give him some advice about not eating the Cattle of the Sun, as well as some information about the current state of disarray in Ithaka. But the major revelation he delivers is that after killing the suitors and regaining control of his kingdom, Odysseus will have to take one more trip. He must go inland far enough that no one has seen or knows about the sea. Once he has gone that far, he is to build a shrine to Poseidon. Then, he will have a gentle death "far from the sea," surrounded by his loved ones.

Tiresias, Homer tells us, is given special powers by Persephone. He alone can still know things that will happen in the world of the living, while the rest of the dead are flitting shadows. He remains, even beyond the grave, a wise old man. Old men in traditional societies are supposed to be closer to the ultimate boundary of death and therefore to the gods and their special knowledge. Tiresias exemplifies this model from the far side of the divide.

Curiously, the most prominent old man in the *Odyssey* is not "real." Disguised as an old beggar, Odysseus himself is the principal character, along with Penelope, in the last third of the poem. The disguised hero's behavior and his treatment by others tell us much about the poem's view of old men. From the time of his arrival at the country outpost of Eumaeus, the king's faithful retainer and keeper of the royal herds, the beggar's vulnerability is always apparent. He is attacked by Eumaeus's dogs as soon as he sets foot on the property. Although he is afterwards treated with great kindness by Eumaeus, when he sets out for the palace, the trouble begins again. He and Eumaeus meet Melanthius, a goatherd, who abuses the old beggar both verbally and physically. Odysseus restrains himself and carries on toward the palace. He is attacked continually in the next few scenes by Irus, another beggar (whom he himself beats in a boxing challenge), by maids in the palace, and by various suitors. Telemachus protects him from physical harm, but not from contemptuous dismissal by the unworthy interlopers. He has, of course, his delicious revenge on all his tormentors, stringing the bow and slaughtering them all.

The figure of the old beggar is important both to Odysseus and Athena inside the poem, as a way of getting Odysseus into the palace without arousing the suitors' suspicions, and to Homer as a storyteller, for the treatment of the beggar becomes a yardstick for measuring the moral character of others in Ithaka. At the same time, our knowledge of the beggar's true identity allows Homer to generate much of the irony that colors the end of the poem: the old man looks feeble, but we know better. Still, the reactions of other characters to the beggar presumably reflect what old beggars might encounter in the palaces of the great in the ninth century B.C.E. in Greece. In fact, no other portrait of a poor old man in Greek literature is so extensive. The *Odyssey* is not meant to be a social commentary on the plight of powerless old men, but the scenes in the royal palace provide a glimpse of how utterly dependent such men would have been on the kindness of strangers. In spite of the more positive examples we have been looking at here, the words most often applied to old age in general in Homeric epic are "harsh," "difficult," sorrowful," and "deadly." Prophets, priests, and kings might have sources of authority that compensated for their loss of physical vitality, but old men who were poor would face a bleak existence.

Although a patriarch of the royal family in Ithaka, Laertes seems to have been reduced in his son's absence to the beggar's level of misery, dressed in rags and scratching in the dirt on his farm. His wretched condition is a measure of how badly out of joint things are in Ithaka, with no young male in charge and the suitors unchecked. Telemachus is unable to do much for his grandfather, who is left on his own out in the country. Odysseus hears about Laertes from his mother in the Underworld:

Your father remains there
on his farm, and never comes to the town. He has
no bed, nor blankets and shining coverlets,
but sleeps on the ground with the servants in the lodge,
in the dirt by the fire, with rags for clothing.
But when the summer comes, and the crops ripen,
anywhere on a rise of the fruit-bearing earth
his bed is thrown on a pile of fallen leaves.
He lies there grieving, and great sadness grows in his mind
as he longs for your return. Harsh old age has come for him.
(Homer, *Odyssey* 11. 187–196)

This portrait is bleak enough and is confirmed in other places in the poem, but when Odysseus actually finds his father in the country, after killing the suitors, we see his exile in a slightly different light. At first the sight of his father appalls Odysseus. He is wearing dirty clothes, ox-hide leggings with patches, and a goatskin cap. He is "worn out with old age." The place where he finds Laertes, however, is a "well-tended plot," and the old man is cultivating a tree. The contrast between his condition and that of the crops also catches his eye:

Old man, you clearly are no beginner when it comes
cultivating an orchard. Things here are well cared-for, nothing
lacks attention, no plant, no figs, no grape vine, no olives,
no pears, no vegetable of any kind goes without your care.
But let me say this, and do not take offense in your heart:
you yourself lack this tender care. You have instead grievous
old age, and wear squalid, unseemly rags. (Homer, *Odyssey* 24. 244–250)

The picture of Laertes in his orchards suggests that although he has been deprived of his regal existence by his son's absence at Troy, he has found some solace in taking care of his farm. His attentive nurture of plants and trees reminds us of Eumeaus, whose rustic outpost, with its stables of animals, is also carefully tended and organized, an emblem of his loyalty to his master. Both men are holding out as best they can in the king's absence, protecting some kind of residual order until Odysseus can return and restore the household and palace. Both have also found a way to foster growth and fecundity amid the overall decline of the royal household—and, in Laertes's case, his own decline into old age. Although he only appears briefly in the poem, Laertes serves as an important but ambiguous symbol. He own debased condition bears witness to his family's (and especially Odysseus's) inability to care for him properly. At the same time, his successful farming hints at another possible venue in which old men can continue to enjoy some efficacy, even when physically diminished.

The picture of old men in both Homeric epics is mixed. Old age in general is usually described in negative terms as painful and difficult. Both the hard treatment that Odysseus receives when disguised as beggar and the diminished condition of Laertes offer glimpses of what awaited old men without family or wealth to protect them. These dark portraits are counterbalanced to some extent by the continued energy and influence of old men like Nestor, Phoenix, Priam, and Laertes. We will have to wait until the very end of the fifth century B.C.E. to see this kind of vitality and force portrayed in an old man.

SEXUALITY IN OLD MEN

As he leans over the walls of Troy and begs Hector to take pity on him as an old father who will lose his son, Priam conjures a disturbing image:

At last my dogs shall rip my raw flesh
before the gates, when some enemy will have struck
with sharp bronze or a spearcast, tearing the life from my limbs,
those dogs I myself have fed at the table to guard the gates,
drinking my blood they will lie in their frenzy in the forecourt.
It is seemly for a young man, killed in battle, slashed with sharp bronze,
to lie exposed. Though he be dead, all that shows is beautiful.
But when dogs disfigure the gray head and beard,
and the private parts of a dead old man,
this is the most pitiful sight for wretched mortals. (Homer, *Iliad* 22. 66–76)

The explicit vision of Priam's mutilated genitals is highly unusual in Homeric poetry. Although sexuality—and sexual antagonism—run in a steady, if submerged, stream through much of Greek literature, direct references to the physical aspects of sexuality are rare outside of Aristophanes, with a few notable exceptions. Neither Hera's seduction of Zeus in book 14 of the *Iliad* nor the tryst between Ares and Aphrodite in book 8 of the *Odyssey* has any explicit description of lovemaking. Even references to males' sexual performance are less frequent than we might expect in the literature of such a competitive, patriarchal culture. The one exception to this latter reticence is the sexuality of old men. Priam's vision of himself naked and defenseless is hardly sexual in itself, but it offers a glimpse into the anxieties that might attend declining physical powers for old men.

A more direct reference to this set of issues is found in the *Homeric Hymn to Aphrodite,* a poem roughly contemporary with the *Odyssey.* The main focus of the story is on the tryst of Aphrodite with Anchises, a Trojan prince, which produces the hero Aeneas. The goddess disguises herself as a young virgin, and pretends to let Anchises seduce her. Afterward, when she reveals her true identity, he is terrified, for the usual consequence for mortal men of having sex with a goddess is impotence at best, and sometimes death. She reassures him that he will retain his virility and offers a short review of mortal/immortal liaisons. Among them is the story of Tithonus, a mortal whom Eos, the goddess of the Dawn, takes for a lover. Hoping to keep her lover virile, Eos asks Zeus to make him immortal but neglects to ask for him to be ageless. Things go well for a while, but eventually Tithonus begins to get older:

But when the first gray hairs sprouted
from his handsome head and well-formed chin,
Eos stayed away from sex with him.
She cared for him, keeping him in her house,
feeding him nectar and ambrosia, and giving him lovely clothes.
But when hateful old age completely overcame him,
and he could no longer move or lift up his limbs,
a plan that seemed best appeared in her heart.
She shut him in a bedroom, and closed the shining doors.
His voice flowed unceasingly, nor was there any force,
such as there once was, in his pliant limbs. (*Homeric Hymn to Aphrodite* 228–238)

The linking of physical decline in old age and sexual failure is explicit here, particularly in the veiled references to impotence ("lift up his limbs," etc.). Also characteristic is the reference to Tithonus's voice. Although the voice flows unceasingly, the surrounding references to physical weakness suggest that it has little force, a strengthless chattering. We remember from the epigraph for this chapter the old men sitting on the walls of Troy:

Oukalegon and Antenor, prudent both,
elders of the people, sat by the Skaian gates,
old men fighting no more, but fine
speakers still, like cicadas, perched
in trees, sending forth delicate voices. (Homer, *Iliad* 3. 148–152)

Old men, like cicadas, have "delicate voices," which seems to imply dry, reedy voices. Hesiod, writing in the seventh century B.C.E., associates the cicada with sexual weakness, its voice sounding most loudly in August, when women are the most lustful and men more prone to impotence.

Greek elegiac poets, working between 650 and 500 B.C.E., tend to be more open than Homer about the sexual decline that accompanies old age in men. Mimnermus, who lived in Colophon on the coast of what is now Turkey, writes often of the pain and indignities of old age for men. In his poetry we find, for the first time in Greek literature, descriptions of the ugliness of old age and its consequences for old men:

What is life, what is pleasure, without Golden Aphrodite?
May I die, when these things no longer matter to me:
hidden love and the gentle gifts of the bedroom.
These alone are the sweet blooms of youth
for men and women. But when painful old age
advances, which makes a man ugly and feeble alike,
dark worries wear away his wits,
and he takes no pleasure in the sun's rays,

being hateful to boys and worthless to women.
So harsh is the old age the gods provide. (Mimnermus, Fragment 1)

For Mimnermus, old age (and so the old man) is "harsh and misshapen," "hateful and without honor," unable to attract either boys or women. It makes a man "unrecognizable." As we have seen, Greek writers usually portray men's love relationships in terms of power, dominance, and submission. In Mimnermus's poetry, the link between physical weakness and sexual failure is made explicit.

Anacreon, the last of the great Greek lyric poets of Ionia (now the coast of Turkey), also writes frequently about the old man as lover. His surviving poetry is almost all about love, seen as an exercise (successful or unsuccessful) of power. In this context, the old man is sometimes portrayed as overcoming his physical shortcomings with experience and craftiness, but more often as rejected as too old:

Already my hair is gray
my head all white;
charming youth has left me;
my teeth are old,
no more time of sweet vigor
is left for me.
And so I weep in fear of
Tartarus, for the murky house
of Hades is fearful, and the road down
is harsh. Once you descend
no way to return. (Anacreon, Fragment 395)

In another poem, Eros seems to summon him to pursue a girl, but he is too old and she is not interested:

Golden-haired Eros throws
a purple ball, calling
me to play with a fancy-sandaled
girl.
She's from well-built Lesbos,
and mocks my white hair,
ogling another girl. (Anacreon, Fragment 358)

Images of hunting are frequent in Greek love elegies, with the male lover as the aggressor. Ibycus, a contemporary of Anacreon who lived and wrote in the Greek settlement in southern Italy, emphasizes the challenges to old men in love by reversing the usual imagery: the speaker, a man "near old age," is the prey now:

Eros again shoots a melting glance
at me from under his dark eyelids,
driving me with every kind of magic
into the capacious nets of Aphrodite.
Oh, I tremble at his approach,

like a champion horse nearing old age,
who enters the race, yoked with swift chariots. (Ibycus, Fragment 287)

Now the speaker, nearing old age, is forced into an erotic contest and fears his powers are no longer sufficient. In these poems of private life as opposed to the grander existence usually portrayed in epic poetry or tragic drama, the physical decline that accompanies old age for men brings to the surface anxieties about sexual performance. In this intimate arena, neither public oratory nor respect for past achievements can offset the sense of failing powers. Although these poems are generally light in tone, deflecting shame with ironic self-deprecation, the underlying anxieties are clear enough.

THE WORST OF EVILS: OLD MEN IN ATHENIAN TRAGEDY

Democratic Athens, our other major source for the lives of old men in Greek culture, was decidedly not a traditional society. Athens in the fifth century B.C.E. was the most urban of Greek cities. The new distribution of political and social power brought on by democratic government would undercut traditional sources of authority and respect for old men. Old men did serve on juries, but there were no offices specifically reserved for them in the political structure of Athens. (And certainly the portrait of old men on juries in Aristophanes's *Wasps* does nothing to enhance their stature.) There are a few instances of old men whose wisdom and advice are valued in Athenian drama, but the usual portrait is much more negative. We have seen how Cadmus and Tiresias in Euripides's *The Bacchae* are made to appear foolish in their enthusiasm for the new god. The chorus of Aeschylus's *Agamemnon* dithers ineffectually while the king is murdered, and the chorus of old men in Euripides's *Children of Herakles* is equally ineffectual. The chorus in Sophocles's *Oedipus at Colonus* characterizes old age as, "powerless, lonely, and devoid of love." The frailty of the old men becomes the vehicle for a hilarious scene in Aristophanes's *Lysistrata,* as the old geezers are routed by women on the Acropolis. The geriatric enthusiasm of the old servant in Euripides's *Electra,* who comes to tell Electra about evidence that her brother has returned, is roundly ridiculed.

If they are not shown as feeble, old men are often portrayed as nasty in Athenian drama. Pheres, the father of Admetus in Euripides's *Alcestis,* refuses to consider dying in place of his son. His ensuing argument with Admetus is an ugly display of intergenerational hatred. Creon in *Oedipus at Colonus* is a bullying, sneaky old man, who does not hesitate to kidnap Oedipus's daughters to get his way. As we will see, the aged Oedipus displays all of these qualities in Sophocles's *Oedipus at Colonus.* But Sophocles's last work is one of two plays that in fact explore possible exceptions to the dreary portrait of old men in Athenian drama, the other being Euripides's *Children of Herakles.* In both works, an old man seems to exhibit all of the negative qualities associated with aging males in fifth-century B.C.E. Athens, but each in his own way finally overcomes his limitations. Looking more closely at the responses of these two dramatists to the experience of old men in classical Athens will help to round out the portrait of the male life course we have been tracing in these pages.

Euripides's *Children of Herakles* was probably first performed in the early years of the Peloponnesian War, between 431 and 425 B.C.E. Although there are no direct references in the play to historical events, the focus on war and the extreme behavior, both positive and negative, that it fosters in communities would resonate strongly within Athens. The war with Sparta had already produced brutalities on both sides: the slaughter by the Plateians, an Athenian ally, of prisoners from Thebes, allies of Sparta who had been guaranteed safe conduct; the retaliation by Sparta two years later, which included killing prisoners of war after they had been promised a fair trial; the killing by Athens of Peloponnesian ambassadors to Thrace, although diplomats were generally considered to be exempt from harm; the decision by Athens to kill all the male citizens and enslave all the women and children of Mytilene, a city in Lesbos that had revolted from alliance with them. (The Athenians relented in time to send another ship and prevent the wholesale slaughter, killing instead a thousand of the city's leading citizens.) According to Thucydides, in his description of the political revolution in Corcyra, a city caught in between warring factions, the pressures of war caused the customary restraints on human behavior to give way in this period.

In Euripides's play, Athens is in a dispute with Argos in the mythical past, and the conduct on both sides is less than honorable. The treatment of prisoners and suppliants is a major focus of the play, issues that would have an inescapably vivid impact on the wartime audience in Athens. Also, the children of Herakles, who are portrayed as suppliants seeking asylum in Athens, were thought to be the ancestors of the major aristocratic families in Sparta and elsewhere in the Peloponnesus. That the king of Athens finally succeeds in rescuing these children would prompt reflection by the audience both on the traditional role of Athens as the savior of suppliants and on the sufferings they themselves were undergoing at Sparta's hands. In short, the play was performed in an atmosphere rich with contemporary referents.

The background for the story would be known to the Athenian audience. Herakles, the son of Zeus and a mortal woman, Alkmene, was hated by Zeus's wife Hera, who made his life as hard as she could, arranging for him to be enslaved to his cousin Eurystheus, the king of Argos, resulting in the famous 12 labors. Eventually, Herakles died in Trachis, and his children were left to fend off the relentless Eurystheus, who continued to pursue them. As the play opens, the children have reached Marathon, outside of Athens. Leading and protecting them are Iolaus, an aged cousin, and Alkmene, their mother. After Iolaus delivers a prologue, filling in the background for the play, Kopreus, an agent of Eurystheus, arrives to demand that Herakles's children return with him to Argos, where they have been condemned to death in a trial. Iolaus protests and refuses to let Kopreus have the children. A tussle ensues, in which Kopreus knocks Iolaus to the ground. The old man's cries for help summon the chorus of citizens of Marathon, who also object to Kopreus's demands, citing the sanctity of suppliants. Demophon, the son of Theseus and king of Athens, and Akamas, his brother, now enter, joining the opposition to Kopreus.

At this point, the audience will have recognized elements of a familiar form, the suppliant play, many examples of which they will have seen in the same theater, including Aeschylus's *Suppliant Women*, Euripides's *Suppliant Women*, and Sophocles's *Philoctetes*. This kind of story requires relatively helpless victims, harsh and relentless pursuers, and noble saviors, all of whom we have already seen in the first scene. Moral questions of fairness, justice, and compassion are foremost in such a story and will be present here. Euripides can count on his audience to know these elements, and he works with the expectations that arise from them.

Children of Herakles is a peculiar play, even by Euripides's standards. Episodic, fast-paced, crowded with incident, the form of the action allows little time for character development or leisurely exploration of knotty moral issues. Nevertheless, the treatment of old men in the play is worth a closer look. Our focus is primarily on the character of Iolaus, the cousin of Herakles's children, descended from the marriage of Alkmene to the mortal Amphitryon. The first thing we notice is that Euripides distorts the accepted genealogy of Herakles's family by making Iolaus an old man, apparently not much different in age from Alkmene, who would in fact be his great aunt. As the action proceeds, we see that the playwright makes an issue of Iolaus's old age and physical weakness. In his first struggle with Kopreus, he is knocked to the ground, a startling event in Athenian drama. Later, when battle has broken out between the forces of Argos and Athens, Iolaus suddenly announces that he will fight:

Iolaus:	I will go with you. We are thinking the same thing, that we should stand by our friends, as is proper, and help them.
Servant:	It is foolish of you to say this.
Iolaus:	Why not join my friends in a fierce battle?
Servant:	A fierce look does no damage, if a strong arm is missing.
Iolaus:	What, are you saying I am not strong enough to pierce a shield?
Servant:	You might be strong enough, if you don't fall down first.
	(Euripides, *Children of Herakles* 680–686)

The exchange continues for another 60 lines, as the chorus and then Alkmene join the servant in an attempt to dissuade Iolaus. "Give way to age," the chorus says, "Yield to the inevitable. Once youth is lost, it cannot be regained." He will not budge and sends the servant to fetch armor left in a nearby temple. Once dressed, he leans on the arm of the servant and totters offstage.

This scene could certainly be played as comic, the tone akin to the geriatric dancing of Cadmus and Tiresias in the *Bacchae*. Iolaus, however, although perhaps a figure of fun in this scene, is not without moral weight. His insistence on the imperative of helping friends and fighting enemies is, first of all, familiar to us as a basic part of the traditional aristocratic code of honor. But his motives for entering the fight here are part of the portrait of him specifically as an old man and reach back to his first speech, which opens the play:

> For a long time, this has been my belief:
> A just man lives for those near him,
> while he who races toward profit
> is useless to the city, harsh to deal with,
> and good only for himself. I know this from experience.
> Though I could live at my ease in Argos,
> I alone, honoring compassion and the bond of blood,
> was a partner for Herakles in most of
> his labors, when he was still alive. Now, since
> he lives among the immortals, I take his children
> under my wing, leading them to the safety I also need.
> (Euripides, *Children of Herakles* 1–11)

Iolaus's words portray him as a model of compassion, reminiscent of Patroclus, in spite of the doughty warrior he later turns out to be. His measure of a just man is his willingness to put the needs of the community before his own, a prominent characteristic, as we have seen, of old men in traditional societies. The Greek word translated here as "compassion" is *aidōs*, which encompasses a wide range of meanings—"shame," "honor," "reverence,"— all reflecting in some way the sense of regard for others and their opinion. Homeric warriors feel *aidōs* if they fail somehow in the eyes of others. Iolaus presents himself as a heroic figure in the mold of Hector, sacrificing his own desires for the good of others.

Iolaus's attitudes are echoed elsewhere in the play. When he learns that Demophon will extend the protection of Athens to the children, he is full of praise for the city:

> We, having fallen into
> the depths of evil, have found in these men
> friends and kinsmen; they alone out of all
> of Greece have stood up for us.
> Children, give your right hand to these men,
> and you, friends, draw near to the children.
> Oh children, we have found the proof of friendship.
> . . .
> Always think of these men as saviors and friends,
> and remember, never lift a hostile spear against this land,
> but consider Athens the dearest city of all.
> We ought to revere these men, who dared to
> take on the great Argives as enemies for us,

who looked on us as wandering suppliants,
but did not forsake us or drive us from their land.
(Euripides, *Children of Herakles* 302–309; 312–319)

Demophon then learns from oracles that to succeed in their struggle to save the children, they must sacrifice a virgin. Makaria, one of Herakles's daughters, volunteers to die, prompting this encomium from Iolaus:

Oh most outstanding of all women
in courage, know that you are most
honored by us in life, and will be so
even more in death! (Euripides, *Children of Herakles* 597–599)

Seen in this context, Iolaus's determination to join the fighting, in addition to being a sign of his—perhaps foolish—defiance of age, is one more act of compassion and sacrifice. Opposed to these gestures is the ruthless determination of Kopreus to bring the children to Argos to be put to death. His arguments would be familiar to Athenians who had lived through the first years of the Peloponnesian War: the strong will always impose their will on the weak; no appeals to compassion or fairness have any bearing on the case. He shows that he is willing to use force himself, bullying Iolaus and throwing him to the ground. And of course in these actions and attitudes, Kopreus only carries out the implacable will of Eurystheus, himself the agent of Hera's anger at Herakles.

After a choral ode, the servant who left for battle with Iolaus returns with joyful news: Hyllus, a son of Herakles, and his army have defeated Eurystheus's Argive forces and taken him prisoner. Hyllus and Iolaus have decided to send Eurystheus back to Marathon, so that Alkmene could see him captured and in her power. All the children are safe and unharmed, but the most miraculous news is that Iolaus has been transformed—temporarily, at least—back into a vigorous young man. He was driving Demophon's chariot and, as he drew close to Eurystheus, he prayed to Zeus and Hebe, Herakles's divine lover and the god of youth, that he might be young again, long enough to conquer Eurystheus. Over his chariot appeared twin stars and,

they hid the chariot in a dark cloud.
Those who would know say it was your son
and Hebe. Iolaus then shown forth from the murky cloud,
the image of a young, strong-armed man. (Euripides, *Children of Herakles* 854–858)

Iolaus never returns to the stage, and we are left to guess how long the rejuvenation will last. The final 100 or so lines of the play are taken up with the exchange between Alkmene and her prisoner, Eurystheus. She is determined to kill him, but everyone else onstage, the chorus and the servant, disagree: Athens is against the killing of the prisoners. Eurystheus offers a defense of sorts for his relentless persecution of Herakles. It was Hera, he says, who insisted that he suffer, and I had to give way to a god. Once Herakles was dead, he had to strike against the children in self-defense, as they were now implacable enemies. Alkmene is completely unmoved by any of this explanation and offers a gruesome solution: she will return Eurystheus to his friends—

after she kills him. Eurystheus at this point refuses to beg for his life, saying he would rather die than be humiliated. But because the Athenians have tried to protect him, he will reveal a prophecy he has heard from the oracle of Apollo: If he dies and his grave is in Attica near the shrine of Athena, his spirit will protect Athens from their enemies. In particular, when the descendents of Herakles's children attack, he will side with Athens as their ally. The play ends with Alkmene apparently ready to have Eurystheus killed.

The play is articulated through the complex interactions between those who show compassion and those who do not. In the end, Iolaus seems to have been granted the extraordinary gift of rejuvenation as a reward for his selfless service to the children of Herakles, and Eurystheus dies on account of his unyielding enmity. Entirely lacking in compassion, Alkmene apparently achieves her revenge on Eurystheus, and the latter's grave will render service to Athens after his death by helping to combat an attack from the descendents of Herakles (that is, the Spartans and their allies). As is often the case in Euripidean drama, discerning coherent moral or ethical principles underlying the action is challenging.

Despite his transformation, Iolaus turns out to be one of the most consistent characters in the play. He steps forward in the prologue and declares himself dedicated to the idea that the good man helps his friends above all else, but the man out only for himself is "useless to the city." This attitude aligns him with a familiar profile, of the old man who puts the good of the family and city above his own welfare. As a reward, he is allowed to become a young man again, at least temporarily, living out the dream so often expressed by Nestor in the *Iliad*, "If only I could be young again, as I was when fighting." Because Euripides appears to have gone to some trouble to make Iolaus older than the myth ordinarily portrays him, and because his feeble body is the focus for some considerable amount of stage business, we might conclude that the playwright is dramatizing some kind of comment in the play on the old men and their struggles.

Looking at this character as a model for how old men can escape the diminished existence normally accorded them in Athenian culture is tricky. The logic (if we may use that term in this case) of the play's action suggests that nobility of character in old men, realized in selfless acts of compassion, can win favor from the gods. But the reward is not in fact enhanced authority and respect *as an old man,* but rather a magical negation of old age itself. Iolaus might be seen as an example of "passive mastery," in that his attitudes and actions induce the gods to reward him, but again, the reward itself seems to cancel out any idea that his existence as an old man is to be understood in a new way. The play envisions no naturalistic alternative to ordinary existence of old men in Athenian society, no new way of understanding all of its pain and limitations. For such a reimagination of an old man's existence, we will have to go to one of the very last tragic plays produced in fifth-century B.C.E. Athens, Sophocles's *Oedipus at Colonus*. As we will see, Sophocles seems, in his last play, to have been responding specifically to *Children of Herakles*.

GREAT CONSUMMATION: SOPHOCLES'S *OEDIPUS AT COLONUS*

Oedipus at Colonus was first performed in 401 B.C.E., five years after Sophocles's death at age 90, and three years after the final defeat of Athens by Sparta in the Peloponnesian War. The play dramatizes the last day of Oedipus's long and painful life. After his horrendous fall from power in Thebes, the subject of *Oedipus Rex*, Oedipus eventually was forced into exile, led by his two daughters, Antigone and Ismene. After wandering for some years, blind and disgraced, he arrives at Colonus, a village near Athens, where he mysteriously disappears in a grove sacred to the Eumenides. In the chronology of the myths about Oedipus and his family (as opposed to the dates of the plays), the events covered in *Oedipus at Colonus* follow those in Sophocles's *Oedipus Rex*, first performed in 428 B.C.E., and precede those in Sophocles's *Antigone*, first performed in 441 B.C.E. and focusing on the aftermath of Oedipus's death.

Although Sophocles did not write these plays as a connected trilogy, there are thematic connections between them, especially between the two Oedipus plays. As we will see, *Oedipus at Colonus* continues and develops the character we see in *Oedipus Rex*. At the same time, Sophocles seems to be responding in some way to Euripides's *Children of Herakles*, offering another answer to the question, "How can an old man be heroic?" Whereas Euripides's solution depends on a magical intervention from the gods, Sophocles marks out new territory, creating a hero who achieves greatness because of his old age, not in spite of it.

As the play opens, we see Antigone leading her aged father onstage near the grove sacred to the Eumenides. In his first words, Oedipus seems far from heroic:

Antigone, child of a blind old man, what
land have we come to, the city of what people?
Who will receive the wandering Oedipus
today, with pitiful gifts?
I ask for little, and come away with less,
but still enough for me.
For my companions, suffering and long years,
along with nobility, my birthright, have taught me acceptance.
But look please, my child, for some place to sit,
near a public space, or the groves of the gods.
Support me and help me to sit down, so we can learn
where we are. For we have come as strangers to learn
from citizens, and we will carry out their wishes fully.
(Sophocles, *Oedipus at Colonus* 1–13)

The figure of a blind old man being led onstage by a child would surely remind Athenians of the entrance of Tiresias in *Oedipus Rex*. The implied comparison might also prompt some questions: Will the aged Oedipus, like the prophet, have some special knowledge from the gods? If so, will that knowledge give Oedipus power that belies his feeble condition? As the play progresses, we will see that the answer to both questions is yes, and that Oedipus's mysterious powers will bring great benefit to Athens.

Antigone eases her father onto a nearby rock at the edge of the grove. She can see that the place where they have stopped is sacred in some way, fragrant with grapes, olives, laurel, and the songs of nightingales filling the air. The city in the distance is Athens, she says, but she does not know anything about where they sit. As she is about to go exploring, a man approaches. Oedipus and Antigone must move immediately, he says, as they have trespassed on ground sacred to the Eumenides. The old man excitedly replies:

Oh, let them receive me, their suppliant, with kindness!
May I never leave this place, my refuge, again.
(Sophocles, *Oedipus at Colonus* 44–45)

After a further exchange, in which we learn that the king of Athens rules Colonus and must decide whether the old man may remain, we discover that Oedipus was given a second prophecy at Delphi. In addition to the dark prediction of murder and incest, Apollo's oracle offered some solace:

The god said that when I had suffered these many evils,
there would be rest for me after a long time,
when I came to my final goal, this place, where
I would find the seat of the awesome goddesses, a haven to strangers.
There I would approach the end of my miserable life,
a blessing to those I live with who took me in,
a curse to those who sent me into exile, drove me out.
And he said to me that the signs for all these things would come
as an earthquake, or thunder, or the lightning bolt of Zeus.
. . .

Now, goddesses,
Grant to me, as Apollo's oracle foretold, some
last trial, some great consummation of my life,
unless I seem to be somehow to be less than worthy,
endlessly enslaved to the worst toils of any man.
Come, sweet daughters of ancient Darkness,
and you Athens, called the most honored
of Pallas Athena's cities,
take pity wretched shadow of
the man Oedipus, no longer the man he was.
(Sophocles, *Oedipus at Colonus* 87–95; 101–110)

These words confirm for us that we are watching a suppliant play, with Oedipus and his daughters as the strangers in need of protection, and the Eumenides and Athens (whose kings ruled Colonus) as the apparent protectors. The entrance of the chorus, elder citizens of Colonus, throws some doubt on the success of the petition. The old men are looking for the trespasser, whom they call "most shameless" of all men, an old wandering fugitive. Oedipus identifies himself as the stranger, prompting pity and revulsion in the chorus at his blindness and ragged clothing. The chorus echoes the demands of the citizen: Oedipus must move out of the sacred precinct. We then watch as Antigone slowly moves her father away from the boundary of the grove, with the chorus anxiously prompting. Once he is properly positioned, the chorus begins to question him: Who is he? Where is he from? How did he become blind?

Oedipus is suddenly frightened, begging them not to ask him anything more about his identity. They persist, and finally he relents:

Oedipus:	Do you know an offspring of Laius?
Chorus:	Oh no!
Oedipus:	From the royal family of Laius?
Chorus:	Oh Zeus!
Oedipus:	The wretched Oedipus?
Chorus:	You're *that* man?
Oedipus:	Rein in your fear, whatever I say . . .
Chorus:	Oh, Ahhhhhhhhhhh
Oedipus:	My terrible fate . . .
Chorus:	Ahhhhhhhhhh (Sophocles, *Oedipus at Colonus* 220–224)

Now Oedipus's past—all the pain and horror of his time in Thebes—has suddenly become a part of the present. He has gone in an instant from being a feeble old stranger to being the most catastrophically notorious man in Greece.

Oedipus's reemergence further imperils his situation, which was hardly promising to begin with. A blind old man, thus lacking any easy way to exercise masculine agency—as Oedipus himself pointed out to Tiresias in *Oedipus Rex*—he is also without access to authority and respect based on his past. Nestor can claim respect from his former glory as a soldier as can Phoenix, based on the nurture he gave to Achilles, but Oedipus has no access to these kinds of authority. His former glory as king of Thebes has been cancelled out by the horrendous revelations of incest and patricide. His position in the family, ordinarily a source of respect for an old man, is compromised beyond repair. Although his daughters/sisters remain loyal to him (an affiliation not highly valued in a patriarchal family in any event), his relationship to his sons, as we will see, disappears in bitterness over the past. By the time he arrives in Colonus and reveals his identity, Oedipus seems to have almost no power, a weak old man with no defenders beyond his daughters, themselves tainted by his past.

The one possible source of leverage remaining to him is the prophecy he reveals, that after his death, he will be a blessing to those who take him in and a curse to those who have driven him out. Once they discover his identity, the chorus demands that he leave immediately. Antigone and then Oedipus himself beg them for mercy. After a vigorous defense of his innocence, in which he portrays himself as merely the victim of the gods and fate, Oedipus returns to the oracle and its predictions:

Do not look at my
hideous face and dishonor me.

For I have come as one sacred and revered,
and bearing a gift for your people. Whenever your ruler
comes, whoever is your leader,
you will hear and know it all.
Meanwhile, do not be unkind to me. (Sophocles, *Oedipus at Colonus* 285–291)

The chorus relents for the moment to await the appearance of Theseus, the king of Athens, who they are sure will come immediately, once he hears that Oedipus is there. Meanwhile, Antigone spots Ismene approaching from a distance. Oedipus's other daughter has been supporting him by bringing him any news from Thebes that might concern him, especially prophecies. She comes this time with ominous news: Eteocles, Oedipus's younger son, has raised an army and driven Polynices, his older brother, out of the kingship of Thebes. The latter has gone to Argos and raised his own army, and war is imminent. She has also heard of another oracle, which says that Thebes must make sure that Oedipus's grave has the proper rites, or disaster awaits that city. The Thebans will not let his body inside the boundaries of the city, for he is ritually polluted from his incest, but they want to have him nearby so that they can bury him properly just outside the boundaries. Creon is on his way, she says, to take him back to Thebes.

With this news, Oedipus begins to look more formidable. Ismene says the oracle has put Thebes in his power. Now the old man suddenly has leverage over those who drove him into exile, but beyond that, the final disposition of his body will also affect his own sons, who are fighting over the kingship of Thebes. This last fact does not soften his resolve. His sons, Ismene tells him, know of his situation and have apparently done nothing, suggesting to him that they value the kingship more than his welfare. This brings forth a powerful speech from the old man, swearing never to help his sons, who did nothing to prevent his exile from Thebes and are not helping him now.

Oedipus's newfound power is characteristic of old men in traditional societies. He can influence events on earth because in his old age he is closer to the gods and impending death, and by virtue of the mysterious powers the oracle has predicted for his grave. His vehement refusal to help his sons is the first stage in his exercising of another weapon attributed to old men in traditional societies, cursing. There will be more spectacular examples to come.

Oedipus now reviews the events of his past in more detail for the chorus, who respond with anguished exclamations of compassion mixed with horror. He maintains his innocence, citing his ignorance and good intentions. Finally, Theseus arrives with his retinue. He questions Oedipus closely about his intentions and his desires, to which Oedipus offers a bargain: if Theseus will give Oedipus sanctuary from the Thebans, he will provide Athens with a great gift:

I come bringing a gift for you,
my own shattered body, not good

to look at, but the gains it offers
are greater than a beautiful form. (Sophocles, *Oedipus at Colonus* 576–579)

Theseus is puzzled at first, but Oedipus explains that if he is buried in Athens or nearby, his grave will be a powerful force for Athens against Thebes in a future conflict. The old man's rage against his sons for what he sees as their betrayal of him will carry a harsh penalty for Thebes if Athens will take him in.

Theseus agrees and pledges that Athens will receive him as a suppliant, guarding him from Creon now and burying him with proper rites after his death. This pledge is put to the test almost immediately. Theseus exits and, after a beautiful choral song in praise of Colonus, Creon arrives, intent on convincing Oedipus to return to Thebes (or near it). At first, Creon promises that he has come in peace and will not use force. He then delivers a smarmy appeal to Oedipus's sense of loyalty to his birthplace. Come home, he says, and end this pitiful exile. Oedipus will hear nothing of it and angrily reviews all of Creon's past offenses against him. The argument descends quickly into threats and name-calling. Creon eventually reveals that he has kidnapped Ismene already and will take Antigone, too, if Oedipus does not come with him. His henchmen grab Antigone, while Oedipus and the chorus of old men protest ineffectually. Creon then orders his men to seize Oedipus, at which point he resorts to his only available weapon, a curse:

May the goddesses of this grove
allow me one more curse:
Oh worst of men, from my ruined eyes
you have dragged away those nearest to me by force.
So may the Sun god who sees all give you
and your offspring a life like mine, to grow old and blind.
(Sophocles, *Oedipus at Colonus* 864–870)

Just as Creon's men are preparing to march Oedipus offstage, Theseus reappears, dashing to the rescue. He has Creon detained and sends his men out to intercept the Thebans who have Ismene and Antigone. While this occurs offstage, Theseus, Oedipus, and Creon exchange taunts. Finally, Theseus's men return with both daughters and there is a tearful reunion. Now Oedipus has one final piece of business with his past. Polynices has come to ask for his blessing. It seems that oracles have predicted that whichever son he supports will win in the coming battle over the kingship of Thebes. Polynices delivers a lengthy apology to Oedipus for his past failures as a son. He is "the worst of all men," he says, and has let his father down. Even so, he begs for forgiveness, and for his father's blessing.

Oedipus responds with his most vitriolic curse, a long and violent denunciation of both sons, almost 50 lines of angry bile. He ends by condemning them to Hell, hoping they will die at each other's hands:

I call down these curses! I call upon the murky depths
of Tartarus, home now of our fathers. May they gather you up!

I call upon these goddesses! I call upon the War god,
who has flung this hatred into your hearts!
Having heard these curses, go, and tell all the
Thebans and all your loyal soldiers, that Oedipus
bequeaths these gifts to his sons! (Sophocles, *Oedipus at Colonus* 1389–1396)

Polynices gives up in the face of this hatred and vows to return to fight his brother without saying anything to his men about Oedipus's curses. Antigone begs him not to go back, but he refuses. He cannot bear the thought of exile, of being laughed at by his brother. Let the fates decide, he says, as he trudges offstage.

Once Polynices has left, the chorus hears thunder in the distance. Oedipus tells his daughters to summon Theseus. The gods are summoning him, as the oracle foretold, and it is time to go. When Theseus arrives, Oedipus explains that the gods are calling him, that Ismene and Antigone may accompany him partway into the grove, but that he, Theseus, alone can witness the final end of his life. He then turns, and in one of the great moments in Western theater, sheds his frailty and confidently leads the way into the grove of the Eumenides, where he is fated to end his life.

After a final choral ode, a messenger enters to tell the story of Oedipus's mysterious disappearance in the grove. As they entered the sacred grove, they heard the voice of the gods calling to Oedipus to hurry, that he was holding them up. After Oedipus said a final farewell to his daughters, he led Theseus farther into the grove while the rest turned tearfully away. When they looked back, Oedipus was gone, and Theseus was kneeling on the ground, raising his hands toward the heavens. They saw no lightning, heard nothing. Oedipus simply disappeared.

Nothing like this ending occurs anywhere else in Greek literature. A few mortals were thought to have been taken up onto Olympus to be gods after their death, Herakles being the most prominent. Oedipus mysteriously disappears, with no clear indication of where he might end up. That the gods call to him certainly suggests that he is somehow with them, but there is no myth that features Oedipus as a god. His grave will be a source of power for the Athenians. The spirits of dead heroes were believed by the Greeks to exert power from their graves, so this part of the story is not unusual, but his disappearance remains mysterious, a "great consummation," as he predicted.

Comprehending the full impact of *Oedipus at Colonus,* one of the longest plays in Athenian tragedy, episodic and full of incident, is challenging. From our perspective here, the play presents a unique hero, an old man who progresses from helpless dependence to triumph. We have said that Sophocles's vision of old age extends and enriches the earlier picture of Oedipus in *Oedipus Rex* and also that its plot seems to recall in some ways Euripides's *Children of Herakles.* Pursuing those parallels will help us to understand how Sophocles, at the very end of the fifth century B.C.E., offers a unique perspective on the experience of old men in Athenian culture.

As we have seen, Oedipus's entrance at the beginning of the play recalls Tiresias in *Oedipus Rex*. Blind, feeble, led by a child, the former king might be said to have chosen, by blinding himself at the end of the earlier play, to follow the perspective on himself and his masculinity exemplified by Tiresias. In Sophocles's last play, we can see the playwright working out the implications of that choice. The younger hero struggled against the will of the gods or fate, as revealed in the oracle at Delphi. He tried to become a different person, through the exertion of his heroic will, than the one doomed to kill his father and create children with his mother. Finally, when he uncovers the truth about who he is and what he has done, the futility of fighting against transcendent powers is affirmed. The old man, in his first words onstage, declares that suffering and old age have taught him acceptance. He will no longer fight against the gods' will. In fact, we soon discover that a prophecy has predicted that he will achieve a "great consummation" in the grove of the Eumenides. His one desire, on hearing that he has found that sacred spot, is to end his life there. Greek heroes, outsized models of masculine ideals, are, like the young Oedipus, usually characterized by defiance of the fact of mortality. Here we have a protagonist who begins by saying that what he seeks is to die as the gods and fate have decreed.

Oedipus's acceptance of the gods' will is in contrast to his angry and assertive response to both Creon and Polynices. The curses he pronounces on both men express the power he possesses as an old man nearing death, and in both cases, the results will be devastating. This power is unlike that of the younger masculine hero, in that it depends not on what the man has done, but where he is in his life. Furthermore, we observe that where Oedipus is physically also becomes important in the play from the very first lines. He has been told that to achieve his great consummation, he must die in a specific place. When the chorus of citizens arrives, they demand that he be moved from where he is sitting to another place. The resulting action has the old man inched around the stage as if he were a bomb ready to explode. Ismene later reports that Creon will soon arrive to attempt to get Oedipus to travel back toward Thebes with him, so that the Thebans can control where he is buried, near but not inside the boundaries of the city. The play's mysterious ending confirms what we heard at the beginning: where Oedipus dies is crucial to the future of Athens and Thebes.

If we map Oedipus's movements onto his attitude and demeanor, we see that when he is pulled, literally or figuratively, toward his Theban past, he becomes angry, vengeful, and recalcitrant. When he moves toward the sacred grove and his destined future, he is calm, accepting, and self-possessed. The entire play thus seems to be informed by a kind of spiritual geography. The past and Thebes as its home draw from Oedipus the defiance and willfulness we associate with younger men in Greek culture. Although his cursing will have powerful results, contact with his past still brings out frustration and shame in the old man. Only when he drives Polynices away, ridding himself of that last connection to Thebes, and turns toward the grove of the Eumenides and the destiny it holds for him, does he achieve the serene confidence that characterizes his final moments on earth. By accepting and even seeking what transcendent powers have planned for him, he achieves another kind of power, one that will commence after his death. He will become a vehicle for the expression of those powers, embracing the identification with Tiresias that he first moved toward by blinding himself at the end of *Oedipus Rex*.

In his realizations of Oedipus, Sophocles has traced the arc of a masculine life from vigorous youth to mature manhood to old age. The hero of the earlier play, in the fullness of his masculine powers, seeks to express his agency as a man by acting out into the world to control people and events in ways that reflect his own will. For him, as for other masculine heroes like Achilles and Ajax, a reckoning eventually comes, when his will to control encounters the transcendent forces of the universe, nature, divine will, and fate. The older Oedipus shows us, for the first time in Greek literature, a fully realized alternative to the ultimately futile masculine drive to control. By accepting and willingly fulfilling what the oracles have predicted, he achieves a new kind of power.

Sophocles's radical revision of accepted ideas about old men has an even greater impact when viewed as a response to Euripides's *Children of Herakles*. Both are suppliant plays, with Athens as the protecting city; both feature a nasty agent for a king who would victimize old men and children for the sake of increased power, and the king of Athens as a dashing rescuer; both feature an aged protagonist who is given new powers through his relationship to the gods; and both have a man who has been told that he will exert power over his enemies from the site of his grave. The parallels seem to be too extensive to be coincidental.

The similarities, however, only point us toward the important ways in which Sophocles has extended and enriched the implications of the earlier play. Where Euripides's Iolaus seems to be rewarded by the gods for his selflessness with a magical but temporary rejuvenation, Oedipus's final triumph is *as an old man*. His mysterious disappearance at the end of the play is only the final stage of an evolution that begins when he blinds himself at the end of *Oedipus Rex*. His serene walk into the grove models a new way for old men to be powerful that is not a temporary escape from who he is but an affirmation of his new understanding of his place in the larger order of the universe.

We cannot end our discussion of Sophocles's last play without noting that the playwright himself was nearing 90 when he composed it. Furthermore, Colonus was in fact Sophocles's birthplace. It is hard not to see the old artist, at the end of his long and productive career as a playwright, soldier, and active politician, commenting in some way on his own life. Like Oedipus, he left a great gift to Athens, in his case, dramatic masterpieces that explore, among many other things, what it meant to be a man during the high point of Athenian culture. When Oedipus walks off stage and into the grove, we may imagine Sophocles right beside him.

CONCLUSION

We began by observing that old men in Greek culture were, like male children, usually measured by how closely they approached the ideal of mature young manhood. As their bodies grew weaker, older men faced the prospect of diminishing authority and respect in their communities. The ability to exert control over their bodies, so essential to Greek ideals of masculinity, slowly left them. As their sons married and moved their wives into the family home, older fathers lost the authority and respect accorded to the head male of household. These challenges seem to have been more acute later in the period we have been exploring, particularly in classical Athens. That observation fits with studies that have been done of aging across many cultures: old men tend to be valued less in societies that are more urbanized and less traditional in their social and political structures. In more traditional societies, on the other hand, older men can retain some of their authority, claiming respect by virtue of their wisdom and experience, as well as their power because of their closeness to death, which was thought to give them greater influence with the gods.

In the Homeric epics, each of which features societies characterized by more traditional, family-centered, and top-down authority structures, we find characters like Nestor, Phoenix, Priam, and Laertes, who command respect because of their wisdom and because of their connection to significant past events. The story of Tithonus in the *Homeric Hymn to Aphrodite*, roughly contemporary with the *Odyssey*, and the Greek elegiac poets Mimnermus, Anacreon, and Ibycus, all working a little less than two centuries later than Homer, reflect in their poems the anxieties about sexual vigor that preoccupied Greek men as they entered old age. The effect of changes in Greek political and social organizations, which eventually led to the radical break with the past represented by Athenian democracy, may be evident in the greater openness about male sexuality in these poets, although some of the difference may be the result of the less formal nature of the poetry itself.

Finally, in Athenian drama of the fifth century B.C.E., we see the influence of political and social changes that led to a loosening of traditional lines of authority. The portrait of old men in these plays is considerably more negative than in earlier works. Old men tend to be shown as physically feeble and lacking in authority. The choruses made up of old men bluster and complain, but accomplish little. Old men like Cadmus and Tiresias in Euripides's *The Bacchae* or Iolaus before his transformation in *Children of Herakles* are meant to be laughed at in their attempts to exert themselves in pursuit of goals thought more appropriate for young men. The one significant exception to this trend is the kind of old man represented by Tiresias in Sophocles's *Oedipus Rex* and reborn in the aged Oedipus in *Oedipus at Colonus*. In these two characters, Sophocles develops an entirely different way of looking at the place of old men in Greek society. Rather than trying to compete with younger men for power, this kind of old man chooses to avoid the eventual showdown with the transcendent powers of the universe over which no mortal is thought to have any real power. By seeing themselves as conduits for powers beyond their control or understanding, both Tiresias and Oedipus achieve a new kind of authority, as old men, in the willing expression of that power.

Afterword

In pursuit of our original questions, we have explored many complex, sophisticated works of art. Although the very richness of these sources makes summarizing a challenge, a few clear ideas have emerged. All of the stories we have studied reinforce the observation that the universe, as the Greeks saw it, was fundamentally *gendered.* Human civilization was the result of imposing intelligence, in the form of limits, on the undifferentiated powers of the natural world. That intelligence, in turn, was understood to be a natural endowment of men, who were the agents of civilization. Women, on the other hand, were closer by their biological makeup to the forces of nature and so had to be controlled by men in order for human civilization to function smoothly. Thus independent women like Medea and Clytemnestra were frightening, not only because they might kill particular men (or women) but also, on a deeper level, because they threatened the right order of the universe.

The need to control others as a prerequisite for male agency presupposed self-control. That imperative, in turn, included both the physical and emotional dimensions of a man's bodily self. The need to preserve bodily integrity was reflected in male standards for both war and sexual behavior with partners of either sex: to be penetrated was to be unmanly. Control of one's emotions was equally important. Odysseus is the first and most famous example of the power over others that self-control can afford. Anonymity in the *Odyssey* prevents a man from winning fame that can live after one's death, the one bulwark against oblivion available to mortal men. Even so, Odysseus never reveals his identity to strangers until he has earned their respect through his actions. He *endures* namelessness to hoard power. He does not tell his own wife who he is when he returns to Ithaka after 20 years, although getting back to her has been a primary motivation for him to keep struggling to get back. He does not trust her to keep his secrets, and so he exercises control over his own emotions in the face of her despair.

Most of the male heroes in our stories are conspicuous examples of these masculine traits. At the same time, many of our stories suggest, in one way or another, that to be a fully mature man required the integration of some qualities the Greeks identified as feminine. Thus to escape the consequences of his selfishness and self-destructive rage, Achilles must integrate into his perspective traits associated with his lost friend, Patroclus. He must recognize that what connects humans to one another is at least as important as what distinguishes them from one another. Oedipus, after his catastrophic fall from king to outcast, begins to recover his will to survive by reaching toward the perspective of Tiresias. On the last day of his life, he completes his transformation from hypermasculine hero to a more feminine, inward stance toward the universe. Pentheus's transformation is seen in a much darker context, but the limitations of his ideas about masculinity are clear enough.

The emergence of the world's first democracy, with its radical challenges to traditional assumptions about the distribution of power within a society, prompted deep intellectual, social, and political ferment in Athenian culture. The plays of Aeschylus, Sophocles, and Euripides explore and illuminate the profound consequences of these changes for the Greeks' understanding of masculinity. The traditional aristocratic hero, with his fierce independence and competitive drive, becomes in these dramas a lightning rod for the conflicts between older, hierarchical measures of human worth and the greater emphasis on cooperative values in the newly emerging democracy. The aristocratic hero, the epitome of manliness, was always a problematical force within his social group, whether it be the Greek army at Troy or the king's household in Ithaka. As long as the imperatives of his will happened to coincide with the needs of the community, he could be a force for good in his community. His masculine drive for power, however, could also tear that community apart. In the context of Athenian democracy, with its strong challenges to received ideas about how to evaluate a human life and the place of human society in the larger scheme of the universe, the old-fashioned hero became yet more problematic. Oedipus, who believes he is wholly dedicated to the saving of Thebes and its citizens, ends up throwing the community into frightening uncertainty. Ajax, when faced with the consequences of his homicidal rage, driven by his sense of failure as a man, can no longer bear to live among his fellow Greeks. His suicide then provokes a crisis that nearly tears the Greek army apart. The inherent conflict between the male drive for power and control and the need for human cooperation to ensure a healthy community was always at the center of Greek ideas about masculinity.

Fundamental to all expressions of masculine power as the Greeks understood it was the conflict between masculine agency and the challenges posed by aging. Men were the creators and guardians of human civilization. They had to learn how to exert control over themselves and others so that the world could function as it should. The natural process of aging, with its inevitable decline in physical and mental powers, challenged men's agency within their communities. In more traditional societies, like those in the Homeric epics, older men could retain some influence, because their experience was felt to give them wisdom not available to younger men, and because their closeness to death also suggested that they were closer to the gods and their power. Democratic Athens again provides a different perspective. Because many of the traditional assumptions about status and worth were challenged, old men had less access to continuing influence. Athenian tragedy, as we have seen, is filled with portraits of foolish, ineffectual old men.

The final and most important limitation on masculine agency was, of course, the fact of human mortality. Male power was always exercised in the face of transcendent forces, the gods, fate, and forces of nature, but the limit of death remained the most vivid symbol of the ultimately futile masculine drive for control. Thus Achilles, the most famous Greek hero, whose life defines so much of what the Greeks thought about manhood, must grow into a mature understanding of himself as a man who must die. His semidivine heritage gives him the hope that he, unlike his fellow warriors, can somehow escape the confining limit of death. But the *Iliad* also insists on the fact that without the limit of death, human life would be meaningless and morally trivial. The Greeks were the first to recognize and work out fully the implications of the fact that it is the limit of human mortality that requires us to have virtues. Homeric gods, all-powerful, all-knowing, and ageless, are inevitably comic figures when we see them on Olympus. Only by injecting themselves into the world of death and change can they do anything meaningful. The tension between human greatness and the oblivion of death is at the heart of the Greek tragic perspective, which endures in some of the greatest works of Western art.

As the Greeks saw it, to be a man was to be defined by your ability to exert power in a world articulated through transcendent forces ultimately beyond human control. The apparent futility of this perspective was outweighed by the nobility that came with the struggle. The very meaning of human life was, in fact, determined by its inherent limits. These ideas persist in Western culture today. The drive to control the natural world through scientific knowledge has characterized Western cultures at least since the Renaissance. Astronauts, who travel beyond the boundaries of ordinary human experience, physically replicate the symbolic journeys of Achilles or Odysseus. The stubborn persistence of assumptions about the "natural" capacities of men and women, and the fierce conflicts over their validity characterize most modern cultures in one form or another.

We may not want to perpetuate Greek ideals of manliness; we may find their beliefs about the gendered nature of the universe to be unjust or confining. Whatever we finally decide about these issues, however, we abandon at our peril their insatiable curiosity and drive to see things clearly and think about them deeply.

Further Reading

CHAPTER ONE

Alvin Gouldner's *Enter Plato* (New York: Basic Books, 1965) is a stimulating interpretation of ancient Greek culture as a whole. Joseph Roisman's *The Rhetoric of Manhood* (Berkeley: University of California Press, 2005) is an excellent study of attitudes toward masculinity in Athenian oratory. The best contemporary English translations of Homer's *Iliad* are Robert Fagles, *Homer: The Iliad* (New York: Penguin Books, 1990) and Richmond Lattimore, *The Iliad of Homer* (Chicago: University of Chicago Press, 1951). See also a more recent translation by Stanley Lombardo, *Homer: Iliad* (Indianapolis/Cambridge: Hackett Publishing Company, 1997), a more radically contemporary version with an excellent introduction by Sheila Murnaghan. The best contemporary English translation of *The Epic of Gilgamesh* is by Maureen Gallery Kovacs, *The Epic of Gilgamesh* (Stanford: Stanford University Press, 1990). Good general discussions of Homeric epic can be found in Seth Schein, *The Mortal Hero: An Introduction to Homer's Iliad* (Berkeley: University of California Press, 1984), Mark Edwards, *Homer: Poet of the* Iliad (Baltimore: Johns Hopkins University Press, 1987), and Charles Beye, *Ancient Epic Poetry* (Ithaca: Cornell University Press, 1993). On the *Iliad* in particular, E. T. Owen's interpretative reading, *The Story of the Iliad* (Toronto: University of Toronto Press, 1946) is still the best introduction to the story. Jasper Griffin, *Homer on Life and Death* (Oxford: Oxford University Press, 1980) is a good place to begin reading about the impact of mortality on the heroic vision of life. For an introductory discussion of *The Epic of Gilgamesh*, see Thorkild Jacobsen, *The Treasures of Darkness* (New Haven, CT: Yale University Press, 1976) and Kovacs 1985. For a more detailed discussion of the issues raised in this chapter, particularly the second self, as they apply to *The Epic of Gilgamesh*, Homer's *Iliad*, and Virgil's *Aeneid*, see Thomas Van Nortwick, *Somewhere I Have Never Travelled: The Second Self and the Hero's Journey in Ancient Epic* (New York: Oxford University Press, 1992). For an excellent introduction to the *Homeric Hymn to Demeter*, see Helene Foley, *The*

Homeric Hymn to Demeter: Translation, Commentary, and Interpretive Essays
(Princeton: Princeton University Press, 1994).

CHAPTER TWO

The best source for childhood in Athens is Mark Golden, *Children and Childhood in Classical Athens* (Baltimore: Johns Hopkins Press, 1990). On the relationship of fathers and sons, see Barry Strauss, *Fathers and Sons in Athens* (Princeton: Princeton University Press, 1993). Stephen Tracy, *The Story of the Odyssey* (Princeton: Princeton University Press, 1990), is a full and helpful interpretation of the *Odyssey.* The best English translations of the *Odyssey* are Robert Fagles, *Homer: The Odyssey* (New York: Penguin Books, 1996), Richmond Lattimore, *The Odyssey of Homer* (Chicago: University of Chicago Press, 1965), and Stanley Lombardo *Homer: Odyssey* (Indianapolis/ Cambridge: Hackett Publishing Company, 2000), all with excellent introductions on the poem. For an insightful and stimulating reading of the *Homeric Hymn to Hermes,* see Lewis Hyde, *Trickster Makes This World* (New York: Farrar, Straus and Giroux, 1998), pp. 203–225. The introduction to Ruby Blondell, Mary-Kay Gamel, Nancy Rabinowitz, and Bella Zweig, *Women on the Edge: Four Plays by Euripides* (London: Routledge, 1999) has an excellent section on the staging of dramas in Athens. For an introduction to Sophocles, see Ruth Scodel *Sophocles* (Boston: Twayne Publishers, 1984), and Cedric Whitman, *Sophocles* (Cambridge, MA: Harvard University Press, 1951). David Grene's English translation of Sophocles's *Philoctetes,* in David Grene and Richmond Lattimore, *The Complete Greek Tragedies: Sophocles II* (Chicago: University of Chicago Press, 1957), is excellent. See also Carl Phillips, *Sophocles' Philoctetes* (New York: Oxford University Press, 2003), a more recent version with an thoughtful introduction by Diskin Clay.

CHAPTER THREE

C. John Herington, *Aeschylus* (New Haven, CT: Yale University Press, 1986) is a fine general introduction to Aeschylus. The best English translations of the *Oresteia* trilogy are Robert Fagles, *Aeschylus: The Oresteia* (New York: Penguin Books, 1966) and Alan Shapiro and Peter Burian, *Aeschylus: The Oresteia* (New York: Oxford University Press, 2003). Both have helpful introductions on the plays. On Euripides's *Medea,* see William Allan, *Euripides: Medea* (London: Duckworth, 1970), Emily McDermott, *Euripides' Medea: The Incarnation of Disorder* (University Park: Pennsylvania State University Press, 1989), and Blondell, Gamel, Rabinowitz, and Zweig, *Women on the Edge* (London: Routledge, 1999). For English translations of *Medea,* see Rex Warner's version in David Grene and Richmond Lattimore, *The Complete Greek Tragedies: Euripides I* (Chicago: University of Chicago Press, 1957), and Ruby Blondell's translation of *Medea* in Blondell, Gamel, Rabinowitz, and Zweig, 1999. The latter has excellent introductory material on the background for Athenian drama in general and Euripidean drama in particular.

CHAPTER FOUR

On the Homeric warrior and his place in Homeric society, see James Redfield, *Nature and Culture in the* Iliad: *The Tragedy of Hector* (Chicago: University of Chicago Press,1975), Griffin 1980, pp. 81–143, and Schein 1984, pp. 67–88. John Moore's English translation of Sophocles's *Ajax* in Grene and Lattimore, *Sophocles II,* (Chicago: University of Chicago Press, 1957) is excellent. A more recent translation, Herbert Golder and Richard Pevear, *Sophocles: Aias* (New York: Oxford University Press, 1999), is also very good. Richard Crawley and Donald Lateiner, *Thucydides: The History of the Peloponnesian War* (New York: Barnes and Noble, 2006) is the best place to begin reading Thucydides. Lateiner's introduction is excellent.

CHAPTER FIVE

W.K.C. Guthrie, *The Greeks and Their Gods* (London: Methuen, 1950) is a good survey of Greek religion. See also Jon Mikalson *Ancient Greek Religion* (London: Blackwell, 2005). The best translation of Sophocles's *Oedipus Rex* is in Robert Fagles, *Sophocles: The Three Theban Plays* (New York: Penguin Books, 1982), with an excellent introduction by Bernard Knox. For a brilliant and powerfully-written study of *Oedipus Rex*, see Bernard Knox, *Oedipus at Thebes: Sophocles' Tragic Hero and His Time* (New Haven, CT: Yale University Press, 1957). On *Oedipus Rex* as an exploration of a masculine life, see Thomas Van Nortwick, *Oedipus: The Meaning of a Masculine Life* (Norman: University of Oklahoma Press, 1998). The best English translation of Euripides's *Bacchae* is by William Arrowsmith, in David Grene and Richmond Lattimore *The Complete Greek Tragedies: Euripides V* (Chicago: University of Chicago Press, 1959), with a provocative introduction. On Euripides's drama, see Douglas Conacher, *Euripidean Drama; Myth, Theme and Structure* (Toronto: University of Toronto Press, 1967).

CHAPTER SIX

Thomas Falkner's *The Poetics of Old Age in Greek Epic, Lyric, and Tragedy* (Norman: University of Okalahoma Press, 1995) is the best study of old age in Greek literature, with chapters devoted to Homer's *Odyssey,* Greek lyric poetry, Euripides's *Children of Herakles,* and Sophocles's *Oedipus at Colonus.* For a fuller discussion of the ideas in this chapter about *Oedipus at Colonus,* see Thomas Van Nortwick, *Oedipus: The Meaning of a Masculine Life* 1998. The best translation of Sophocles's *Oedipus at Colonus* is in Fagles 1982. The best translation of Euripides's *Children of Herakles* is Henry Taylor and Robert Brooks *Euripides: The Children of Herakles* (New York: Oxford University Press, 1981).

Index

ABOUT THE AUTHOR

THOMAS VAN NORTWICK is Nathan A. Greenberg Professor of Classics at Oberlin College, where he has taught since 1974. He holds a B.A. in History and a Ph.D. in Classics from Stanford University and an M.A. in Classics from Yale University. He has published scholarly articles on Greek and Latin literature, and three books, *Somewhere I Have Never Travelled: The Second Self and the Hero's Journey in Ancient Epic, Compromising Traditions: The Personal Voice in Classical Scholarship,* and *Oedipus: The Meaning of a Masculine Life.* He is also a contributing editor of *North Dakota Quarterly.*